USING MATHEMATICS
Book 4

ANDRIA P. TROUTMAN
Professor, University of South Florida
Tampa, Florida

JAMES J. BEZDEK
Professor of Education, North Texas State University
Denton, Texas

CATHERINE TOBIN
Educational Consultant
Newtonville, Massachusetts

TEACHER–CONSULTANTS

Philip E. Bertoni
Teacher, John F. Kennedy High School
Anaheim Union High School District
La Palma, California

Lula P. Smith
Teacher, Mahalia Jackson School
Chicago Public Schools
Chicago, Illinois

Caroline L. Chin
Teacher, Nathan Hale School
Boston Public Schools
Roxbury, Massachusetts

Alma E. Wright
Teacher, Trotter School
Boston Public Schools
Boston, Massachusetts

LAIDLAW BROTHERS • PUBLISHERS
A Division of Doubleday & Company, Inc.
RIVER FOREST, ILLINOIS

Irvine, California   Chamblee, Georgia   Dallas, Texas   Toronto, Canada

The USING MATHEMATICS Program

USING MATHEMATICS Kindergarten

USING MATHEMATICS	Book 1	USING MATHEMATICS	Book 5
USING MATHEMATICS	Book 2	USING MATHEMATICS	Book 6
USING MATHEMATICS	Book 3	USING MATHEMATICS	Book 7
USING MATHEMATICS	Book 4	USING MATHEMATICS	Book 8

ACKNOWLEDGMENTS

EDITORIAL STAFF

Project Director: Albert F. Kempf   *Staff Editor:* David B. Spangler   *Production Director:* LaVergne G. Niequist
Art Director: Gloria J. Muczynski   *Assistant to the Art Director:* Dennis Horan   *Production Supervisor:* Mary C. Steermann
Production Associates: Anthony Giometti, Robert A. Porché, Jr.   *Photo Researcher:* William A. Cassin

ILLUSTRATORS

George Hamblin; Paul Hazelrigg; Rick Incrocci; Sergei Itomlenskis/John D. Firestone & Associates, Inc.; Dick Martin;
Donald C. Meighan; Keith Neely; Joseph Rogers; Sam Sirdofsky

PHOTOGRAPHERS

Cover photograph by H. Armstrong Roberts; other photographs credited where each photograph appears.

ISBN 0-8445-1204-4

23456789 10 11 12 13 14 15   10987654

1 Using Numbers

2 Addition and Subtraction

3 Multiplication

4 Division

5 Problem Solving

6 Geometry

7 Measurement

8 Addition and Subtraction

9 Multiplication

10 Division

11 Fractions and Decimals

12 Fractions and Decimals (+, -)

13 Graphs and Probability

Review and Practice   314-351

1 Using Numbers

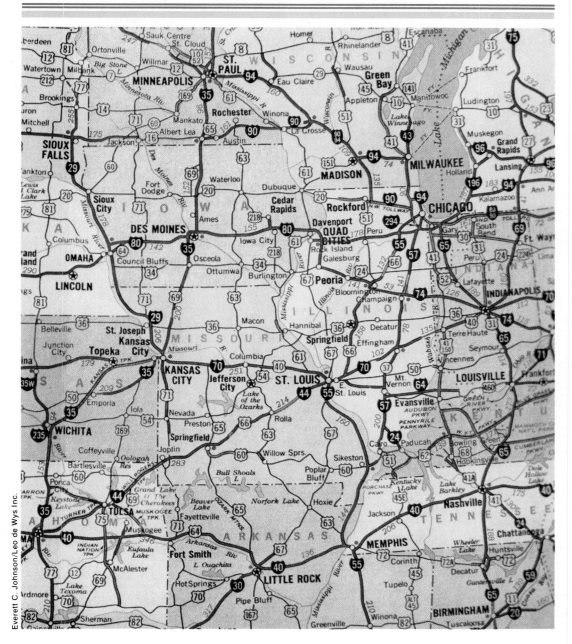

Everett C. Johnson/Leo de Wys Inc.

Comparing Numbers

Who is taller?

50 is greater than 48.

50 > 48

Who is shorter?

48 is less than 50.

48 < 50

< and > both point to the smaller number.

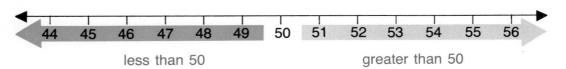

less than 50   greater than 50

Exercises

Write < or > for each ●.

1. 47 ● 50

2. 55 ● 50

3. 49 ● 50

4. 52 ● 50

5. 60 ● 50

6. 40 ● 50

7. 72 ● 50

8. 36 ● 50

8

9. 5 ● 8

10. 9 ● 7

11. 10 ● 6

12. 12 ● 15

13. 20 ● 30

14. 23 ● 32

15. 70 ● 50

16. 75 ● 58

17. 27 ● 17

18. 36 ● 46

19. 55 ● 52

20. 29 ● 31

21. 19 ● 91

22. 45 ● 54

23. 72 ● 70

24. 63 ● 59

25. 80 ● 79

26. 90 ● 50

27. 26 ● 18

28. 43 ● 39

Each problem has several answers. Write any three of them.

29. The fewest players on a team is 9. The most is 14. How many players can be on a team?

30. The speed limit is 55 miles per hour. At what speeds may a car travel?

31. 30 problems are on a test. You need 26 problems correct for an A. What scores get an A?

32. A dozen eggs sell for less than 98¢ but more than 72¢. What could be the price?

Find a number for □.

33. 12 > □

34. 26 < □

35. 84 < □

36. 55 > □

37. □ < 31

38. □ > 73

39. □ > 65

40. □ < 19

Which Is Taller?

Pikes Peak
14,110 feet

Mount Evans
14,264 feet

Hundreds

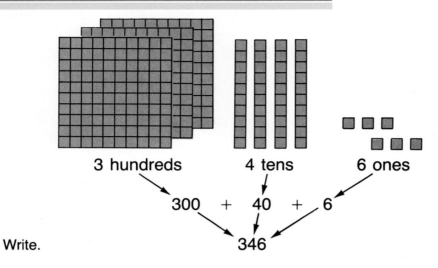

3 hundreds   4 tens   6 ones

300 + 40 + 6

Write.

346

Read.   *three hundred forty-six*

Exercises

Write the numeral.

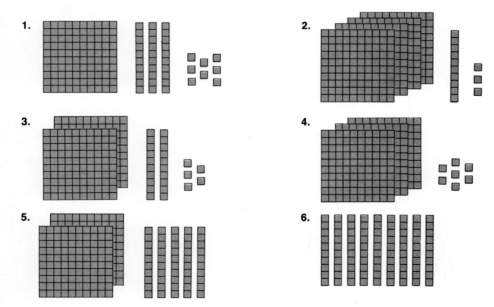

1.

2.

3.

4.

5.

6.

10

What is the score?

7.

8.

Write the numeral.

9. 7 hundreds, 4 tens, 8 ones

10. 3 hundreds, 9 tens, 5 ones

11. 2 hundreds, 0 tens, 3 ones

12. 9 hundreds, 6 tens, 0 ones

13. 8 tens, 4 ones

14. 5 hundreds, 1 ten, 7 ones

15. 6 hundreds, 3 tens, 0 ones

16. 8 hundreds, 2 tens, 1 one

17. 4 hundreds, 0 tens, 5 ones

18. 9 hundreds, 9 tens, 9 ones

19. 700 + 30 + 2

20. 100 + 90 + 3

21. 200 + 7

22. 600 + 50

23. 400 + 60 + 8

24. 40 + 1

25. 900 + 20 + 5

26. 500 + 10 + 6

27. 800 + 90 + 4

28. 900 + 70 + 9

Write < or > for each ●.

29. 300 ● 500

30. 350 ● 530

31. 700 ● 600

32. 708 ● 609

33. 426 ● 428

34. 699 ● 711

35. 780 ● 790

36. 388 ● 288

11

Thousands

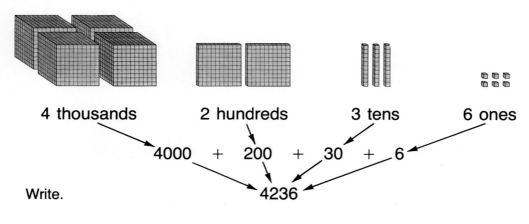

4 thousands   2 hundreds   3 tens   6 ones

4000 + 200 + 30 + 6

Write.   4236

Read.   *four thousand two hundred thirty-six*

Exercises

What is the score?

1.
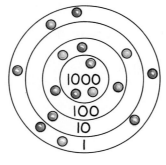

2.
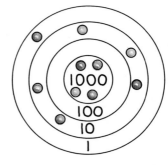

Write the numeral.

3. 6 thousands, 7 hundreds, 1 ten, 3 ones

4. 8 thousands, 0 hundreds, 5 tens, 2 ones

5. 5 thousands, 4 hundreds, 0 tens, 9 ones

6. 9 thousands, 9 hundreds, 4 tens, 8 ones

12

7. 5000 + 400 + 30 + 7

8. 7000 + 800 + 50 + 2

9. 4000 + 900 + 60

10. 2000 + 400 + 6

11. 6000 + 20 + 9

12. 8000 + 40

13. 3000 + 500 + 70 + 1

14. 1000 + 900 + 20 + 7

15. 9000 + 100 + 90 + 1

16. 7000 + 6

17. 2000 + 300

18. 5000 + 800 + 30 + 2

You can compare numbers by comparing the digits.

	Compare the thousands.	Compare the hundreds.	Compare the tens.	Compare the ones.
5276 ● 5259	5276 5259 same	5276 5259 same	5276 5259 7 > 5, so 5276 > 5259.	
4317 ● 4509	4317 4509 same	4317 4509 3 < 5, so 4317 < 4509.		

Write < or > for each ●.

19. 3186 ● 3181

20. 7503 ● 7812

21. 6492 ● 5917

22. 8157 ● 8139

23. 1926 ● 1924

24. 4733 ● 4753

25. 2940 ● 2960

26. 5700 ● 5500

27. 8717 ● 9717

28. 6003 ● 6001

29. 9030 ● 9070

30. 5762 ● 5769

Large Numbers

Believe it or not! There are about 491,500 words in the English language.

Hundred Thousands	Ten Thousands	Thousands	Hundreds	Tens	Ones
HTh	TTh	Th	H	T	O
4	9	1,	5	0	0

491,500 = 400,000 + 90,000 + 1000 + 500

value of the 4 ⟶

value of the 9 ⟶

value of the 1 ⟶

value of the 5 ⟶

four hundred ninety-one thousand, five hundred

A **comma** is used to make the numeral easier to read.

There are also about 312,750 special terms in the English language. Tell the value of each digit and then read 312,750.

Exercises

Name the value of the colored digit.

1. 48,026

2. 75,361

3. 20,755

4. 39,040

5. 38,579

6. 17,433

7. 391,642

8. 285,979

9. 106,824

10. 150,271

11. 950,431

12. 973,605

Name the number that comes between these numbers.

13. 52,899, ___, 52,901

14. 63,999, ___, 64,001

15. 98,079, ___, 98,081

16. 253,999, ___, 254,001

17. 700,000, ___, 700,002

18. 599,998, ___, 600,000

Write the numeral.

19. 20,000 + 7000 + 500 + 40 + 9

20. 60,000 + 3000 + 80 + 4

21. 300,000 + 70,000 + 1000 + 200 + 3

22. 700,000 + 5000 + 30

23. 800,000 + 10,000 + 700 + 6

24. 100,000 + 60,000 + 40 + 9

25. There are *ten thousand, eighty* minutes in a week.

26. It is about *two hundred eighty-six thousand* miles to the moon.

27. The distance around the earth at the equator is about *forty thousand, seventy-five* kilometers.

28. Your heart beats about *one hundred nine thousand, four hundred forty* times a day.

29. Light travels about *one hundred eighty-six thousand* miles each second.

30. A spaceship travels about *seventeen thousand, two hundred thirty* miles each hour.

Write < or > for each ⬤.

31. 17,643 ⬤ 17,651

32. 705,832 ⬤ 704,971

33. 82,075 ⬤ 82,078

34. 592,316 ⬤ 582,507

Addition Facts

This week Larry mowed 8 lawns. Cary mowed 7 more lawns than that. How many lawns did Cary mow?

Here are two ways to find the answer.

$$7 + 8 = 15 \qquad \begin{array}{r} 7 \\ +8 \\ \hline 15 \end{array}$$

↑——— sum ———↑

Cary mowed 15 lawns.

Camerique

Exercises

1. $3 + 6 = \square$ 2. $4 + 9 = \square$ 3. $0 + 8 = \square$

4. $6 + 6 = \square$ 5. $5 + 8 = \square$ 6. $9 + 1 = \square$

7. $\begin{array}{r} 4 \\ +5 \\ \hline \end{array}$ 8. $\begin{array}{r} 6 \\ +4 \\ \hline \end{array}$ 9. $\begin{array}{r} 8 \\ +4 \\ \hline \end{array}$ 10. $\begin{array}{r} 7 \\ +7 \\ \hline \end{array}$ 11. $\begin{array}{r} 7 \\ +4 \\ \hline \end{array}$ 12. $\begin{array}{r} 3 \\ +8 \\ \hline \end{array}$

13. $\begin{array}{r} 5 \\ +7 \\ \hline \end{array}$ 14. $\begin{array}{r} 7 \\ +0 \\ \hline \end{array}$ 15. $\begin{array}{r} 8 \\ +6 \\ \hline \end{array}$ 16. $\begin{array}{r} 3 \\ +9 \\ \hline \end{array}$ 17. $\begin{array}{r} 6 \\ +7 \\ \hline \end{array}$ 18. $\begin{array}{r} 9 \\ +9 \\ \hline \end{array}$

19. $\begin{array}{r} 1 \\ +8 \\ \hline \end{array}$ 20. $\begin{array}{r} 7 \\ +5 \\ \hline \end{array}$ 21. $\begin{array}{r} 4 \\ +8 \\ \hline \end{array}$ 22. $\begin{array}{r} 8 \\ +7 \\ \hline \end{array}$ 23. $\begin{array}{r} 2 \\ +9 \\ \hline \end{array}$ 24. $\begin{array}{r} 8 \\ +8 \\ \hline \end{array}$

25. $\begin{array}{r} 9 \\ +6 \\ \hline \end{array}$ 26. $\begin{array}{r} 7 \\ +6 \\ \hline \end{array}$ 27. $\begin{array}{r} 5 \\ +5 \\ \hline \end{array}$ 28. $\begin{array}{r} 6 \\ +9 \\ \hline \end{array}$ 29. $\begin{array}{r} 9 \\ +4 \\ \hline \end{array}$ 30. $\begin{array}{r} 7 \\ +9 \\ \hline \end{array}$

31. $\begin{array}{r} 8 \\ +5 \\ \hline \end{array}$ 32. $\begin{array}{r} 0 \\ +7 \\ \hline \end{array}$ 33. $\begin{array}{r} 6 \\ +8 \\ \hline \end{array}$ 34. $\begin{array}{r} 9 \\ +7 \\ \hline \end{array}$ 35. $\begin{array}{r} 8 \\ +9 \\ \hline \end{array}$ 36. $\begin{array}{r} 9 \\ +8 \\ \hline \end{array}$

37. $5 + 6 = \square$

38. $6 + 5 = \square$

Are the answers the same?

39. $3 + 7 = \square$

40. $7 + 3 = \square$

Are the answers the same?

41. $9 + 5 = \square$

42. $5 + 9 = \square$

Are the answers the same?

Study these ways of adding three numbers.

$$
\begin{array}{l}
5 \\
3 \\
+6 \\
\hline 14
\end{array}
\quad 8 \quad 6
$$

$$
\begin{array}{l}
5 \quad 5 \\
3 \\
+6 \\
\hline 14
\end{array}
\quad 9
$$

$$
3 + 4 + 6 \\
7 \qquad 6 \\
13
$$

$$
3 + 4 + 6 \\
3 \qquad 10 \\
13
$$

43. $3 + 6 + 3 = \square$

44. $8 + 0 + 3 = \square$

45. $6 + 1 + 9 = \square$

46.
$$
\begin{array}{r}
5 \\
4 \\
+5 \\
\end{array}
$$

47.
$$
\begin{array}{r}
7 \\
8 \\
+0 \\
\end{array}
$$

48.
$$
\begin{array}{r}
4 \\
5 \\
+2 \\
\end{array}
$$

49.
$$
\begin{array}{r}
3 \\
2 \\
+6 \\
\end{array}
$$

50.
$$
\begin{array}{r}
5 \\
5 \\
+5 \\
\end{array}
$$

51.
$$
\begin{array}{r}
6 \\
3 \\
+7 \\
\end{array}
$$

Find the cost.

52.

53.

54.

55.

Mystery Triangle

Write a different digit for each ● so that the sum of the numbers is 20. (There are several correct answers.)

Extra Practice—Set A, page 315

17

Addition (2-digit)

On a bike hike there were 13 boys and 24 girls. How many children went?

Charles E. Schmidt/Taurus

Add the ones.			Add the tens.		
T	O		T	O	
1	3		1	3	
+2	4		+2	4	
	7		3	7	

37 children went.

Exercises

1.	40 +36	2.	62 +16	3.	50 +20	4.	12 +83	5.	70 +10	6.	33 +15
7.	41 +37	8.	27 +62	9.	45 +43	10.	74 + 5	11.	34 +12	12.	27 +52
13.	10 +40	14.	46 +22	15.	65 +10	16.	30 + 9	17.	52 +14	18.	17 +61
19.	39 +60	20.	52 +17	21.	76 +10	22.	60 +20	23.	61 +34	24.	81 +18
25.	12 +83	26.	45 +21	27.	13 +56	28.	24 +34	29.	53 +41	30.	72 + 6

31. 52 +42	32. 34 +31	33. 62 + 5	34. 11 +18	35. 13 +63	36. 24 +75
37. 64 +33	38. 81 + 6	39. 47 +42	40. 85 +13	41. 73 + 6	42. 50 +36

43. They rode 15 miles before lunch and 12 miles after lunch. How far did they ride?

44. They passed 16 signs. There were 23 signs ahead. How many signs were there?

45. Diane brought $12. Mark brought $4 more than that. How much money did Mark bring?

46. There were 60 people in a club. Then 16 more joined. How many are in the club now?

47. 30 30 +30	48. 31 46 +21	49. 50 14 +24	50. 22 31 +14	51. 32 20 +16	52. 24 13 +52

53. Some bikers rode 14 miles on Monday, 21 miles on Tuesday, and 13 miles on Wednesday. How far did they ride in the 3 days?

54. There are 23 girls, 25 boys, and 21 parents in a biking club. How many people are in the club?

How Many Bikes?

There are 11 blue bikes. There are 3 times as many red bikes as blue bikes. There are 12 more green bikes than red bikes.

1. How many red bikes are there?

2. How many green bikes are there?

3. How many bikes are there in all?

Addition (2-digit)

Coreen made 14 masks. Alice made 18 masks. How many masks did they make?

Add the ones.	Add the tens.

```
   T O          T O
   [1]           1
   1 4          1 4      4
 + 1 8   + 8  + 1 8
     2    [1]2  3 2
```

They made 32 masks.

Exercises

1.	37 +46	2.	29 +44	3.	18 +36	4.	27 +67	5.	45 +25	6.	28 +44
7.	53 +19	8.	16 +47	9.	77 +18	10.	53 + 9	11.	15 +78	12.	59 +25
13.	38 +24	14.	42 +39	15.	29 +61	16.	14 +16	17.	63 + 8	18.	28 +36
19.	34 +37	20.	45 +15	21.	48 + 7	22.	65 +28	23.	49 +39	24.	16 +58

25. 45 +36	26. 72 + 9	27. 57 +14	28. 13 +59	29. 28 +34	30. 27 +47
31. 56 +26	32. 44 +49	33. 78 + 8	34. 67 + 5	35. 33 +38	36. 79 +18

37. Cindy spent 59¢ for a coin purse and 38¢ for a key case. How much did she spend in all?

38. Chen Chu used 24 white beads and 29 red beads. How many beads did she use in all?

39. Frank made 16 key cases one week and 18 the next. How many did he make altogether?

40. A wallet costs $7 and a purse costs $28 more than that. How much does the purse cost? How much do both cost?

41. 36 14 +45	42. 51 7 +33	43. 26 50 + 8	44. 49 25 +15	45. 40 29 +17	46. 54 16 +18

47. How many points did Karen make altogether?

48. How many points did the 3 pupils make in Round 1?

49. How many points did the 3 pupils make altogether?

Points

Pupil	Round 1	Round 2	Round 3
Karen	15	8	5
Tony	16	6	10
Kevin	4	11	9

What Is Missing?

1. 2 4 +6 ■ ‾‾‾‾ 9 3	2. ■ 6 +2 5 ‾‾‾‾ 5 ■	3. 1 7 +■ ■ ‾‾‾‾ 6 5	4. 2 ■ +■ 5 ‾‾‾‾ 8 0	5. 3 ■ +4 9 ‾‾‾‾ ■ 8

Subtraction Facts

Brent Jones

Hans had 17 cars. He gave 9 of them to Bernard. How many cars does Hans have left?

Here are two ways to find the answer.

Hans had ⟶ 17
He gave away ⟶ − 9
$17 - 9 = 8$ ⟵ He has left ⟶ 8

8 is called the **difference.**

Bernard gave back 5 cars. How many cars does Hans have now?

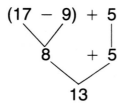

Work inside the
( ) first.

$$(17 - 9) + 5$$
$$8 \quad + 5$$
$$13$$

Exercises

1. $10 - 5 = \square$ 2. $13 - 7 = \square$ 3. $11 - 0 = \square$ 4. $14 - 8 = \square$

5. $16 - 7 = \square$ 6. $10 - 9 = \square$ 7. $13 - 5 = \square$ 8. $11 - 7 = \square$

9.
$$\begin{array}{r} 15 \\ -\ 6 \\ \hline \end{array}$$
10.
$$\begin{array}{r} 12 \\ -\ 7 \\ \hline \end{array}$$
11.
$$\begin{array}{r} 14 \\ -\ 9 \\ \hline \end{array}$$
12.
$$\begin{array}{r} 15 \\ -\ 7 \\ \hline \end{array}$$
13.
$$\begin{array}{r} 13 \\ -\ 6 \\ \hline \end{array}$$
14.
$$\begin{array}{r} 15 \\ -\ 9 \\ \hline \end{array}$$

15.	16.	17.	18.	19.	20.
12 − 5	14 − 7	10 − 0	11 − 5	16 − 8	16 − 9

21.	22.	23.	24.	25.	26.
14 − 6	12 − 6	15 − 8	10 − 6	17 − 8	18 − 9

27. Marta bought paper for 4¢. She paid for it with a dime. How much change did she get back?

28. A game cost $17. Les has $8. How much more money does Les need in order to buy the game?

29. Team A scored 14 points. Team B scored 5 points. Team A is how many points ahead?

30. Marilyn had 16 stamps. She used 9 of them. How many stamps does she have left?

31. $(13 - 7) + 3 = \square$ 32. $(6 + 9) - 9 = \square$ 33. $(12 - 8) - 4 = \square$

34. $(8 + 6) - 7 = \square$ 35. $(13 - 6) + 9 = \square$ 36. $(17 - 8) - 8 = \square$

37. Peggy had 9 model airplanes. She made 6 more. Then she gave 4 of them to her brother. How many does she have now?

38. Rod spent 9¢ from the 18¢ he had with him. Then he lost 2 pennies. How much money does he have now?

Looking Ahead

40 = 4 tens
3 tens + 1 ten
40 = 3 tens + 10 ones

36 = 3 tens + 6 ones
2 tens + 10 ones
36 = 2 tens + 16 ones

Can you rename these?

1. 24 = ___ ten + 14 ones

2. 78 = 6 tens + ___ ones

3. 59 = ___ tens + 19 ones

4. 67 = 5 tens + ___ ones

5. 81 = ___ tens + 11 ones

6. 40 = 3 tens + ___ ones

Subtraction (2-digit)

A truck driver is taking milk from Rockford to Chicago. The distance is 89 miles. He stops for lunch in Elgin. How far has he driven?

Subtract the ones.			Subtract the tens.	
T	O		T	O
8	9		8	9
−3	8		−3	8
	1		5	1

He has driven 51 miles.

The distance from Rockford to Chicago is 47 miles more than the distance from Rockford to Dixon. Explain how to find the distance from Rockford to Dixon.

Exercises

1.	19 − 9	**2.**	48 −13	**3.**	80 −30	**4.**	24 −10	**5.**	68 −45	**6.**	97 − 7
7.	57 −24	**8.**	73 −43	**9.**	97 −73	**10.**	85 − 4	**11.**	59 −28	**12.**	83 −83
13.	64 −23	**14.**	88 −45	**15.**	93 −60	**16.**	76 −65	**17.**	59 −27	**18.**	18 −10
19.	64 −33	**20.**	37 −37	**21.**	75 −50	**22.**	66 −56	**23.**	29 − 7	**24.**	82 −51

24

25. 37 − 5	26. 96 −43	27. 48 −21	28. 56 −34	29. 96 − 6	30. 78 −77
31. 98 −65	32. 89 −65	33. 68 −27	34. 59 −32	35. 47 −47	36. 85 − 4

37. Mr. Fahl sold 13 of his 97 chickens. How many did he have left?

38. Gertrude gathered 79 eggs on Thursday and 45 on Friday. How many more eggs did she gather on Thursday?

39. Joe has 56 milk cans to load on a truck. He just loaded 25 of them. How many does he still have to load?

40. Mrs. Farmer has 40 black cows. The rest are brown. She has 96 cows in all. How many brown cows does she have?

41. It is 38 miles from Chicago to Joliet. It is 58 miles from Chicago to Kankakee. How much farther is it from Chicago to Kankakee?

42. There are 35 gallons of water in a tank. You take out 15 gallons. Then you put 9 gallons back in. How much water is in the tank now?

Looking Ahead

73 = 7 tens + 3 ones

= 6 tens + 1 ten + 3 ones

= 6 tens + 13 ones

Rename these.

1. 56 = 4 tens + _____ ones

2. 82 = 7 tens + _____ ones

3. 45 = _____ tens + 15 ones

4. 91 = _____ tens + 11 ones

Subtraction (2-digit)

A lunch costs 75¢. Beth has only 58¢. How many more cents does she need for a lunch?

To subtract the ones, rename 75 as 6 tens and 15 ones.

Rename.	Subtract the ones.	Subtract the tens.
T O	T O	T O
6 15	6 15	6 15
7 5	7 5	7 5
−5 8	−5 8	−5 8
	7	1 7

Beth needs 17¢ more for lunch.

Exercises

1.   30
    −16

2.   73
    −25

3.   51
    −23

4.   44
    −15

5.   80
    −61

6.   73
    − 6

7.   53
    −29

8.   34
    − 7

9.   82
    −36

10.   95
    −77

11.   20
    − 4

12.   81
    −17

13.   50
    −25

14.   46
    −39

15.   61
    −26

16.   32
    − 7

17.   53
    −28

18.   60
    −32

19.   34
    − 8

20.   90
    −33

21.   42
    −18

22.   96
    −67

23.   41
    −24

24.   54
    −46

25.   72
    −24

26.   73
    −24

27.   51
    −19

28.   86
    −58

29.   23
    −17

30.   85
    − 8

| **31.** 70
$\underline{-17}$ | **32.** 92
$\underline{-29}$ | **33.** 65
$\underline{-46}$ | **34.** 84
$\underline{-\ 5}$ | **35.** 78
$\underline{-\ 9}$ | **36.** 77
$\underline{-59}$ |

37. 35 pupils went on a trip. Only 19 brought lunch. How many did not bring lunch?

38. Cal brought 97¢. He spent 88¢ on lunch. How much did he have left?

39. There are 54 math books and 39 science books. How many more math books are there than science books?

40. 20 pupils are needed to play softball. So far, only 9 have signed up to play. How many more pupils are needed?

41. How far is it from Camp to Boon?

42. To get from Dole to Ada, you can go through Boon or through Enid. Which way is shorter?

43. How much shorter is it?

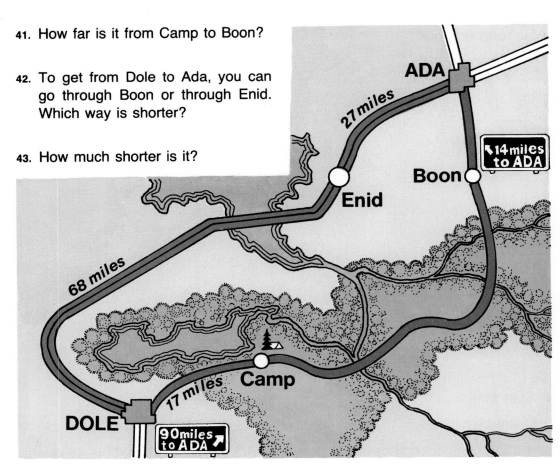

Extra Practice—Set A, page 316

Odds and Evens

even numbers

| 0 | 2 | 4 | 6 |

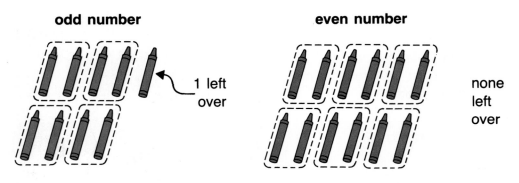

Ed Hoppe Photography

| 1 | 3 | 5 |

odd numbers

See what happens when you count by twos.

odd number

1 left over

even number

none left over

Exercises

Odd or even?

1.

2.

3.

4. Start with 0.

   Count by twos.

   Are the numbers odd or even?

5. Start with 1.

   Count by twos.

   Are the numbers odd or even?

28

6. Write the even numbers from 0 through 30.
   Look at the ones digits. Are they odd or even?

7. Write the odd numbers from 1 through 29.
   Look at the ones digits. Are they odd or even?

Odd or even?

8. 16   9. 30   10. 89   11. 100   12. 75

13. 212   14. 323   15. 642   16. 97   17. 476

18. 501   19. 1000   20. 1278   21. 5111   22. 4444

23. 23,517   24. 60,764   25. 219,510 26. 102,481 27. 999,999

Adding Makes It Happen

Both numbers are even.

1. 8   2. 20   3. 34   4. Are the sums
   +4   + 6   +12   odd or even?

Both numbers are odd.

5. 7   6. 15   7. 41   8. Are the sums
   +3   + 9   +25   odd or even?

One number is odd. The other is even.

9. 8   10. 11   11. 52   12. Are the sums
   +5   + 6   +17   odd or even?

Ordinals

OCTOBER						
Sun.	Mon.	Tue.	Wed.	Thur.	Fri.	Sat.
				1	2	3
4	5	6	7	8	9	10
11	12	13	14	15	16	17
18	19	20	21	22	23	24
25	26	27	28	29	30	31

The 6th day of every week is Friday.

The first of October is a Thursday.

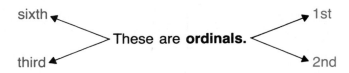

The 3rd day of every week is Tuesday.

The second of October is a Friday.

Exercises

Tell the ordinals for these days of a week.

1. Monday

2. Saturday

3. Tuesday

4. Wednesday

5. Sunday

6. Thursday

Name the dates for these days of October.

7. 2nd Saturday

8. 1st Wednesday

9. 4th Thursday

10. 3rd Sunday

11. 2nd Tuesday

12. 5th Friday

13. 4th Friday

14. 5th Saturday

15. 3rd Monday

30

You are riding west (◄—) on Broadway. Which avenue would you come to first?

16. 3rd or 5th

17. 7th or 4th

18. 10th or 12th

19. 2nd or 6th

20. 8th or 7th

21. 23rd or 25th

Suppose you are riding east (—►). Which avenue would you come to first?

22. 5th or 2nd

23. 3rd or 4th

24. 14th or 18th

25. 4th or 1st

26. 6th or 8th

27. 22nd or 26th

28. John was the 6th pupil to come into the room. How many pupils came in before John?

29. 10 pupils ran a race. Cheryl won 4th place. How many pupils ran slower than Cheryl?

Do You Know?

The discovery made on October 12th

Another name for October 31st

Which month of the year is October?

Number Patterns

What should the next picture show?   3, 13, 23, ___, ___

$+10 +10 +10$

What should the next picture show?   8, 6, 4, ___, ___

$-2 -2 -2$

Exercises

Complete each number pattern.

1. 47, 48, 49, ___, ___

2. 506, 507, 508, ___, ___

3. 93, 92, 91, ___, ___

4. 1703, 1702, 1701, ___, ___

5. 10, 12, 14, ___, ___

6. 304, 306, 308, ___, ___

7. 66, 64, 62, ___, ___

8. 106, 104, 102, ___, ___

9. 20, 25, 30, ___, ___

10. 85, 90, 95, ___, ___

11. 75, 70, 65, ___, ___

12. 1015, 1010, 1005, ___, ___

13. 70, 80, 90, ___, ___

14. 530, 520, 510, ___, ___

15. 40, 30, 20, ___, ___

16. 7005, 7015, 7025, ___, ___

Think of 2, 3, 5, 8, ___.

17. Can you find a pattern so the last number is 12?

18. Can you find a pattern so the last number is 13?

Addition-Subtraction Practice

Add or subtract. Watch the signs!

1. 5
   +6

2. 13
   − 9

3. 84
   −42

4. 9
   +5

5. 56
   +27

6. 14
   − 6

7. 54
   −27

8. 17
   − 9

9. 40
   +35

10. 57
    +26

11. 95
    −81

12. 8
    +7

13. 63
    + 6

14. 16
    − 8

15. 75
    +18

16. 42
    +54

17. 80
    −16

18. 56
    −33

19. 62
    −38

20. 6
    +4

21. 61
    −54

22. 13
    +72

23. 39
    +17

24. 12
    − 7

25. 48
    +46

26. 79
    − 8

27. 73
    −67

28. 9
    +9

29. 69
    +24

30. 81
    −67

31. 56
    −27

32. 35
    +24

33. 67
    + 9

34. 67
    −47

35. 36
    +59

36. 48
    −39

37. 45
    +25

38. 92
    −65

39. 27
    +27

40. 95
    −79

41. 70
    − 8

42. 18
    +68

43. Jane read 57 pages in a book. To complete the book, she needs to read 39 more pages. How many pages are in the book?

44. Jim has worked all but 7 of the 25 problems on a test. How many problems has he worked?

45. 41 pupils rode on Bus A. Only 19 pupils rode on Bus B. How many more pupils rode on Bus A than on Bus B?

46. You had 19¢. Then Mother gave you 45¢. Now you can buy a pen and have 9¢ left. How much does the pen cost?

CHAPTER REVIEW

Write the numeral.

1. 2 hundreds, 0 tens, 8 ones   2. 900 + 70 + 4

3. 3 thousands, 7 hundreds, 1 ten, 5 ones   4. 8000 + 10 + 6

5. 600,000 + 50,000 + 200 + 80   6. 40,000 + 3000 + 6

Write < or > for each ●.

7. 8 ● 5   8. 30 ● 40   9. 399 ● 401

10. 715 ● 709   11. 5082 ● 5081   12. 9132 ● 9098

Add.

13. 9   14. 56   15. 37   16. 68   17. 54   18. 27
    +7   +30   +19   + 6   +39   +28

Subtract.

19. 17   20. 89   21. 42   22. 80   23. 75   24. 83
    − 8   −29   −17   −43   − 6   −76

Odd or even?

25. 12   26. 231   27. 5703   28. 38,356

Name the following in this word: **encyclopedia**

29. 4th letter   30. 7th letter   31. 10th letter

Complete each number pattern.

32. 15, 17, 19, ___, ___   33. 83, 73, 63, ___, ___

2 Addition and Subtraction

Grant Heilman

Adding Three Numbers

What is the cost of all these items?

$$28 + 15 + 49 = \square$$

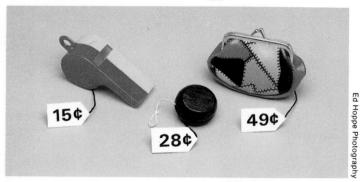

15¢

28¢

49¢

Ed Hoppe Photography

Add the ones. **Add the tens.**

The cost is 92¢.

Exercises

1.	15	2.	22	3.	13	4.	42	5.	31	6.	21
	30		41		20		11		24		52
	+43		+16		+45		+34		+24		+ 5

7.	15	8.	27	9.	19	10.	28	11.	8	12.	26
	23		25		7		15		37		36
	+60		+34		+12		+53		+49		+22

13.	14.	15.	16.	17.	18.
19	14	39	10	35	9
51	32	26	15	28	29
+20	+47	+18	+26	+33	+19

19. 30 + 23 + 14 = □   20. 16 + 14 + 20 = □   21. 38 + 6 + 41 = □

22. 10 + 15 + 29 = □   23. 46 + 38 + 12 = □   24. 61 + 18 + 7 = □

25. 35 + 28 + 17 = □   26. 4 + 29 + 18 = □   27. 68 + 12 + 19 = □

Find the cost.

28. Pen, Pencil, Crayons

29. Sharpener, Eraser, Ruler

30. Scissors, Pencil, Ruler

31. Pen, Pencil, Eraser

32. Crayons, Eraser, Ruler

33. Scissors, Sharpener, Ruler

34. Pen, Crayons, Sharpener

Price List

Scissors	....	59¢
Pen	....	35¢
Pencil	....	8¢
Crayons	....	43¢
Sharpener	....	21¢
Eraser	....	24¢
Ruler	....	16¢

35. Alan made scores of 24, 19, and 28 on three tests. What was his total score for all the tests?

36. Rita had 29¢. Then she got 40¢ for bottles. She still needs 26¢ to buy a ball. How much does the ball cost?

Try These

1.	2.	3.	4.	5.
1 5	3 3	1 5	4 0	4 4
2 2	2 4	8	1 7	1 9
3 8	1 7	2 1	1 8	3 3
+ 1 6	+ 2	+ 4 9	+ 3 2	+ 2 6
▪ ▪	▪ ▪	▪ ▪	▪ ▪ ▪	▪ ▪ ▪

Addition (3-digit)

Jack climbed up 279 feet on the bean stalk. Then he climbed up another 168 feet. How many feet did he climb up?

Add the ones.	Add the tens.	Add the hundreds.

```
    H T O                    H T O                    H T O
     ⬚1⬚                    ⬚1⬚ 1                   1 1
    2 7 9    9             2 7 9       1 T          2 7 9
  + 1 6 8  + 8           + 1 6 8       7 T        + 1 6 8
      7    1 7             4 7     + 6 T            4 4 7
                                  1 4 T
```

He climbed up 447 feet.

Exercises

1. 221	2. 543	3. 728	4. 493	5. 803
+385	+146	+ 31	+366	+187

38

6. 600
   +399

7. 619
   +237

8. 204
   +697

9. 589
   +236

10. 158
    + 8

11. 760
    +194

12. 639
    + 35

13. 124
    +286

14. 157
    +686

15. 630
    +280

16. 238
    + 65

17. 589
    +209

18. 259
    +351

19. 299
    +523

20. 203
    +482

21. 793
    +107

22. 395
    +345

23. 198
    +222

24. 699
    + 9

25. 159
    +774

26. 487
    +436

27. 674
    +263

28. 608
    +192

29. 408
    +480

30. 749
    + 65

31. 808
    +109

32. 257
    +487

33. 265
    +388

34. 388
    +389

35. 897
    + 6

36. 286 flights go to Utah, and 415 flights go to Colorado. How many flights are there?

37. There are 525 airmail letters and 388 airmail packages. How many pieces of mail are there?

38. One adult ticket costs $229. One student ticket costs $178. What is the cost for both?

39. 143 people will be on Flight 102. There will be 97 people more than that on Flight 336. How many people will be on Flight 336? How many people will be on both flights?

40. 256
    34
    +307

41. 173
    240
    +456

42. 307
    176
    +185

43. 190
    208
    +358

44. 83
    456
    +379

Rounding

32¢ is about 30¢
37¢ is about 40¢
Both cost about 70¢

Da-Ming **rounded** both numbers to the nearest ten.

Closer to 30 or to 40?

Closer to 30 or to 40?

Closer to 30 or to 40?

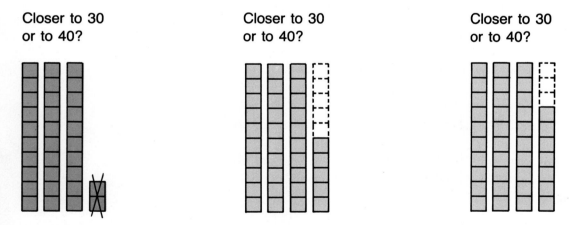

Here is an easy way to round to the nearest ten. Look at the *ones digit*.

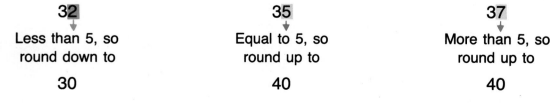

32
Less than 5, so round down to

30

35
Equal to 5, so round up to

40

37
More than 5, so round up to

40

To round to the nearest hundred, look at the *tens digit*.

446	450	483
Less than 5, so round down to	Equal to 5, so round up to	More than 5, so round up to
400	500	500

Exercises

Round to the nearest ten.

1. 33
2. 45
3. 18
4. 61
5. 9

6. 38
7. 15
8. 54
9. 82
10. 26

11. 75
12. 8
13. 11
14. 98
15. 79

Round to the nearest hundred.

16. 122
17. 574
18. 814
19. 250
20. 449

21. 115
22. 752
23. 278
24. 360
25. 943

26. 509
27. 649
28. 91
29. 825
30. 450

	Number	Round to the nearest hundred.	Round to the nearest ten.
31.	6485		
32.	23,652		
33.	140,753		

A score was rounded and given as 70.

34. What was the smallest score possible?

35. What was the largest score possible?

41

Estimating Sums

Guess the combined weight of the two monkeys.

A good guess is an **estimate.**

To estimate the sum of 48 and 33, round both numbers to the nearest 10. Then add the new numbers "in your head."

$$
\begin{array}{rlr}
48 & \text{—— is about ——} & 50 \\
+33 & \text{—— is about ——} & +30 \\
\hline
& \text{the sum is about ——} & 80
\end{array}
$$

The two monkeys weigh about 80 pounds.

Guess the combined weight of the two lions.

$$
\begin{array}{rlr}
485 & \text{—— to the nearest 100 ——} & 500 \\
+424 & \text{—— to the nearest 100 ——} & +400 \\
\hline
& \text{an estimate ——} & 900
\end{array}
$$

The two lions weigh about 900 pounds.

Exercises

Estimate each sum.

1. $\begin{array}{r} 32 \\ +17 \end{array} \longrightarrow \begin{array}{r} 3\ 0 \\ +\ 2\ 0 \\ \hline \blacksquare\ \ \blacksquare \end{array}$

2. $\begin{array}{r} 59 \\ +25 \end{array}$

3. $\begin{array}{r} 15 \\ +82 \end{array}$

4. $\begin{array}{r} 64 \\ +18 \end{array}$

5. $\begin{array}{r} 21 \\ +14 \end{array}$

6. $\begin{array}{r} 11 \\ +54 \end{array}$

7. $\begin{array}{r} 32 \\ +73 \end{array}$

8. $\begin{array}{r} 49 \\ +67 \end{array}$

9. $\begin{array}{r} 85 \\ +39 \end{array}$

10. $\begin{array}{r} 45 \\ +18 \end{array}$

11. $\begin{array}{r} 24 \\ +19 \end{array}$

12. $\begin{array}{r} 45 \\ +43 \end{array}$

13. $\begin{array}{r} 62 \\ +68 \end{array}$

14. $\begin{array}{r} 97 \\ +34 \end{array}$

15. $\begin{array}{r} 532 \\ +378 \end{array} \longrightarrow \begin{array}{r} 5\ 0\ 0 \\ +\ 4\ 0\ 0 \\ \hline \blacksquare\ \ \blacksquare\ \ \blacksquare \end{array}$

16. $\begin{array}{r} 155 \\ +611 \end{array}$

17. $\begin{array}{r} 230 \\ +250 \end{array}$

18. $\begin{array}{r} 787 \\ +139 \end{array}$

19. $\begin{array}{r} 481 \\ +320 \end{array}$

20. $\begin{array}{r} 673 \\ +142 \end{array}$

21. $\begin{array}{r} 496 \\ +378 \end{array}$

22. $\begin{array}{r} 225 \\ +175 \end{array}$

23. $\begin{array}{r} 680 \\ +120 \end{array}$

24. $\begin{array}{r} 533 \\ +240 \end{array}$

25. $\begin{array}{r} 724 \\ +149 \end{array}$

26. $\begin{array}{r} 387 \\ +493 \end{array}$

27. $\begin{array}{r} 561 \\ +276 \end{array}$

28. $\begin{array}{r} 99 \\ +150 \end{array}$

29. There are 37 boys and 44 girls. Estimate how many children there are.

30. He spent $399 for a ring and $513 for a necklace. Estimate how much he spent.

31. $\begin{array}{r} 691 \\ +\ 72 \end{array}$

32. $\begin{array}{r} 937 \\ +\ 57 \end{array}$

33. $\begin{array}{r} 553 \\ +\ 88 \end{array}$

34. $\begin{array}{r} 745 \\ +\ 65 \end{array}$

35. $\begin{array}{r} 487 \\ +\ 24 \end{array}$

Can You Estimate These?

1. $\begin{array}{r} 37 \\ 45 \\ +14 \end{array}$

2. $\begin{array}{r} 97 \\ 45 \\ 96 \\ +47 \end{array}$

3. $\begin{array}{r} 324 \\ 324 \\ +137 \end{array}$

4. $\begin{array}{r} 352 \\ 343 \\ +347 \end{array}$

Calculator Addition

A calculator cannot solve problems by itself. It can only do what you tell it to do. By pushing keys in the proper order, you can tell a calculator to add two numbers like 157 and 482.

Push the keys in this order.	The display will show this.
C	0
1 5 7	157
+	157
4 8 2	482
=	639

Ed Hoppe Photography

Estimate each sum. Then find the sum with a calculator.

1. 83 +37	**2.** 97 +42	**3.** 302 +477	**4.** 644 +267	**5.** 178 +608
6. 718 +189	**7.** 532 +378	**8.** 870 + 44	**9.** 394 +488	**10.** 423 +298
11. 607 + 86	**12.** 586 +307	**13.** 711 +279	**14.** 478 +492	**15.** 431 + 77

Use a calculator to find each sum. Then turn the calculator upside down to find the word for each blank.

16. The _____ said, " _____ my _____ ."
19,908 + 15,101   6888 + 220   187 + 806

17. _____ ate the _____ and left the _____ .
6 + 28   894 + 99   222,333 + 77,123,660

44

SKILLS REVIEW

Write the numeral.

1. 5000 + 700 + 20 + 8

2. 800 + 6

3. 2000 + 900 + 1

4. 3000 + 40 + 7

5. 300,000 + 2000 + 10

6. 40,000 + 900

Write < or > for each ●.

7. 28 ● 31

8. 71 ● 69

9. 598 ● 612

10. 513 ● 499

11. 7142 ● 7139

12. 3999 ● 4001

Odd or even?

13. 16

14. 100

15. 2465

16. 4998

Subtract.

17. 80
   −30

18. 66
   − 4

19. 90
   −77

20. 36
   −19

21. 85
   −27

22. 92
   −89

23. 77
   −76

24. 90
   −24

25. 74
   −38

26. 81
   −35

27. 79
   −69

28. 63
   −36

29. A bank is 78 feet tall. A drugstore is 59 feet tall. How much taller is the bank?

30. Tammy mowed 18 lawns in June and 25 lawns in July. How many lawns did she mow?

31. A pen costs 64¢. Sean has 29¢. How much more does he need to buy the pen?

32. You buy a 37¢ marker. You give the clerk 50¢. How much change should you get?

Subtraction (3-digit)

354 pupils attend this school. Only 172 of the pupils are going on a field trip. How many pupils are not going?

Subtract the ones.	Rename.	Subtract the tens.	Subtract the hundreds.

H	T	O
3	5	4
−1	7	2
		2

	2	15
3	5	4
−1	7	2
		2

	2	15
3	5	4
−1	7	2
	8	2

	2	15
3	5	4
−1	7	2
1	8	2

Rename 3 hundreds, 5 tens as 2 hundreds, 15 tens.

182 pupils are not going.

Exercises

1. $\begin{array}{r} 800 \\ -600 \\ \hline \end{array}$
2. $\begin{array}{r} 413 \\ -140 \\ \hline \end{array}$
3. $\begin{array}{r} 702 \\ -201 \\ \hline \end{array}$
4. $\begin{array}{r} 492 \\ -339 \\ \hline \end{array}$
5. $\begin{array}{r} 847 \\ -\ 61 \\ \hline \end{array}$

6. $\begin{array}{r} 713 \\ -452 \\ \hline \end{array}$
7. $\begin{array}{r} 674 \\ -158 \\ \hline \end{array}$
8. $\begin{array}{r} 487 \\ -\ 29 \\ \hline \end{array}$
9. $\begin{array}{r} 570 \\ -430 \\ \hline \end{array}$
10. $\begin{array}{r} 632 \\ -324 \\ \hline \end{array}$

11. 949
    −578

12. 296
    − 41

13. 839
    −779

14. 436
    −345

15. 811
    − 7

16. 250
    −129

17. 781
    − 56

18. 263
    −136

19. 924
    −318

20. 243
    − 35

21. 369
    −175

22. 653
    −471

23. 727
    − 8

24. 885
    −695

25. 924
    −644

26. 607
    −564

27. 309
    − 27

28. 820
    −507

29. 440
    −435

30. 911
    −291

31. 484 pupils attend Gingerwood School. There are 276 girls. How many boys are there?

32. 130 pupils are 9 years old, and 114 pupils are 8 years old. How many more are 9 years old?

33. Our class collected 306 cans. The other class collected 12 cans less than that. How many did the other class collect?

34. 555 tickets were printed. Only 185 tickets were sold. How many were not sold?

35. How much does the father weigh?

36. How much does the girl weigh?

37. How much does the mother weigh?

38. If the mother and father got on the scale, what would the reading be?

Extra Practice—Set B, page 318

47

Subtraction (3-digit)

Bowling Scores

Mrs. Valdez	214
Juan Valdez	136

By how many pins did Mrs. Valdez win the game?

Rename and subtract the ones.	**Rename and subtract the tens.**	**Subtract the hundreds.**
H|T|O	H|T|O	H|T|O
0 14	10	10
2 1̸ 4̸	1 0̸ 14	1 0̸ 14
− 1 3 6	2̸ 1̸ 4̸	2̸ 1̸ 4̸
8	− 1 3 6	− 1 3 6
	7 8	7 8

Mrs. Valdez won by 78 pins.

The best score you can get is 300. By how many pins did Mrs. Valdez miss that score?

```
  2 10              9                9
               2 1̶0̶ 10          2 1̶0̶ 10
  3̸ 0̸ 0          3̸ 0̸ 0̸          3̸ 0̸ 0̸
− 2 1 4        − 2 1 4          − 2 1 4
                                  8 6
```

How is 300 renamed?

Why is 300 renamed first?

How is 10 tens renamed?

Why is 10 tens renamed?

How is the answer found?

48

Exercises

1. 750
   − 275

2. 312
   − 134

3. 520
   − 475

4. 200
   − 126

5. 941
   − 78

6. 648
   − 259

7. 400
   − 326

8. 632
   − 393

9. 900
   − 452

10. 504
    − 487

11. 573
    − 175

12. 624
    − 359

13. 367
    − 78

14. 801
    − 492

15. 410
    − 136

16. 842
    − 365

17. 917
    − 128

18. 654
    − 279

19. 500
    − 492

20. 672
    − 195

21. 301
    − 3

22. 605
    − 378

23. 802
    − 619

24. 540
    − 248

25. 230
    − 136

26. 800
    − 249

27. 526
    − 197

28. 100
    − 87

29. 536
    − 438

30. 700
    − 635

There are 834 beans in the jar.

31. Who should get first prize?

32. By how many beans did that person miss?

33. Who should get third prize?

34. Who made the poorest guess?

35. By how many beans did that person miss?

36. Bob's guess was how many beans closer to 834 than Nancy's guess?

Guess how many beans are in the jar. →

NAME	GUESS
Cindy	765
Kevin	819
Nancy	799
Jack	867
Bob	850

49

Checking Subtraction

Jim had a roll of 50 pennies. He used 12 for a pen. How many were left?

Later he put back 12 pennies. Did that fill the roll?

Subtract	Check
50	38
−12	+12
38	50

Here is a shorter way to check subtraction.

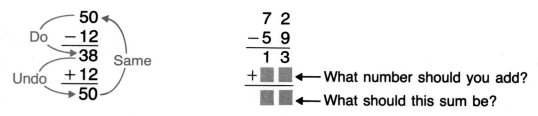

Do
50
−12
38
Undo
+12
50
Same

7 2
−5 9
1 3
+ ■ ■ ←— What number should you add?
■ ■ ←— What should this sum be?

Exercises

Subtract and check.

1.
  4 7
− 2 4
■ ■
+ 2 4
■ ■

2.
  67
−46

3.
  59
−23

4.
  75
−31

5.
  25
−12

6.
  92
−57

7.
  61
−34

8.
  50
−25

9.
  80
−15

10.
  1 0 0
− 8 6
■ ■
+ 8 6
■ ■ ■

11.
  230
−191

12.
  452
−371

13.
  407
− 32

14.
  900
−384

15.
  868
−379

16.
  254
−127

17.
  200
− 9

18.
  650
−322

19. 800
      − 269

20. 776
      − 288

21. 193
       − 27

22. 482
      − 396

23. 500
      − 263

Look at the four sentences at the right. Notice that the same three numbers are used in each sentence.

The four sentences make up a **family.**

$$136 + 89 = 225$$
$$225 − 89 = 136$$
$$89 + 136 = 225$$
$$225 − 136 = 89$$

Write a numeral for each □.

24. $74 + 97 = □$

25. $171 − 97 = □$

26. $97 + □ = 171$

27. $171 − □ = 97$

28. $116 + □ = 205$

29. $205 − 89 = □$

30. $□ + 116 = 205$

31. $□ − 116 = 89$

32. $□ + 289 = 587$

33. $587 − 289 = □$

34. $□ + 298 = 587$

35. $587 − □ = 289$

36. The sum of two numbers is 600. One of the numbers is 368. Find the other number.

37. When you subtract this number from 75, you get 56. Find the number.

38. When you subtract 17 from this number, you get 296. Find the number.

39. The difference between two numbers is 88. One of the numbers is 34. Find the other number.

Who Am I?

1. I am the smallest number in my family. The other two are 75 and 68.

2. I am the largest number in my family. The other two are 489 and 498.

Extra Practice—Set A, page 319   51

Estimating Differences

About how many more records were sold on Monday than on Tuesday?

To estimate the difference between 85 and 57, round both numbers. Then subtract the new numbers.

Records Sold	
Monday	85
Tuesday	57
Wednesday	71

$$85 \longrightarrow \text{to the nearest 10} \longrightarrow 90$$
$$-57 \longrightarrow \text{to the nearest 10} \longrightarrow -60$$
$$\text{an estimate} \longrightarrow 30$$

About 30 more records were sold on Monday.

425 records must be put in order. So far, 287 are in order. Estimate how many records are left to put in order.

$$425 \longrightarrow \text{to the nearest 100} \longrightarrow 400$$
$$-287 \longrightarrow \text{to the nearest 100} \longrightarrow -300$$
$$\text{an estimate} \longrightarrow 100$$

About 100 records are left.

Exercises

Estimate each difference.

1. $\begin{array}{r} 68 \\ -44 \\ \hline \end{array} \longrightarrow \begin{array}{r} 7\,0 \\ -4\,0 \\ \hline \blacksquare\ \blacksquare \end{array}$

2. $\begin{array}{r} 41 \\ -29 \\ \hline \end{array}$

3. $\begin{array}{r} 82 \\ -15 \\ \hline \end{array}$

4. $\begin{array}{r} 72 \\ -59 \\ \hline \end{array}$

5. $\begin{array}{r} 92 \\ -34 \\ \hline \end{array}$

6. $\begin{array}{r} 28 \\ -11 \\ \hline \end{array}$

7. $\begin{array}{r} 43 \\ -22 \\ \hline \end{array}$

8. $\begin{array}{r} 68 \\ -59 \\ \hline \end{array}$

9. $\begin{array}{r} 87 \\ -63 \\ \hline \end{array}$

10. $\begin{array}{r} 55 \\ -24 \\ \hline \end{array}$

11. $\begin{array}{r} 76 \\ -33 \\ \hline \end{array}$

12. $\begin{array}{r} 82 \\ -49 \\ \hline \end{array}$

13. $\begin{array}{r} 63 \\ -58 \\ \hline \end{array}$

14. $\begin{array}{r} 81 \\ -57 \\ \hline \end{array}$

15. 593 → 600
    −238   −200
    ▪▪▪

16. 321
    −182

17. 775
    −425

18. 607
    −290

19. 426
    −172

20. 339
    −203

21. 930
    −120

22. 578
    −255

23. 621
    −613

24. 651
    −449

25. 350
    −150

26. 896
    −619

27. 468
    −389

28. 223
    −190

29. José had $91. Then he spent $38. Estimate how much he had left.

30. A trip is 663 miles long. So far we have gone 358 miles. Estimate how much farther we have to go.

31. 492
    − 28

32. 734
    − 53

33. 281
    − 49

34. 537
    − 64

35. 121
    − 46

36. How many tickets were sold?

37. Estimate how many tickets are still in the roll.

800 tickets

Extra Practice—Set B, page 319   53

Calculator Subtraction

A calculator isn't intelligent; you are. You do the thinking and let the calculator do the work.

Here is how to tell the calculator to subtract 487 from 725.

Push the keys in this order.	The display will show this.
C	0
7 2 5	725
−	725
4 8 7	487
=	238

Estimate each difference. Then find the difference with a calculator.

1. 97
 −69

2. 52
 −17

3. 840
 −398

4. 421
 −179

5. 687
 −408

6. 714
 − 75

7. 865
 −239

8. 742
 −156

9. 603
 −594

10. 230
 − 90

11. 471
 −294

12. 740
 −408

13. 525
 − 32

14. 693
 −309

15. 809
 − 89

Use a calculator to find each difference. Then turn the calculator upside down to find the word for each blank.

16. Why $\dfrac{}{100 - 49}$ $\dfrac{}{5837 - 299}$ sleeping under an $\dfrac{}{1000 - 290}$ tank?

17. $\dfrac{}{595 - 250}$ wants to $\dfrac{}{76 - 38}$ up $\dfrac{y}{803 - 93}$ in the morning.

54

Addition-Subtraction Practice

Add or subtract. Watch the signs!

1. $\begin{array}{r} 345 \\ +198 \end{array}$	2. $\begin{array}{r} 906 \\ +\ 87 \end{array}$	3. $\begin{array}{r} 666 \\ -385 \end{array}$	4. $\begin{array}{r} 591 \\ -287 \end{array}$	5. $\begin{array}{r} 600 \\ -312 \end{array}$
6. $\begin{array}{r} 720 \\ +180 \end{array}$	7. $\begin{array}{r} 470 \\ -324 \end{array}$	8. $\begin{array}{r} 809 \\ -222 \end{array}$	9. $\begin{array}{r} 788 \\ +199 \end{array}$	10. $\begin{array}{r} 734 \\ -\ 38 \end{array}$
11. $\begin{array}{r} 563 \\ -247 \end{array}$	12. $\begin{array}{r} 499 \\ +\ 9 \end{array}$	13. $\begin{array}{r} 518 \\ -429 \end{array}$	14. $\begin{array}{r} 625 \\ +285 \end{array}$	15. $\begin{array}{r} 720 \\ -207 \end{array}$
16. $\begin{array}{r} 700 \\ -521 \end{array}$	17. $\begin{array}{r} 436 \\ -429 \end{array}$	18. $\begin{array}{r} 307 \\ +370 \end{array}$	19. $\begin{array}{r} 421 \\ -\ 59 \end{array}$	20. $\begin{array}{r} 341 \\ +599 \end{array}$
21. $\begin{array}{r} 867 \\ -866 \end{array}$	22. $\begin{array}{r} 678 \\ -158 \end{array}$	23. $\begin{array}{r} 400 \\ -\ 8 \end{array}$	24. $\begin{array}{r} 399 \\ +111 \end{array}$	25. $\begin{array}{r} 945 \\ -376 \end{array}$
26. $\begin{array}{r} 433 \\ +367 \end{array}$	27. $\begin{array}{r} 300 \\ -188 \end{array}$	28. $\begin{array}{r} 470 \\ -353 \end{array}$	29. $\begin{array}{r} 805 \\ +\ 98 \end{array}$	30. $\begin{array}{r} 203 \\ -144 \end{array}$
31. $\begin{array}{r} 602 \\ -\ 5 \end{array}$	32. $\begin{array}{r} 507 \\ +207 \end{array}$	33. $\begin{array}{r} 500 \\ -355 \end{array}$	34. $\begin{array}{r} 948 \\ -888 \end{array}$	35. $\begin{array}{r} 540 \\ +180 \end{array}$
36. $\begin{array}{r} 532 \\ +369 \end{array}$	37. $\begin{array}{r} 600 \\ -579 \end{array}$	38. $\begin{array}{r} 766 \\ -\ 68 \end{array}$	39. $\begin{array}{r} 259 \\ +678 \end{array}$	40. $\begin{array}{r} 404 \\ -197 \end{array}$
41. $\begin{array}{r} 34 \\ 34 \\ +24 \end{array}$	42. $\begin{array}{r} 17 \\ 28 \\ +39 \end{array}$	43. $\begin{array}{r} 56 \\ 9 \\ +21 \end{array}$	44. $\begin{array}{r} 490 \\ 77 \\ +139 \end{array}$	45. $\begin{array}{r} 8 \\ 607 \\ +\ 99 \end{array}$

Solving Problems

1. What is the cost of the apples and 1 orange?

2. What is the cost of 3 oranges?

3. The cereal costs how much more than the beans? Check your answer.

4. Round each cost in the picture to the nearest 10 cents.

5. Estimate how much more the noodles cost than the crackers. Then subtract to find out how much more.

6. Estimate the cost of the crackers and 1 can of soup. Then find the actual cost.

7. Find the total weight of the sand and the bricks.

8. The water is heavier than the bricks. Find how much heavier. Check your answer.

9. What is the weight of 2 bags of cement?

10. Round each weight to the nearest 100 pounds.

11. Estimate the total weight of the bricks and the water.

12. The sand is heavier than the bricks. Estimate how much heavier.

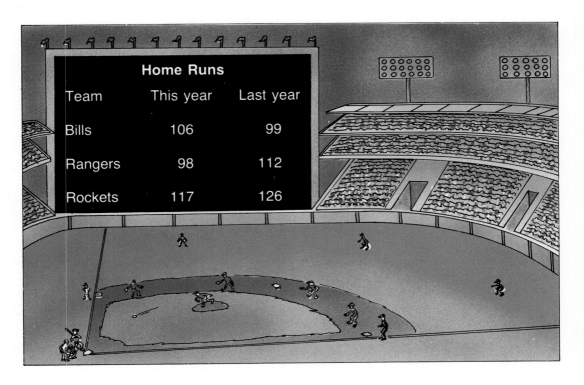

Home Runs		
Team	This year	Last year
Bills	106	99
Rangers	98	112
Rockets	117	126

13. How many more home runs did the Rockets hit last year than this year?

14. How many home runs did the Rangers hit in the 2 years?

15. Did the Bills or the Rockets hit fewer home runs last year? How many fewer?

16. The Bills wanted to hit 130 home runs this year. They missed that goal by how many home runs?

17. "Spanky" Spellman hit 28 home runs for the Rockets this year. How many home runs were hit by the rest of the team?

18. Two years ago the Bills hit 25 more home runs than they hit last year. How many home runs did they hit two years ago?

19. How many home runs did the 3 teams hit this year?

20. How many home runs did the 3 teams hit last year?

21. How many more home runs did the 3 teams hit last year than this year?

22. Which two teams were closest in the number of home runs they hit this year?

CHAPTER REVIEW

Add.

1. 15
    46
  + 19

2. 28
    27
  + 25

3. 507
  + 216

4. 678
  + 32

5. 467
  + 486

Round to the nearest ten.

6. 28   7. 7   8. 99   9. 65

Round to the nearest hundred.

10. 387   11. 226   12. 450   13. 908

Estimate each sum or difference.

14. 538
   + 329

15. 118
   + 662

16. 391
   − 99

17. 752
   − 367

18. 406
   − 239

Subtract.

19. 228
   − 163

20. 436
   − 18

21. 752
   − 367

22. 406
   − 239

23. 700
   − 248

Subtract and check.

24. 86
   − 27

25. 90
   − 21

26. 784
   − 696

27. 800
   − 92

28. 444
   − 148

29. 188 girls and 235 boys went to summer camp. How many children went to camp?

30. 504 pupils go to Adams School. Today 26 pupils are absent. How many pupils are in school?

3 Multiplication

L.L.T. Rhodes/Taurus

Multiplication Facts

To find how many, you can *add* or *multiply*.

By adding

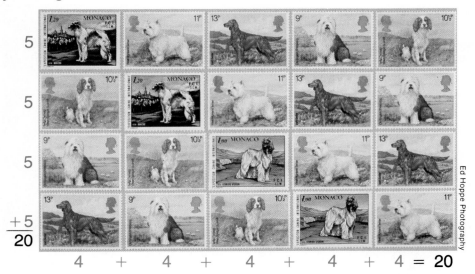

5
5
5
+5
20

4 + 4 + 4 + 4 + 4 = 20

By multiplying

4 rows of 5   5 columns of 4

$4 \times 5 = 20$ $5 \times 4 = 20$

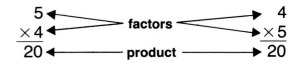

5
×4   factors   4
20   product   ×5
               20

There are 20 stamps.

Exercises

1. $1 \times 4 = \square$ 2. $8 \times 1 = \square$ 3. $0 \times 6 = \square$ 4. $7 \times 0 = \square$

5. $7 \times 1 = \square$ 6. $0 \times 9 = \square$ 7. $1 \times 9 = \square$ 8. $1 \times 0 = \square$

60

9. 7
×2

10. 2
×7

11. 2
×8

12. 8
×2

13. 9
×2

14. 2
×9

15. 3
×3

16. 3
×0

17. 4
×3

18. 3
×4

19. 5
×3

20. 3
×5

21. 6
×3

22. 7
×3

23. 3
×8

24. 8
×3

25. 3
×9

26. 9
×3

27. 4
×4

28. 1
×4

29. 4
×5

30. 6
×4

31. 7
×4

32. 4
×8

33. 9
×4

34. 4
×9

35. 5
×5

36. 0
×5

37. 6
×5

38. 7
×5

39. 5
×8

40. 9
×5

41. 6
×6

42. 6
×1

43. 6
×7

44. 7
×6

45. 8
×6

46. 6
×8

47. 9
×6

48. 6
×9

49. 7
×7

50. 7
×8

51. 8
×7

52. 9
×7

53. 7
×9

54. 8
×8

55. 8
×9

56. 9
×9

57. 9 players are on each team. There are 8 teams. How many players are there in all?

58. 8 people can sit in each row. How many people can sit in 8 rows?

59. Last week the Cubs scored only 9 runs. The Mets scored 4 times that many runs. How many runs did the Mets score?

61

Multiplication Table

×	0	1	2	3	4	5	6	7	8	9
0	0	0	0	0	0	0	0	0	0	0
1	0	1	2	3	4	5	6	7	8	9
2	0	2	4	6	8	10	12	14	16	18
3	0	3	6	9	12	15	18	21	24	27
4	0	4	8	12	16	20	24	28	32	36
5	0	5	10	15	20	25	30	35	40	45
6	0	6	12	18	24	30	36	42	48	54
7	0	7	14	21	28	35	42	49	56	63
8	0	8	16	24	32	40	48	56	64	72
9	0	9	18	27	36	45	54	63	72	81

Find 7 in the left column. Find 8 in the top row. Follow the arrows. Where do they meet?

$$7 \times 8 = 56$$

Find 8×7 in the table. Is $8 \times 7 = 7 \times 8$?

Exercises

1. Cards **A** and **E** have the same answer.
   Which other pairs of cards have the same answer?

A	**B**	**C**	**D**	**E**	**F**	**G**	**H**
4	9	9	6	5	7	6	8
×5	×6	×7	×8	×4	×9	×9	×6

Multiply.

2. 3
   ×7

3. 5
   ×7

4. 2
   ×8

5. 0
   ×9

6. 6
   ×8

7. 3
   ×1

8. 1
   ×8

9. 9
   ×7

10. 7
    ×4

11. 1
    ×1

12. 8
    ×0

13. 6
    ×9

14. 7
   ×3

15. 6
   ×1

16. 5
   ×5

17. 8
   ×9

18. 4
   ×6

19. 7
   ×8

20. 4
   ×4

21. 0
   ×2

22. 9
   ×3

23. 5
   ×8

24. 5
   ×6

25. 8
   ×5

26. 5
   ×0

27. 4
   ×7

28. 8
   ×6

29. 4
   ×9

30. 7
   ×7

31. 7
   ×6

32. 9
   ×9

33. 4
   ×8

34. 6
   ×3

35. 6
   ×6

36. 0
   ×7

37. 3
   ×2

38. 1
   ×9

39. 8
   ×8

40. 5
   ×9

41. 6
   ×7

42. 7
   ×5

43. 9
   ×6

44. 9
   ×8

45. 6
   ×5

46. 8
   ×4

47. 0
   ×6

48. 8
   ×7

49. 7
   ×9

Here are two ways to multiply 4, 2, and 3.

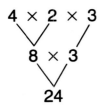

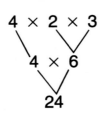

50. Are the answers the same?

51. Does it matter which two numbers you multiply first?

Multiply.

52. 1 × 2 × 3 = ☐

53. 5 × 1 × 2 = ☐

54. 5 × 0 × 6 = ☐

55. 2 × 2 × 2 = ☐

56. 3 × 3 × 3 = ☐

57. 0 × 9 × 8 = ☐

58. 4 × 2 × 5 = ☐

59. 6 × 4 × 2 = ☐

60. 9 × 3 × 3 = ☐

Multiplying 10's and 100's

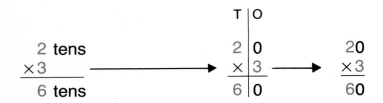

2 tens
×3
6 tens

	T	O
	2	0
×		3
	6	0

20
×3
60

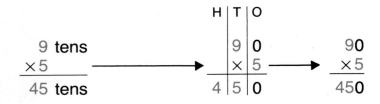

9 tens
×5
45 tens

H	T	O
	9	0
	×	5
4	5	0

90
×5
450

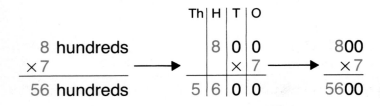

8 hundreds
×7
56 hundreds

Th	H	T	O
	8	0	0
		×	7
5	6	0	0

800
×7
5600

Exercises

1.   6 tens   ⟶   60
      ×3   ×3
     18 tens

2.   10
    ×8

3.   40
    ×7

4.   50
    ×3

5.   40
    ×1

6.   20
    ×2

7.   40
    ×3

8.   20
    ×6

9.   90
    ×2

10.   90
     ×3

11.   50
     ×7

12.   60
     ×6

13.   80
     ×5

14.   70
     ×9

| 15. | 30
×2 | 16. | 20
×4 | 17. | 30
×3 | 18. | 70
×1 | 19. | 10
×5 |

20. 6 hundreds → 600
      ×3   ×3
    18 hundreds

| 21. | 100
×8 | 22. | 400
×7 | 23. | 900
×2 |

| 24. | 300
×5 | 25. | 200
×3 | 26. | 300
×8 | 27. | 500
×4 | 28. | 200
×7 |

| 29. | 600
×5 | 30. | 800
×4 | 31. | 700
×6 | 32. | 700
×7 | 33. | 400
×9 |

| 34. | 900
×6 | 35. | 800
×8 | 36. | 500
×5 | 37. | 800
×9 | 38. | 900
×9 |

39. A store ordered 7 boxes of bolts. Each box had 20 bolts. How many bolts were ordered?

40. Each package of art paper has 100 sheets. How many sheets of art paper are in 9 packages?

Money Math

Complete the table.

	Number of dollars	Number of dimes	Number of pennies
	2	20	200
1.	7		
2.		40	
3.			500
4.	8		
5.	6		

Extra Practice—Set B, page 320

Multiplication (2-digit by 1-digit)

To find how many lights there are, you could add or multiply.

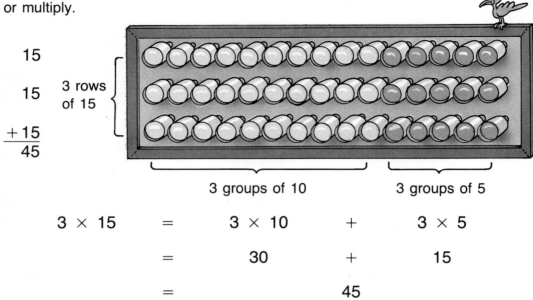

```
  15
  15    3 rows
+ 15    of 15
  45
```

3 groups of 10   3 groups of 5

$3 \times 15 \quad = \quad 3 \times 10 \quad + \quad 3 \times 5$

$= \quad 30 \quad + \quad 15$

$= \quad 45$

You can also do the multiplication this way.

Multiply the ones by 3.

```
  T │ O
  ⊡ │
  1   5      5
×     3    × 3
      5    ⊡ 5
```

Multiply the tens by 3.

```
  T │ O
  1─┐      1 ten
  1   5    × 3
×     3    3 tens
  4   5  + 1 ten
           4 tens
```

Exercises

1.	2.	3.	4.	5.	6.
12	11	13	14	15	21
×4	×7	×3	×2	×2	×4

7. 46
×2

8. 15
×4

9. 28
×3

10. 48
×2

11. 14
×7

12. 15
×6

13. 17
×5

14. 19
×5

15. 14
×5

16. 13
×5

17. 11
×8

18. 15
×5

19. 16
×4

20. 25
×3

21. 18
×5

22. 12
×8

23. 29
×3

24. 24
×4

25. 13
×7

26. 14
×6

27. 16
×5

28. 16
×6

29. 19
×4

30. 39
×2

31. You are carrying 4 boxes of rulers. Each box has 24 rulers. How many rulers are you carrying?

32. A radio costs $14. A clock radio costs 5 times that much. How much does a clock radio cost?

33. 10 cows and 15 chickens are in a barnyard. How many legs do they have in all?

34. Give three other combinations of cows and chickens that have that many legs in all.

How Much Money?

1. You have just enough money to buy 3 pencils and 2 rulers. How much do you have?

2. Lynn has enough money to buy 2 packs of paper. She does not have enough to buy 3 bottles of glue. How much does she have?

3. Jim has only dimes and nickels. He can buy 3 rulers. He does not have enough for 6 pencils. How much does he have?

Extra Practice—Set C, page 320

67

Multiplication (2-digit by 1-digit)

24 Cans   24 Cans   24 Cans   24 Cans   24 Cans

How many cans are in the 5 boxes?

Find the product like this.

Multiply the ones by 5.	**Multiply the tens by 5.**

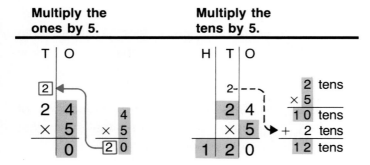

There are 120 cans.

Exercises

Complete.

1. 12 tens = ___ + 20

2. 17 tens = ___ + 70

3. 28 tens = ___ + 80

4. 45 tens = ___ + 50

Multiply.

5.	6.	7.	8.	9.	10.
17	25	39	42	71	26
×2	×4	×3	×4	×6	×6

11. 19 $\times 4$	12. 46 $\times 2$	13. 34 $\times 3$	14. 28 $\times 6$	15. 55 $\times 7$	16. 38 $\times 7$
17. 15 $\times 6$	18. 21 $\times 8$	19. 49 $\times 2$	20. 59 $\times 9$	21. 86 $\times 7$	22. 14 $\times 7$
23. 52 $\times 3$	24. 74 $\times 9$	25. 64 $\times 6$	26. 81 $\times 5$	27. 62 $\times 7$	28. 25 $\times 4$
29. 67 $\times 4$	30. 37 $\times 6$	31. 49 $\times 7$	32. 58 $\times 8$	33. 17 $\times 8$	34. 49 $\times 8$
35. 46 $\times 5$	36. 44 $\times 8$	37. 37 $\times 7$	38. 97 $\times 6$	39. 28 $\times 9$	40. 67 $\times 9$

41. 7 scout troops went camping. Each troop had 24 scouts. How many scouts went camping?

42. 86 scouts went on a hike. Each scout drank 3 cups of water. How much water did they drink altogether?

43. The scouts had 12 tents. Each tent needed 8 stakes. The scouts brought along 15 more stakes than they needed. How many stakes did they bring along?

What Is Missing?

1.
```
    4 ■
  ×   3
 ─────
  1 3 2
```

2.
```
  ■ 6
  × 4
 ─────
 1 0 4
```

3.
```
    8 3
  ×   ■
 ─────
  4 1 5
```

4.
```
    9 ■
  ×   7
 ─────
  6 7 2
```

5.
```
  ■ 0
  × 8
 ─────
 5 6 ■
```

6.
```
    5 7
  ×   ■
 ─────
  2 2 8
```

7.
```
  ■ 6
  × 6
 ─────
 9 6
```

8.
```
    9 ■
  ×   3
 ─────
  2 9 7
```

Extra Practice—Set A, page 321

69

Multiplication (3-digit by 1-digit)

A factory can make 130 yo-yos each hour. How many yo-yos can be made in 7 hours?

Multiply the ones by 7.	Multiply the tens by 7.	Multiply the hundreds by 7.

H	T	O
1	3	0
	×	7
		0

② →

H	T	O
1	3	0
	×	7
	1	0

3 T
× 7
②1 T

2- - - -

H	T	O
1	3	0
	×	7
9	1	0

1 H
× 7
7 H
+ 2 H
9 H

910 yo-yos can be made.

Exercises

1. 230
   ×2

2. 905
   ×1

3. 203
   ×4

4. 250
   ×3

5. 164
   ×4

6. 178
   ×2

7. 312
   ×3

8. 150
   ×5

9. 319
   ×2

10. 207
    ×4

11. 283 ×3	12. 400 ×2	13. 180 ×5	14. 196 ×5	15. 129 ×7
16. 309 ×3	17. 189 ×4	18. 119 ×8	19. 256 ×3	20. 171 ×5
21. 128 ×7	22. 154 ×6	23. 140 ×5	24. 102 ×9	25. 117 ×8
26. 247 ×3	27. 138 ×6	28. 137 ×7	29. 108 ×9	30. 678 ×1
31. 118 ×8	32. 127 ×6	33. 120 ×8	34. 106 ×7	35. 296 ×3

36. Last month Mr. Wong sold 125 yo-yos. This month he sold 6 times that many yo-yos. How many did he sell this month?

37. Yo-yos come in 5 colors. A store has 148 of each color. How many does the store have?

38. Ruby won a yo-yo contest. She was given $200 when she won and will get $125 a year for the next 6 years. How much money did she win in all?

39. 144 yo-yos come in a box. One store ordered 5 boxes and another store ordered 4 boxes. How many yo-yos were ordered by the 2 stores?

Who Am I?

1. I am an odd number between 254 and 261. Multiply me by 4 and the ones digit is 8.

2. I am an odd number between 117 and 126. Multiply me by 4 and the ones digit is 0.

3. I am a number between 70 and 75. Multiply me by 6 and the ones digit is 6.

4. I am a number between 152 and 156. Multiply me by 5 and the answer is an even number.

Multiplication (3-digit by 1-digit)

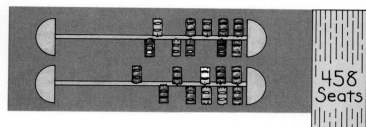
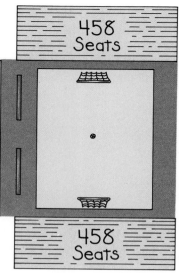

458 Seats

458 Seats

458 Seats

How many seats are in each section?

How many sections are there?

Let's find how many seats there are altogether.

Multiply the ones by 3.	Multiply the tens by 3.	Multiply the hundreds by 3.

H	T	O
	☐2	
4	5	8
	×	3
		4

H	T	O
☐1	2	
4	5	8
	×	3
	7	4

Th	H	T	O
	1	2	
	4	5	8
		×	3
1	3	7	4

$$\begin{array}{r} 4 \text{ H} \\ \times\,3 \\ \hline 1\,2 \text{ H} \\ +\ \ 1 \text{ H} \\ \hline 1\,3 \text{ H} \end{array}$$

There are 1374 seats altogether.

Exercises

Multiply.

1. 278
   ×3

2. 633
   ×2

3. 202
   ×8

4. 572
   ×4

5. 543
   ×9

6. 435
   ×6

7. 712
   ×7

8. 604
   ×4

9. 822
   ×8

10. 197
    ×3

72

11. 641
    ×2

12. 172
    ×8

13. 347
    ×7

14. 253
    ×9

15. 241
    ×4

16. 249
    ×7

17. 487
    ×6

18. 396
    ×2

19. 475
    ×6

20. 732
    ×5

21. 504
    ×8

22. 307
    ×4

23. 203
    ×8

24. 209
    ×7

25. 306
    ×6

26. 293
    ×7

27. 458
    ×9

28. 267
    ×5

29. 187
    ×7

30. 659
    ×8

31. 895
    ×5

32. 932
    ×6

33. 567
    ×4

34. 748
    ×8

35. 462
    ×9

Calculator Multiplication

To multiply 572 by 9 on a calculator,
do this.

Push the keys in this order.	The display will show this.
C	0
5 7 2	572
×	572
9	9
=	5148

Use a calculator to multiply these numbers.

1. 747
   ×4

2. 509
   ×8

3. 476
   ×6

4. 913
   ×5

5. 626
   ×7

6. 350
   ×3

7. 527
   ×6

8. 809
   ×9

9. 677
   ×8

Extra Practice—Set A, page 322

Solving Problems

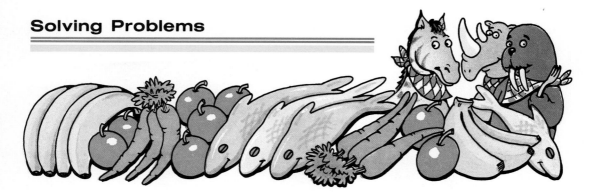

The table shows how much food is used at a zoo. Find the number of pounds of

Kind of food	Pounds used each week
Fish	130
Apples	260
Carrots	190
Bananas	875

1. apples used in 6 weeks

2. carrots used in 8 weeks

3. fish used in 7 weeks

4. bananas used in 4 weeks

5. How many more pounds of apples are used each week than carrots?

6. Derrick got 5 darts in the 50 ring. How many points was that?

7. André threw 4 darts. He got all of them in the 75 ring. How many points was that?

8. With 3 darts Gino got a bull's-eye and two 50's. How many points did he score?

9. 800 points are needed to win. Heidi threw 3 darts, and they all hit the bull's-eye. How many more points did she need to win?

watch
battery

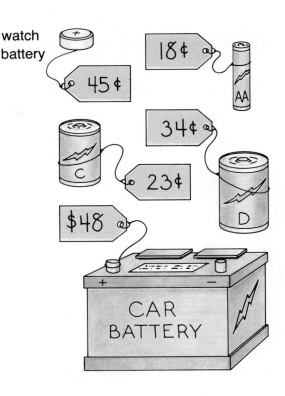

18¢ AA

34¢

45¢

23¢

C

D

$48

CAR
BATTERY

10. How much would 3 C batteries cost?

11. How much more does a D battery cost than a AA battery?

12. A flashlight should work for 18 hours on a set of batteries. How long should it work on 5 sets?

13. A car battery should last 3 years. How many days is that? (1 year is 365 days.)

14. You bought a battery for a watch and 2 AA batteries. How much did they cost?

15. Kathy bought 6 C batteries. Jeff bought 4 D batteries. Who spent more? How much more?

16. Mr. Kent wants to put new batteries in his 3 cars. How much will the batteries cost?

17. A watch should run for 18 months on 1 battery. How long should it run on 6 batteries?

18. A calculator used 4 AA batteries. How much would it cost to put new batteries in the calculator?

19. First-class postage was 8¢ an ounce in 1971. In 1981 it was 18¢ an ounce. How much more did it cost to mail a 4-ounce parcel in 1981 than in 1971?

20. An art teacher had 9 boxes of crayons and ordered 14 more boxes. Each box held 8 crayons. How many crayons did she have for art class?

21. Jane is 14 years old today. Her grandmother is 5 times that old. In what year was her grandmother born?

22. 84 tomatoes were in a basket. Mike took 3 dozen tomatoes out of the basket. How many were left in the basket? (1 dozen is 12.)

75

Add or subtract. Watch the signs!

1. 493
   +273

2. 91
   − 28

3. 113
   − 64

4. 26
   +97

5. 881
   + 73

6. 60
   − 27

7. 65
   +38

8. 759
   +149

9. 724
   − 526

10. 447
    +387

11. 202
    − 69

12. 900
    − 799

13. 32
    +78

14. 368
    +279

15. 730
    − 343

16. 804
    + 59

17. 433
    − 338

18. 525
    − 336

19. 653
    +247

20. 800
    − 146

21. Fay had 436 baseball cards. She bought 57 more. How many does she have now?

22. It is 943 miles from Denver to Chicago. Ms. Colbey left Denver for Chicago. She drove 476 miles. How far is she from Chicago?

23. How much do both TV's cost?

24. How much more does the color TV cost than the black-and-white TV?

25. Mr. Cable has $350. How much more does he need to buy the color TV?

Faster and Faster

The numeral with each picture tells the speed in **miles per hour** (mi/h).

Copy and complete.

Object	Miles traveled in		
	2 hours	5 hours	8 hours
Swimmer			
Runner			
Jackrabbit			
Train			
Plane			
Sound			

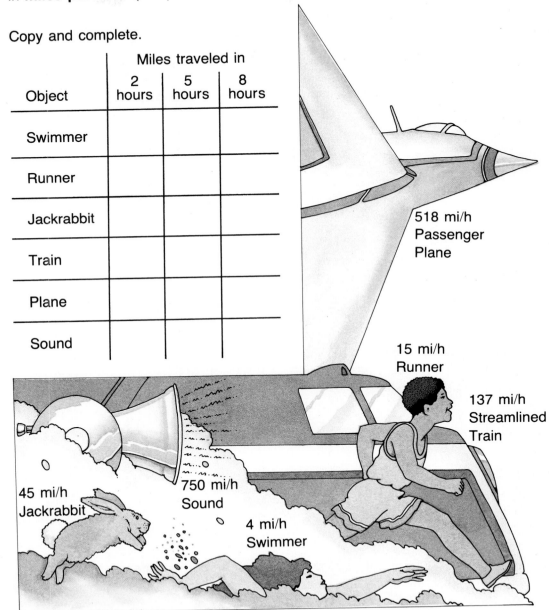

518 mi/h
Passenger
Plane

15 mi/h
Runner

137 mi/h
Streamlined
Train

45 mi/h
Jackrabbit

750 mi/h
Sound

4 mi/h
Swimmer

77

CHAPTER REVIEW

1. $5 \times 7 = \square$ 2. $6 \times 8 = \square$ 3. $4 \times 9 = \square$ 4. $7 \times 6 = \square$

5. 8
    $\times 8$

6. 7
    $\times 6$

7. 5
    $\times 9$

8. 7
    $\times 7$

9. 9
    $\times 9$

10. 4 people came in each car. There were 5 cars. How many people came?

11. Gina put 6 pictures in each row. She made 8 rows. How many pictures were there?

12. 10
    $\times 7$

13. 90
    $\times 6$

14. 100
    $\times 8$

15. 300
    $\times 3$

16. 700
    $\times 5$

17. 11
    $\times 9$

18. 32
    $\times 3$

19. 46
    $\times 2$

20. 25
    $\times 2$

21. 23
    $\times 4$

22. 35
    $\times 3$

23. 57
    $\times 6$

24. 68
    $\times 4$

25. 21
    $\times 9$

26. 46
    $\times 8$

27. A family spends $74 each week for food. How much does it spend for food in 4 weeks?

28. The 4th grade uses 3 rooms. There are 37 pupils in each room. How many 4th graders are there?

29. 110
    $\times 7$

30. 350
    $\times 2$

31. 113
    $\times 7$

32. 408
    $\times 2$

33. 241
    $\times 7$

34. 209
    $\times 5$

35. 348
    $\times 9$

36. 406
    $\times 3$

37. 279
    $\times 5$

38. 586
    $\times 4$

39. You are in school about 125 hours each month. How many hours are you in school in 9 months?

40. 319 pupils attend Meir School. Each pupil uses 6 books. How many books are needed?

78

4 Division

Division

12 apples are put into packages of 3 each.

4 packages

number of apples	divided by	number of apples in each group	is equal to	number of groups
12	÷	3	=	4

Twelve divided by three is equal to four.

Exercises

1. There are ___ grapes.

2. ___ grapes are in each group.

3. How many groups are there?

4. 18 ÷ 6 = ☐

5. There are ___ plums.

6. ___ plums are in each row.

7. How many rows are there?

8. 10 ÷ 5 = ☐

80

Write a division sentence to tell how many groups.

9.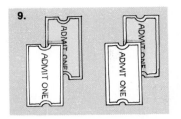

10.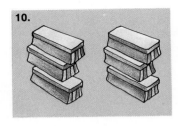

11.

12.

13.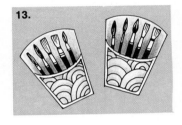

14.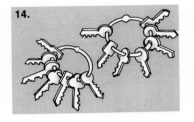

15.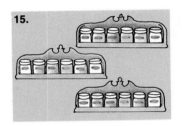

16.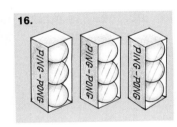

17.

18.

19.

20.

21.

81

Division

The same number of pigs will be put into each pen. You can use division to tell how many will be put into each pen.

number of pigs	divided by	number of pens	is equal to	number of pigs in each pen
12	÷	4	=	3

Exercises

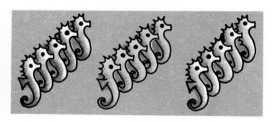

1. There are ___ turtles.

2. ___ groups have the same number.

3. How many are in each group?

4. 8 ÷ 2 = ☐

5. There are ___ sea horses.

6. ___ groups have the same number.

7. How many are in each group?

8. 15 ÷ 3 = ☐

Write a division sentence to tell how many in each group.

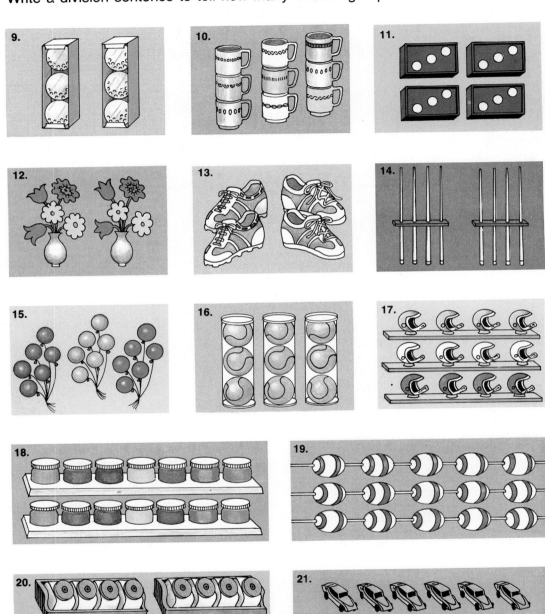

9.

10.

11.

12.

13.

14.

15.

16.

17.

18.

19.

20.

21.

Multiplication and Division

Join 3 groups of 5 each.

Separate 15 into groups of 5.

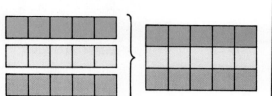 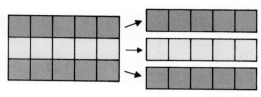

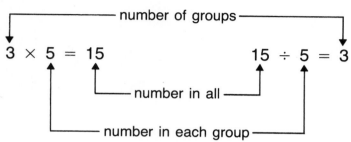

number of groups

$3 \times 5 = 15$ $15 \div 5 = 3$

number in all

number in each group

You can think of multiplication to help you do division.

Exercises

Write a numeral for each □.

1.

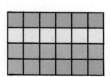

□ × 6 = 24   24 ÷ 6 = □

2.

□ × 9 = 27   27 ÷ 9 = □

3.

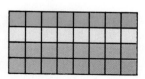

□ × 8 = 32   32 ÷ 8 = □

4.

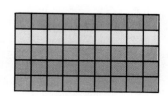

□ × 9 = 45   45 ÷ 9 = □

84

5. What do you notice about the three numbers used in each of the facts shown at the right?

The four facts make up a **family.**

$$4 \times 8 = 32$$
$$32 \div 8 = 4$$
$$8 \times 4 = 32$$
$$32 \div 4 = 8$$

Write a numeral for each □.

6. $5 \times 4 = \square$

7. $20 \div 4 = \square$

8. $4 \times 5 = \square$

9. $20 \div 5 = \square$

10. $2 \times 9 = \square$

11. $18 \div 9 = \square$

12. $9 \times 2 = \square$

13. $18 \div 2 = \square$

14. $3 \times 8 = \square$

15. $24 \div 8 = \square$

16. $8 \times 3 = \square$

17. $24 \div 3 = \square$

18. $7 \times 3 = \square$

19. $21 \div 3 = \square$

20. $\square \times 7 = 21$

21. $21 \div 7 = \square$

22. $4 \times 7 = \square$

23. $28 \div 7 = \square$

24. $\square \times 4 = 28$

25. $28 \div 4 = \square$

26. $6 \times 7 = \square$

27. $42 \div 7 = \square$

28. $\square \times 6 = 42$

29. $42 \div 6 = \square$

30. $\square \times 7 = 35$

31. $35 \div 7 = \square$

32. $\square \times 5 = 35$

33. $35 \div 5 = \square$

34. $\square \times 8 = 48$

35. $48 \div 8 = \square$

36. $\square \times 6 = 48$

37. $48 \div 6 = \square$

38. $\square \times 9 = 72$

39. $72 \div 9 = \square$

40. $\square \times 8 = 72$

41. $72 \div 8 = \square$

Multiplication–Division Families

1. The two smallest numbers in a family are 6 and 9. Find the other number.

2. The two largest numbers in a family are 56 and 8. Find the other number.

85

Division Facts

36 books are to be put into stacks of 4 books each. How many stacks will there be?

dividend ÷ divisor = quotient

$$36 \div 4 = \square$$

Think

How many 4's are in 36?

$$\square \times 4 = 36$$

$$9 \times 4 = 36, \text{ so } 36 \div 4 = 9.$$

There will be 9 stacks.

Jacqueline Durand

Exercises

Name the following for 48 ÷ 6 = 8:

1. dividend

2. divisor

3. quotient

Divide.

4. $8 \div 4 = \square$

5. $18 \div 2 = \square$

6. $18 \div 6 = \square$

7. $15 \div 5 = \square$

8. $16 \div 4 = \square$

9. $21 \div 3 = \square$

10. $21 \div 7 = \square$

11. $24 \div 3 = \square$

12. $9 \div 9 = \square$

13. $14 \div 7 = \square$

14. $12 \div 2 = \square$

15. $18 \div 3 = \square$

16. $6 \div 2 = \square$

17. $30 \div 5 = \square$

18. $28 \div 4 = \square$

19. $28 \div 7 = \square$

20. $6 \div 6 = \square$

21. $6 \div 1 = \square$

22. $36 \div 9 = \square$

23. $24 \div 4 = \square$

24. $27 \div 3 = \square$

25. $7 \div 1 = \square$

26. $20 \div 4 = \square$

27. $36 \div 6 = \square$

28. $32 \div 8 = \square$

29. $32 \div 4 = \square$

30. $7 \div 7 = \square$

31. $25 \div 5 = \square$

32. $40 \div 5 = \square$

33. $45 \div 9 = \square$

34. $45 \div 5 = \square$

35. $42 \div 6 = \square$

36. $42 \div 7 = \square$

37. $48 \div 6 = \square$

38. $9 \div 1 = \square$

39. $56 \div 7 = \square$

40. $56 \div 8 = \square$

41. $49 \div 7 = \square$

42. $48 \div 8 = \square$

43. $64 \div 8 = \square$

44. $54 \div 6 = \square$

45. $72 \div 8 = \square$

46. $63 \div 9 = \square$

47. $72 \div 9 = \square$

48. $81 \div 9 = \square$

49. 48 seats are in a music room. There are 8 seats in each row. How many rows are there?

50. 54 tickets were sold by 6 pupils. Each pupil sold the same number. How many tickets did each sell?

Don't Get Cornered!

Complete so that the "middle" number is the product of the "corner" numbers.

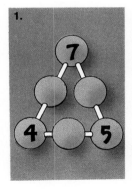

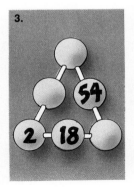

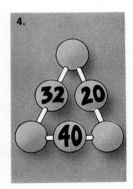

Using a Table

A multiplication table can be used to show division.

×	0	1	2	3	4	5	6	7	8	9
0	0	0	0	0	0	0	0	0	0	0
1	0	1	2	3	4	5	6	7	8	9
2	0	2	4	6	8	10	12	14	16	18
3	0	3	6	9	12	15	18	21	24	27
4	0	4	8	12	16	20	24	28	32	36
5	0	5	10	15	20	25	30	35	40	45
6	0	6	12	18	24	30	36	42	48	54
7	0	7	14	21	28	35	42	49	56	63
8	0	8	16	24	32	40	48	56	64	72
9	0	9	18	27	36	45	54	63	72	81

$$40 \div 8 = 5$$

Find 8 in the top row. Follow the red arrow down to 40. Then follow the blue arrow to the left.

$$40 \div 8 = 5$$ can be written as

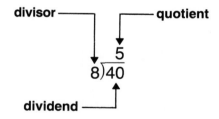

$$\overset{5}{8)\overline{40}}$$ is read "forty divided by eight is equal to five."

Exercises

Name the following for $\overset{6}{7)\overline{42}}$:

1. dividend

2. divisor

3. quotient

In these exercises the divisor is 1.

4. $1\overline{)2}$ 5. $1\overline{)8}$ 6. $1\overline{)6}$ 7. $1\overline{)5}$ 8. $1\overline{)9}$

9. When you divide any number by 1, what will the quotient be?

In these exercises the dividend is 0.

10. $5\overline{)0}$ 11. $2\overline{)0}$ 12. $7\overline{)0}$

13. When you divide 0 by some other number, what will the quotient be?

Divide.

14. $3\overline{)9}$ 15. $3\overline{)12}$ 16. $8\overline{)16}$ 17. $2\overline{)12}$ 18. $9\overline{)27}$

19. $1\overline{)1}$ 20. $9\overline{)9}$ 21. $1\overline{)7}$ 22. $3\overline{)21}$ 23. $6\overline{)0}$

24. $6\overline{)48}$ 25. $9\overline{)18}$ 26. $7\overline{)28}$ 27. $3\overline{)24}$ 28. $6\overline{)24}$

29. $7\overline{)63}$ 30. $8\overline{)56}$ 31. $5\overline{)25}$ 32. $9\overline{)36}$ 33. $7\overline{)49}$

34. $9\overline{)72}$ 35. $7\overline{)35}$ 36. $4\overline{)32}$ 37. $5\overline{)45}$ 38. $6\overline{)30}$

39. $6\overline{)54}$ 40. $3\overline{)0}$ 41. $9\overline{)81}$ 42. $6\overline{)42}$ 43. $8\overline{)64}$

44. There are enough eggs so that each camper can get 4 eggs. How many campers are there?

45. Only 6 campers want eggs. Each of them will get the same number of eggs. How many will each get?

Remainders

14 bottles of milk are put into boxes of 4 bottles each. How many boxes are there? How many bottles are left over?

You can also answer the questions by dividing 14 by 4.

Estimate the quotient.			Multiply and subtract.	Write the remainder.
Can I fill 1 box?	$1 \times 4 = 4$	Yes		
2 boxes?	$2 \times 4 = 8$	Yes	$$4\overline{)14} \atop \begin{array}{r} 3 \\ -12 \\ \hline 2 \end{array}$$	$$4\overline{)14} \atop \begin{array}{r} 3 \\ -12 \\ \hline 2 \end{array}$$ R2
3 boxes?	$3 \times 4 = 12$	Yes		
4 boxes?	$4 \times 4 = 16$	No		

The estimate is 3.

remainder (number left)

There are 3 boxes and 2 bottles left over.

Exercises

Write a digit for each ▦. Then write the remainder for each ☐.

$1 \times 6 = 6$
$2 \times 6 = 12$
$3 \times 6 = 18$
$4 \times 6 = 24$
$5 \times 6 = 30$
$6 \times 6 = 36$
$7 \times 6 = 42$
$8 \times 6 = 48$
$9 \times 6 = 54$

1. ▦ R☐
$$6\overline{)23} \atop \begin{array}{r} -18 \\ \hline 5 \end{array}$$

2. ▦ R☐
$$6\overline{)50} \atop \begin{array}{r} -48 \\ \hline 2 \end{array}$$

$1 \times 7 = 7$
$2 \times 7 = 14$
$3 \times 7 = 21$
$4 \times 7 = 28$
$5 \times 7 = 35$
$6 \times 7 = 42$
$7 \times 7 = 49$
$8 \times 7 = 56$
$9 \times 7 = 63$

3. ▦ R☐
$$7\overline{)11} \atop \begin{array}{r} -7 \\ \hline 4 \end{array}$$

4. ▦ R☐
$$7\overline{)29} \atop \begin{array}{r} -28 \\ \hline 1 \end{array}$$

5. ▦ R☐
$$7\overline{)34} \atop \begin{array}{r} -28 \\ \hline 6 \end{array}$$

6. ▦ R☐
$$7\overline{)68} \atop \begin{array}{r} -63 \\ \hline 5 \end{array}$$

7.
$$\frac{8}{5)47}$$
$$-40$$
$$\overline{7}$$

Are enough
5's subtracted?

7 is not the remainder.

8.
$$\frac{8}{5)45}$$
$$-40$$
$$\overline{5}$$

Are enough
5's subtracted?

5 is not the remainder.

9.
$$\frac{8}{5)42}$$
$$-40$$
$$\overline{2}$$

Are enough
5's subtracted?

2 is the remainder.

10. Can the remainder be larger than the divisor?

11. Can the remainder be equal to the divisor?

12. If you divide by 5, what do you know about the remainder?

Find the quotient and the remainder.

13. $3)\overline{11}$　　14. $2)\overline{13}$　　15. $6)\overline{24}$　　16. $8)\overline{45}$　　17. $6)\overline{8}$

18. $3)\overline{25}$　　19. $4)\overline{30}$　　20. $3)\overline{20}$　　21. $5)\overline{29}$　　22. $4)\overline{36}$

23. $9)\overline{70}$　　24. $9)\overline{16}$　　25. $5)\overline{8}$　　26. $8)\overline{21}$　　27. $7)\overline{17}$

28. $5)\overline{39}$　　29. $7)\overline{35}$　　30. $9)\overline{21}$　　31. $6)\overline{35}$　　32. $8)\overline{31}$

33. $9)\overline{38}$　　34. $8)\overline{56}$　　35. $6)\overline{43}$　　36. $5)\overline{43}$　　37. $7)\overline{41}$

38. $6)\overline{55}$　　39. $7)\overline{54}$　　40. $8)\overline{63}$　　41. $9)\overline{79}$　　42. $9)\overline{88}$

43. A room has 40 desks. You put them in as many rows of 7 each as possible. How many rows can you make? How many desks are left?

44. 60 pupils form teams of 9 players each. The rest of the pupils will keep score. How many teams are there? How many pupils will keep score?

SKILLS REVIEW

Subtract.

1.	2.	3.	4.	5.
64 −41	79 −38	56 − 8	42 −29	85 −76

6.	7.	8.	9.	10.
547 −236	233 −107	455 − 17	206 − 36	292 −286

11.	12.	13.	14.	15.
842 −654	308 −259	773 −498	400 − 72	600 −156

Multiply.

16.	17.	18.	19.	20.
10 ×8	30 ×4	60 ×7	200 ×4	700 ×5

21.	22.	23.	24.	25.
32 ×3	46 ×2	18 ×4	56 ×8	24 ×5

26.	27.	28.	29.	30.
421 ×2	130 ×4	305 ×3	107 ×9	118 ×4

31.	32.	33.	34.	35.
148 ×5	123 ×8	295 ×3	139 ×6	450 ×2

36. How much more does it cost to buy the 10-speed bicycle than the 3-speed bicycle?

37. How much would it cost to buy both bicycles?

38. 5 people each buy a 10-speed bicycle. How much do they spend in all?

3-speed $129

10-speed $178

Estimating the Tens Digit

3 pupils will share the money equally. About how much money will each pupil get?

To answer the question, think about dividing 84 by 3.

$$\begin{array}{c|c} \text{T} & \text{O} \\ \hline \blacksquare & \\ 3)\overline{8} & 4 \end{array}$$

Could each pupil get 1 dime?   1 ten $\times$ 3 = 30

Could each pupil get 2 dimes?   2 tens $\times$ 3 = 60

Could each pupil get 3 dimes?   3 tens $\times$ 3 = 90

Each pupil can get between 20¢ and 30¢.

Here is a fast way to estimate the tens digit.

3)8̄ is about 2.
Use 2 as the
tens digit.

5)6̄ is about 1.
Use 1 as the
tens digit.

2)7̄ is about 3.
Use 3 as the
tens digit.

Exercises

Estimate the tens digit.

1. 4)56̄   2. 2)76̄   3. 6)90̄   4. 4)80̄   5. 5)95̄

6. 3)69̄   7. 2)92̄   8. 4)88̄   9. 7)91̄   10. 3)72̄

Division (2-digit by 1-digit)

4 pupils will share 92 crayons equally. How many crayons will each pupil get?

You can use these steps to divide 92 by 4.

Estimate the tens digit.	Multiply and subtract.	Bring down the ones. Estimate the ones digit.	Multiply and subtract.

4)92
 	
4)9 is about 2.
Use 2 as the tens digit.
	T | O
	  2
	4)9 | 2
	−8
	  1
		T | O
		  2
		4)9 | 2
		−8 ↓
		  1 | 2
		
		4)12 is 3.
		Use 3 as the ones digit.
			T | O
			  2 | 3
			4)9 | 2
			−8
			  1 | 2
			 −1 | 2
			    0

Each pupil will get 23 crayons.

You can use these steps to divide 60 by 2.

Estimate the tens digit.	Multiply and subtract.	Bring down the ones. Estimate the ones digit.	Multiply and subtract.

2)60
 	
2)6 is 3.
Use 3 as the tens digit.
	T | O
	  3
	2)6 | 0
	−6
	  0
		T | O
		  3
		2)6 | 0
		−6 ↓
		    0
		
		2)0 is 0.
		Use 0 as the ones digit.
			T | O
			  3 | 0
			2)6 | 0
			−6
			    0
			  − 0
			    0

Exercises

Estimate the ones digit.

1.
$$\begin{array}{r} 1\blacksquare \\ 4\overline{)56} \\ -4 \\ \hline 16 \end{array}$$

2.
$$\begin{array}{r} 3\blacksquare \\ 2\overline{)76} \\ -6 \\ \hline 16 \end{array}$$

3.
$$\begin{array}{r} 1\blacksquare \\ 6\overline{)90} \\ -6 \\ \hline 30 \end{array}$$

4.
$$\begin{array}{r} 3\blacksquare \\ 3\overline{)90} \\ -9 \\ \hline 0 \end{array}$$

5.
$$\begin{array}{r} 1\blacksquare \\ 5\overline{)95} \\ -5 \\ \hline 45 \end{array}$$

Divide.

6. $4\overline{)56}$ 7. $3\overline{)72}$ 8. $5\overline{)60}$ 9. $4\overline{)64}$ 10. $2\overline{)36}$

11. $2\overline{)28}$ 12. $4\overline{)48}$ 13. $7\overline{)84}$ 14. $3\overline{)39}$ 15. $2\overline{)80}$

16. $8\overline{)96}$ 17. $3\overline{)42}$ 18. $5\overline{)85}$ 19. $7\overline{)91}$ 20. $5\overline{)75}$

21. $3\overline{)60}$ 22. $6\overline{)72}$ 23. $9\overline{)90}$ 24. $3\overline{)63}$ 25. $8\overline{)88}$

26. $2\overline{)28}$ 27. $3\overline{)87}$ 28. $7\overline{)98}$ 29. $3\overline{)90}$ 30. $4\overline{)52}$

31. There are 70 frankfurters. Each person will get 2 frankfurters. How many people are there?

32. 52 cards are in a deck. All cards are dealt to 4 players. How many cards does each player get?

33. Olga has 85 cents. It is all in nickels. How many nickels does she have?

34. 99 magazines are put into stacks of 9 each. How many stacks are there?

35. 4 pencils are in each box. There are 60 pencils in all. How many boxes are there?

36. 80 seeds are planted in 5 rows. Each row has the same number of seeds. How many seeds are in each row?

Division (2-digit by 1-digit)

You have 88 beads. How many rings like this can you make? How many beads will you have left over?

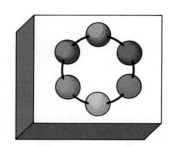

You can answer the questions by dividing 88 by 6 as shown below.

Estimate the tens digit.	Multiply and subtract.	Bring down the ones. Estimate the ones digit.	Multiply and subtract. Write the remainder.

6)88

6)8 is about 1.
Use 1 as the tens digit.

$$\begin{array}{r} 1 \\ 6\overline{)8} \\ -6 \\ \hline 2 \end{array}\ 8$$

$$\begin{array}{r} 1 \\ 6\overline{)8} \\ -6\downarrow \\ \hline 2 \end{array}\ 8$$

6)28 is about 4.
Use 4 as the ones digit.

$$\begin{array}{r} 1\ 4\ R4 \\ 6\overline{)8}\ 8 \\ -6 \\ \hline 2\ 8 \\ -2\ 4 \\ \hline 4 \end{array}$$

You can make 14 rings and have 4 beads left over.

Exercises

Complete each division.

1.
$$\begin{array}{r} 1\ 3\ R\blacksquare \\ 6\overline{)8}\ 0 \\ -6 \\ \hline 2\ 0 \\ -\blacksquare\blacksquare \\ \hline \blacksquare \end{array}$$

2.
$$\begin{array}{r} 4\ \blacksquare\ R\blacksquare \\ 2\overline{)8}\ 7 \\ -8 \\ \hline 7 \\ -\blacksquare \\ \hline \blacksquare \end{array}$$

3.
$$\begin{array}{r} 2\ \blacksquare\ R\blacksquare \\ 2\overline{)5}\ 9 \\ -4 \\ \hline \blacksquare\ \blacksquare \\ -\blacksquare\ \blacksquare \\ \hline \blacksquare \end{array}$$

4.
$$\begin{array}{r} 2\ \blacksquare \\ 3\overline{)6}\ 0 \\ -6 \\ \hline \blacksquare \\ -\blacksquare \\ \hline \blacksquare \end{array}$$

96

Divide.

5. $2\overline{)29}$ 6. $4\overline{)44}$ 7. $2\overline{)33}$ 8. $4\overline{)75}$ 9. $2\overline{)30}$

10. $3\overline{)34}$ 11. $5\overline{)62}$ 12. $4\overline{)67}$ 13. $3\overline{)47}$ 14. $6\overline{)80}$

15. $8\overline{)85}$ 16. $3\overline{)54}$ 17. $7\overline{)77}$ 18. $8\overline{)94}$ 19. $5\overline{)91}$

20. $6\overline{)83}$ 21. $7\overline{)80}$ 22. $2\overline{)91}$ 23. $3\overline{)70}$ 24. $6\overline{)90}$

25. $5\overline{)71}$ 26. $3\overline{)80}$ 27. $5\overline{)85}$ 28. $6\overline{)95}$ 29. $3\overline{)76}$

30.

How many paper clips could you buy? How much money would you have left?

31.

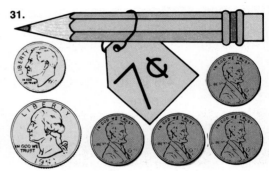

How many pencils could you buy? How much money would you have left?

32.

How many marbles could you buy? How much money would you have left?

33.

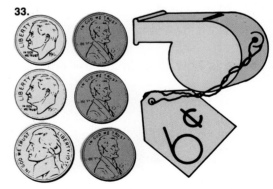

How many whistles could you buy? How much money would you have left?

Estimating in Division

4 pupils will share 512 baseball cards equally.
About how many will each get?

H | T | O   Could each pupil get 100 cards?   **1 hundred × 4 = 400**

             Could each pupil get 200 cards?   **2 hundreds × 4 = 800**

?

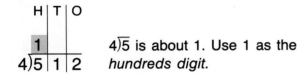

Each pupil can get between 100 and 200 cards.

Here is a fast way to estimate the hundreds digit.

H | T | O

1

4)5 | 1 | 2

4)5̄ is about 1. Use 1 as the
hundreds digit.

Suppose 6 pupils share 512 baseball cards equally.
About how many will each get?

H | T | O   Could each pupil get 100 cards?   **1 hundred × 6 = 600**

?

6)5 | 1 | 2

Since the quotient is less than 100,
there will be no hundreds digit.

Here is how to estimate the first digit in the quotient.

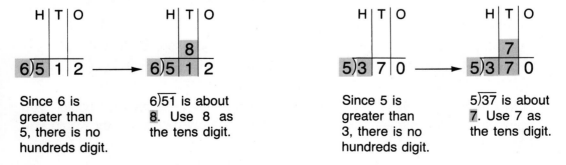

Since 6 is
greater than
5, there is no
hundreds digit.

6)5̄1̄ is about
8. Use 8 as
the tens digit.

Since 5 is
greater than
3, there is no
hundreds digit.

5)3̄7̄ is about
7. Use 7 as
the tens digit.

Exercises

Estimate the hundreds digit.

1. $2\overline{)312}$ 　 2. $4\overline{)732}$ 　 3. $2\overline{)896}$ 　 4. $3\overline{)615}$

5. $5\overline{)575}$ 　 6. $3\overline{)963}$ 　 7. $4\overline{)916}$ 　 8. $7\overline{)854}$

Estimate the first digit and tell its place value.

Example: $8\overline{)424}$ 　 Use 5 as the tens digit. 　 9. $2\overline{)186}$ 　 10. $3\overline{)144}$

11. $2\overline{)458}$ 　 12. $3\overline{)258}$ 　 13. $4\overline{)736}$ 　 14. $5\overline{)395}$

15. $6\overline{)366}$ 　 16. $5\overline{)870}$ 　 17. $8\overline{)224}$ 　 18. $6\overline{)414}$

19. $3\overline{)736}$ 　 20. $8\overline{)624}$ 　 21. $7\overline{)588}$ 　 22. $9\overline{)747}$

About How Many?

Choose the letter for the correct answer.

Artstreet

Bill Wilkinson/Joan Kramer and Associates

1. A company has 546 bicycle wheels. That is enough to make about how many bicycles?

   a. between 100 and 200
   b. between 200 and 300
   c. between 300 and 400

2. A company has 246 tricycle wheels. That is enough to make about how many tricycles?

   a. between 800 and 900
   b. between 70 and 80
   c. between 80 and 90

99

Division (3-digit by 1-digit)

How many trucks are needed to carry 756 cars?

You can use these steps to divide 756 by 6.

Estimate the hundreds digit.	Multiply and subtract.	Estimate the tens digit. Multiply and subtract.	Estimate the ones digit. Multiply and subtract.

6)756

6)7 is about 1.
Try 1 as the
hundreds digit.

	H	T	O
		1	
6)	7	5	6
	−6		
		1	

	H	T	O
		1	2
6)	7	5	6
	−6	↓	
		1	5
	−1	2	
			3

	H	T	O
		1	2	6
6)	7	5	6
	−6		↓
		1	5
	−1	2	↓
			3	6
		−3	6
			0

126 trucks are needed.

100

Exercises

Complete each division.

```
       2 3 ▩              4 1 ▩  R▩            2 ▩ ▩              1 ▩ ▩  R▩
1. 3)7 1 7          2. 2)8 3 5          3. 3)8 6 1          4. 4)6 9 0
     -6                  -8                  -6                  -4
     ‾‾‾                  ‾‾                  ‾‾                  ‾‾
     1 1                    3                 2 ▩                ▩ ▩
       -9                  -2                 -▩ ▩               -▩ ▩
       ‾‾                  ‾‾                 ‾‾‾                 ‾‾‾
        2 ▩                  1 ▩               ▩ ▩                 ▩ ▩
       -▩ ▩                -▩ ▩               -▩ ▩                -▩
       ‾‾‾                 ‾‾‾                ‾‾‾                 ‾‾‾
         ▩                   ▩                  ▩                   ▩
```

Divide.

5. 4)844   6. 2)648   7. 4)924   8. 4)847

9. 2)512   10. 7)799   11. 5)692   12. 6)810

13. 4)744   14. 5)845   15. 3)845   16. 2)873

17. 6)960   18. 2)730   19. 5)968   20. 3)981

21. 6)714   22. 2)857   23. 3)837   24. 7)938

25. 8)940   26. 5)835   27. 3)815   28. 6)886

29. A factory needs 620 tires for its new cars. Each new car comes with 5 tires. How many cars does the factory have?

30. 634 pennies are put into stacks of 5 pennies each. How many stacks are there? How many pennies are left over?

31. Elsie and her 3 friends will share 627 trading cards equally. How many cards will each person get? How many cards will be left over?

32. Mrs. Moy's 3-day trip is 762 miles long. She will drive the same number of miles each day. How many miles will she drive each day?

Division (3-digit by 1-digit)

An art class made the same number of snow-flakes each day. In 3 days they made 135 snow-flakes. How many did they make each day?

You can use these steps to divide 135 by 3.

Estimate the hundreds digit.	Estimate the tens digit.	Multiply and subtract.	Estimate the ones digit. Multiply and subtract.
$3\overline{)135}$	$3\overline{)135}$		
Since 3 is greater than 1, there is no hundreds digit.	$3\overline{)13}$ is about 4. Use 4 as the tens digit.	H|T|O 　　4 3)1 3 5 −1 2 　　1	H|T|O 　　4 5 3)1 3 5 −1 2 ↓ 　　1 5 　−1 5 　　　0

They made 45 snowflakes each day.

Exercises

Complete each division.

1.
```
      7 8  R▇
  3)2 3 6
   −2 1
      2 6
     −2 4
        ▇
```

2.
```
       7 ▇
  4)3 1 2
    −2 8
       3 ▇
      −▇ ▇
         ▇
```

3.
```
       8 ▇  R▇
  2)1 7 5
    −1 6
       1 5
      −▇ ▇
         ▇
```

4.
```
        ▇ ▇
  7)4 8 3
    −▇ ▇
       ▇ ▇
      −▇ ▇
         ▇
```

Divide.

5. $2\overline{)156}$ 6. $3\overline{)177}$ 7. $4\overline{)184}$ 8. $5\overline{)765}$

9. $6\overline{)135}$ 10. $7\overline{)187}$ 11. $8\overline{)192}$ 12. $9\overline{)168}$

13. $6\overline{)300}$ 14. $4\overline{)456}$ 15. $7\overline{)350}$ 16. $6\overline{)426}$

17. $4\overline{)948}$ 18. $9\overline{)237}$ 19. $5\overline{)280}$ 20. $8\overline{)248}$

21. $3\overline{)881}$ 22. $7\overline{)497}$ 23. $5\overline{)355}$ 24. $6\overline{)430}$

25. $9\overline{)612}$ 26. $7\overline{)617}$ 27. $8\overline{)680}$ 28. $9\overline{)791}$

29. Each bag weighs 9 pounds. How many bags are there?

30. How much would it cost to buy 1 tire?

31. Abe has 239 pennies to trade for nickels. How many nickels will he get? How many pennies will be left?

32. You and 6 friends share 851 pennies equally. How many pennies will each get? How many pennies will be left?

What Is Missing?

1.
```
        ■ 9
  5)2 ■ ■
  -2 0
     4 ■
    -■ ■
        0
```

2.
```
        ■ 6
  3)2 ■ ■
  -2 4
     1 ■
    -■ ■
        0
```

3.
```
  ■ ■
6)■ 0 2
 -3 6
  ■ ■
 -■ ■
     0
```

4.
```
       7 ■ R■
  ■)3 1 ■
  -■ 8
     ■ ■
    -3 6
        3
```

Extra Practice—Set A, page 325   103

Checking Division

You can tell if a division answer is correct by checking. Check this way when the remainder is 0.

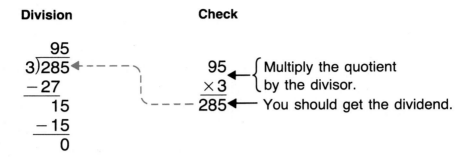

Division

$$\begin{array}{r} 95 \\ 3\overline{)285} \\ -27 \\ \hline 15 \\ -15 \\ \hline 0 \end{array}$$

Check

$$\begin{array}{r} 95 \\ \times 3 \\ \hline 285 \end{array}$$ { Multiply the quotient by the divisor.

285 ← You should get the dividend.

Check this way when the remainder is not 0.

$$\begin{array}{r} 86 \text{ R3} \\ 6\overline{)519} \\ -48 \\ \hline 39 \\ -36 \\ \hline 3 \end{array}$$

$$\begin{array}{r} 86 \\ \times 6 \\ \hline 516 \end{array}$$ { Multiply the quotient by the divisor.

+3 ← Add the remainder.

519 ← You should get the dividend.

Exercises

If the division is correct, write *Yes.* If the division is wrong, work it correctly.

1.
$$\begin{array}{r} 27 \\ 2\overline{)56} \\ -4 \\ \hline 16 \\ -16 \\ \hline 0 \end{array}$$
$$\begin{array}{r} 27 \\ \times 2 \\ \hline 54 \end{array}$$

2.
$$\begin{array}{r} 83 \text{ R2} \\ 5\overline{)422} \\ -40 \\ \hline 22 \\ -20 \\ \hline 2 \end{array}$$
$$\begin{array}{r} 83 \\ \times 5 \\ \hline 415 \\ +2 \\ \hline 417 \end{array}$$

3.
$$\begin{array}{r} 84 \text{ R1} \\ 7\overline{)589} \\ -56 \\ \hline 29 \\ -28 \\ \hline 1 \end{array}$$
$$\begin{array}{r} 84 \\ \times 7 \\ \hline 588 \\ +1 \\ \hline 589 \end{array}$$

Check. If the division is wrong, work it correctly.

4. $\begin{array}{r} 36 \text{ R1} \\ 2\overline{)73} \end{array}$ 5. $\begin{array}{r} 155 \\ 4\overline{)620} \end{array}$ 6. $\begin{array}{r} 44 \text{ R3} \\ 6\overline{)267} \end{array}$ 7. $\begin{array}{r} 3 \\ 3\overline{)90} \end{array}$

8. $\begin{array}{r} 212 \\ 4\overline{)856} \end{array}$ 9. $\begin{array}{r} 223 \\ 6\overline{)332} \end{array}$ 10. $\begin{array}{r} 94 \text{ R7} \\ 6\overline{)759} \end{array}$ 11. $\begin{array}{r} 221 \text{ R3} \\ 4\overline{)987} \end{array}$

Divide. Then check.

12. $8\overline{)63}$ 13. $7\overline{)50}$ 14. $4\overline{)87}$ 15. $6\overline{)96}$

16. $5\overline{)80}$ 17. $2\overline{)91}$ 18. $3\overline{)84}$ 19. $2\overline{)60}$

20. $2\overline{)332}$ 21. $4\overline{)864}$ 22. $5\overline{)480}$ 23. $3\overline{)148}$

24. $5\overline{)854}$ 25. $8\overline{)256}$ 26. $4\overline{)314}$ 27. $4\overline{)770}$

28. $8\overline{)400}$ 29. $2\overline{)570}$ 30. $3\overline{)819}$ 31. $6\overline{)725}$

32. $8\overline{)97}$ 33. $7\overline{)432}$ 34. $8\overline{)472}$ 35. $9\overline{)510}$

36. $9\overline{)999}$ 37. $8\overline{)797}$ 38. $8\overline{)968}$ 39. $4\overline{)857}$

40. $6\overline{)530}$ 41. $9\overline{)80}$ 42. $3\overline{)687}$ 43. $7\overline{)525}$

44. Vince collected 217 postcards. He can fill each page of a scrapbook with 6 postcards. How many pages can he fill? How many postcards will be left over?

45. Pam, Sue, and Roger share 155 cards equally. Sue also gets the cards that will be left over. How many cards does Pam get? How many cards does Sue get?

46. I am a number between 80 and 90. If you divide me by 7, the remainder is 2. Who am I?

Extra Practice—Set B, page 325

Division Practice

Divide.

1. $1\overline{)9}$ 2. $8\overline{)0}$ 3. $6\overline{)54}$ 4. $7\overline{)56}$

5. $8\overline{)48}$ 6. $7\overline{)49}$ 7. $9\overline{)72}$ 8. $8\overline{)72}$

9. $7\overline{)63}$ 10. $8\overline{)64}$ 11. $9\overline{)81}$ 12. $9\overline{)54}$

13. $5\overline{)29}$ 14. $3\overline{)69}$ 15. $4\overline{)76}$ 16. $2\overline{)99}$

17. $2\overline{)428}$ 18. $5\overline{)745}$ 19. $2\overline{)357}$ 20. $4\overline{)216}$

21. $3\overline{)262}$ 22. $6\overline{)39}$ 23. $5\overline{)560}$ 24. $7\overline{)91}$

25. $4\overline{)856}$ 26. $4\overline{)59}$ 27. $6\overline{)937}$ 28. $5\overline{)425}$

29. $6\overline{)299}$ 30. $8\overline{)95}$ 31. $4\overline{)80}$ 32. $3\overline{)954}$

33. $9\overline{)89}$ 34. $5\overline{)800}$ 35. $7\overline{)427}$ 36. $8\overline{)590}$

37. $8\overline{)649}$ 38. $3\overline{)51}$ 39. $6\overline{)894}$ 40. $3\overline{)759}$

41. $9\overline{)521}$ 42. $7\overline{)623}$ 43. $7\overline{)97}$ 44. $8\overline{)890}$

Choose the letter for the best answer.

45. You put the checkers in stacks of 6 each. How many checkers will be left over?

   a. less than 5   b. less than 6
   c. more than 6   d. can't tell

106

Solving Problems

1. Mr. Gonzalez drove from Atlanta to Tampa in 9 hours. He drove the same number of miles each hour. How far did he drive each hour?

2. Leo and his 4 friends drove from Cheyenne to Dallas. They shared the driving equally. How far did each drive?

3. The Walkers drove from Cheyenne to Omaha to Chicago. How far did they drive?

4. How much farther is it from Chicago to Atlanta than it is from Tampa to Atlanta?

5. The distance from Dallas to Omaha is 107 miles more than the distance from Chicago to Omaha. How far is it from Dallas to Omaha?

6. Ms. O'Hara drove from Atlanta to Albany in 3 days. She drove the same distance each day. How many miles did she drive each day?

7. The distance from Chicago to San Francisco is 4 times as great as the distance from Chicago to Memphis. How far is it from Chicago to San Francisco?

8. Al drove from Chicago to Atlanta. He stopped to rest 9 times, traveling the same distance between stops. How far did he travel between stops? How far did he have to go after the last stop?

CHAPTER REVIEW

Divide.

1. $35 \div 7 = \square$ 2. $56 \div 7 = \square$ 3. $54 \div 6 = \square$

4. $4\overline{)36}$ 5. $1\overline{)7}$ 6. $6\overline{)42}$ 7. $6\overline{)0}$

8. $9\overline{)63}$ 9. $8\overline{)64}$ 10. $9\overline{)72}$ 11. $9\overline{)81}$

12. $2\overline{)19}$ 13. $3\overline{)23}$ 14. $5\overline{)41}$ 15. $7\overline{)54}$

16. $4\overline{)96}$ 17. $4\overline{)80}$ 18. $6\overline{)84}$ 19. $7\overline{)98}$

20. $2\overline{)29}$ 21. $3\overline{)95}$ 22. $8\overline{)94}$ 23. $5\overline{)77}$

24. $4\overline{)932}$ 25. $3\overline{)954}$ 26. $6\overline{)711}$ 27. $7\overline{)860}$

28. $5\overline{)435}$ 29. $2\overline{)189}$ 30. $8\overline{)392}$ 31. $7\overline{)610}$

Divide and check.

32. $3\overline{)78}$ 33. $6\overline{)99}$ 34. $8\overline{)560}$ 35. $5\overline{)784}$

36. Roscoe Street has 84 streetlights. Each block has 3 lights. How many blocks are there?

37. 172 trees will be planted in 6 rows. The same number of trees will be in each row. How many trees will be in each row? How many trees will be left over?

5 Problem Solving

Which Operation?

Problem solving can be fun.

Step 1: Read the problem.

Step 2: Decide which operation to use.

1. Ted has 146 United States stamps. He has 272 foreign stamps. How many stamps does he have?

When joining two groups,
ADD.

2. How many more crayons are in the large box?

When comparing to find how many more are in one group than in another,
SUBTRACT.

3. How many cough drops are there in 4 boxes?

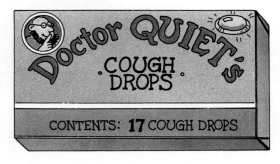

When joining groups of the same size,
MULTIPLY.

4. 120 pupils split into teams. Each team has 8 members. How many teams are there?

When separating a group into smaller groups of the same size,
DIVIDE.

Exercises

Write one of these words to tell which operation to use.

add   *subtract*   *multiply*   *divide*

1. What is the cost of both?

2. How much does 1 bar cost?

3. Ed is 51 years old. Jo is 9 years old. How much younger is Jo?

4. There are 7 days in a week. How many days are in 52 weeks?

5. The art class used 104 sheets of white paper and 78 sheets of red paper. How many sheets of paper were used?

6. Bruno read a 196-page book. Steffi read a book with 4 times that many pages. How many pages are in the book Steffi read?

7. A book has 348 pages. You have read 169 pages. How many pages are left to read?

8. Sancho saved $88. Pedro saved $106 more than that. How much did Pedro save?

9. Jan had 138 seeds. She planted 6 seeds in each row. How many rows were there?

10. Golda has 300 points. Isabel has 78 points less than that. How many points does Isabel have?

11. How many pieces of chalk are in 5 boxes?

12. You have 92 quarters to trade for dollars. How many dollars will you get?

What to Do

After deciding which operation to use, decide what to do to solve the problem.

Step 3: Decide what to do.

These are the problems from page 110.

1. Ted has 146 United States stamps. He has 272 foreign stamps. How many stamps does he have?

ADD

$$146 + 272 = \square \quad \text{or} \quad \begin{array}{r} 146 \\ +272 \\ \hline \end{array}$$

2. How many more crayons are in the large box?

SUBTRACT

$$32 - 8 = \square \quad \text{or} \quad \begin{array}{r} 32 \\ -8 \\ \hline \end{array}$$

3. How many cough drops are there in 4 boxes?

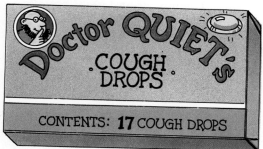

MULTIPLY

$$4 \times 17 = \square \quad \text{or} \quad \begin{array}{r} 17 \\ \times 4 \\ \hline \end{array}$$

4. 120 pupils split into teams. Each team has 8 members. How many teams are there?

DIVIDE

$$120 \div 8 = \square \quad \text{or} \quad 8\overline{)120}$$

Exercises

Show what to do to solve each problem.
(Do not do the computation.)

1. What is the cost of both?

2. How much does 1 bar cost?

3. Ed is 51 years old. Jo is 9 years old. How much younger is Jo?

4. There are 7 days in a week. How many days are in 52 weeks?

5. Mr. Claus had 144 greeting cards. He mailed 86 of them. How many did he have left?

6. Fran hit the bull's-eye 8 times. A bull's-eye is worth 250 points. How many points did she get?

7. Last year we sold 189 buttons. This year we sold 5 times that many buttons. How many did we sell this year?

8. It is 95 miles from Detroit to Cleveland. It is 363 miles from Cleveland to Philadelphia. How far is it from Detroit to Cleveland to Philadelphia?

9. Ms. Klein earns $385 each week. Mrs. Norton earns $199 more than that each week. How much does Mrs. Norton earn each week?

10. There are 328 comic books. Each pupil will get 2 comic books. How many pupils will get comic books?

11. How many bracelets can be made from 234 beads?

12. Herb has $105. How much more does he need to buy the bike?

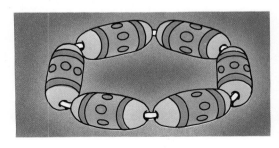

Solving Problems

You are ready for the last two steps in problem solving.

Step 1: Read the problem.

1. Ted has 146 United States stamps. He has 272 foreign stamps. How many stamps does he have?

Step 2: Decide which operation to use.

ADD

Step 3: Decide what to do.

$$146 + 272 = \Box \quad \text{or} \quad \begin{array}{r} 146 \\ +272 \\ \hline \end{array}$$

Step 4: Do the computation.

$$\begin{array}{r} 146 \\ +272 \\ \hline 418 \end{array}$$

Step 5: Answer the problem.

He has 418 stamps.

Step 1: Read the problem.

2. How many more crayons are in the large box?

Step 2: Decide which operation to use.

SUBTRACT

Step 3: Decide what to do.

$$32 - 8 = \Box \quad \text{or} \quad \begin{array}{r} 32 \\ -\ 8 \\ \hline \end{array}$$

Step 4: Do the computation.

$$\begin{array}{r} 32 \\ -\ 8 \\ \hline 24 \end{array}$$

Step 5: Answer the problem.

24 more crayons are in the large box.

Exercises

How many cough drops are there in 4 boxes?

1. Decide which operation to use.

2. Decide what to do.

3. Do the computation.

4. Answer the problem.

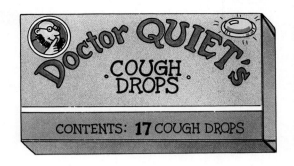

120 pupils split into teams. Each team has 8 members. How many teams are there?

5. Decide which operation to use.

6. Decide what to do.

7. Do the computation.

8. Answer the problem.

Show the computation. Answer the problem.

9. You buy a hamburger for 65¢ and French fries for 28¢. How much do you spend?

10. You can buy 3 bars of soap for 87¢. How much does it cost to buy 1 bar of soap?

11. Ed is 51 years old. Jo is 9 years old. How much younger is Jo?

12. There are 7 days in a week. How many days are in 52 weeks?

13. The trip is 350 miles long. So far we have gone 99 miles. How much farther do we have to go?

14. Mr. Spree had $400. Then he spent $134. How much did he have left?

15. Mother is 32 years old. Grand-mother is 28 years older than Mother. How old is Grandmother?

16. 76 books were sold at the book fair. Each pupil bought 2 books. How many pupils bought books?

17. The little TV costs $106. The big TV costs 4 times that much. How much does the big TV cost?

18. 125 pupils came yesterday and 136 came today. How many pupils came in the 2 days?

115

Solving Problems

1. How many balls are there?

48
BASEBALLS

12
TENNIS BALLS

2. How many fewer points did the Chargers score?

Basketball Scores	
Rockets	81
Chargers	25

3. How many packages of 3 can be made from 450 grapefruits?

4. How many buttons are on 24 cards?

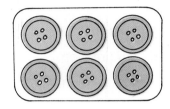

5. How many letters can be stamped? How many stamps would be left?

2 stamps on
a letter

65 stamps

6. How many cups are in 5 gallons of milk?

MILK
1 Gallon
or
16 Cups

7. 58 girls are in the school chorus. There are 76 boys in the chorus. How many pupils are there in the chorus?

8. A store has 9 boxes of crayons. There are 64 crayons in each box. How many crayons are there?

9. July has 31 days. How many weeks does July have? How many extra days are left?

10. Sonya got 98 points on a test. Kim got 79 points. How many more points did Sonya get?

11. What is the cost of both?

12. 75 of these records are top hits. How many records are not top hits?

13. How much shorter is the ribbon than the string?

18 inches   876 inches

14. 46 people can ride in 1 bus. How many can ride in 6 buses?

15. How many bones do you have in your body?

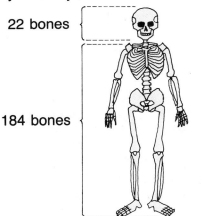

22 bones

184 bones

16. How many posters can be put up with 117 tacks? How many tacks would not be used?

COME TO THE

BOOK FAIR FRIDAY

What Is Missing?

23 boys and girls went camping at Camp Ke de Kaha. Some of them went fishing. The rest went swimming. How many went swimming?

Can you solve the problem?

What else do you need to know?

Exercises

Tell what else you need to know to solve each problem.

1. You go to the store with 75¢. You buy a book. How much money do you have left?

2. 18 papers were delivered on one block and the rest on another block. How many papers were delivered in all?

3. How many apples are there in all?

4. How many blocks is it from home to the store?

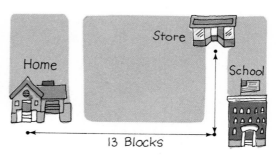

118

5. How much do 8 stamps cost?

6. How much does 1 top cost?

3 tops for

7. How many points have been scored altogether?

8. Does Sarah have enough money to buy the bike?

SALE!
$89

9. How many baseball cards can Milo buy? How much money will he have left?

Baseball Cards
5¢ each

10. Mr. D'Air had 150 balloons. Then he sold some of them. How many balloons did he have left?

11. There are several train sets. How many cars are in all the train sets?

12. What is the cost of both?

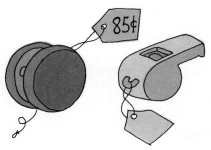

85¢

13. 243 rocks are in some boxes. How many rocks are in each box?

14. Lori is 9 years old. How much older is her mother?

Making Up Problems

You can make up problems by using all the things you see in the picture.

> *Jody*
> What is the cost of both toys?

How would you solve Jody's problem?

> *Nate*
> How much more does the yo-yo cost?

How would you solve Nate's problem?

You do not have to use all the things in the picture. You can also use numbers not shown in the picture.

> *Brad*
> I bought 3 whistles. How much did I spend?

How would you solve Brad's problem?

> *Rosa*
> How many nickels are needed to buy 1 yo-yo?

How would you solve Rosa's problem?

Exercises

Use the picture. Make up a problem in which you must do this.

1. Add

2. Subtract

3. Multiply

4. Divide

5. Add

6. Subtract

7. Multiply

8. Divide

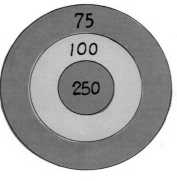

Dart board 98¢

Darts
12¢ each

Score pad
36¢

9. Add

10. Subtract

11. Multiply

12. Divide

Oranges
15¢ each

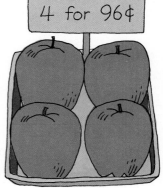

Apples
4 for 96¢

13. Add

14. Subtract

15. Multiply

16. Divide

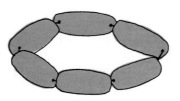

Bracelet
6 beads

Necklace
19 beads

Extra Practice—Set B, page 327

Two-Part Problems

You buy a pen and a comic book. You give the clerk 75¢. How much change should you get?

Here are two ways to solve the problem.

What to do: SUBTRACT cost of pen.

SUBTRACT cost of book.

amount to clerk	cost of pen	cost of book	amount of change

$$(75 - 18) - 39 = \square$$

ADD both costs.

SUBTRACT that from 75.

amount to clerk	cost of both	amount of change

$$75 - (18 + 39) = \square$$

Compute:

75	amount to clerk
− 18	cost of pen
57	amount left

57	
− 39	cost of book
18	amount of change

18	cost of pen
+ 39	cost of book
57	cost of both

75	amount to clerk
− 57	
18	amount of change

Answer: You should get 18¢ change.

Exercises

1. Each of 4 pupils took 12 books to the library. Another pupil took 8 more books. How many books were taken to the library?

2. You worked 9 problems in school and 6 after school. There are still 5 more problems to work. How many problems do you have in all?

3. Mother bought 3 dozen eggs. She used 9 eggs. How many eggs were left?

4. Ken has 14 nickels and 9 pennies. How many cents does he have?

5. You are buying these. You give the clerk 90¢. Find how much change should you get.

6. All the dogs were put into groups of 7 each. How many groups of dogs were there?

34 large dogs

29 small dogs

7. Relay teams were made from 2 classes. Each class had 36 pupils. There were 8 pupils on each team. How many teams were made?

8. Marsha has 6 gerbils. She is buying 4 more. She will put 2 gerbils in each cage. How many cages will there be?

9. Each of 5 children brought 3 balloons to a picnic. Eight of the balloons broke. How many were left?

10. Carol made 6 baskets at 2 points each. She made 3 free throws at 1 point each. How many points did she score?

Problems Without Computation

1. A boy with a red shirt plays the drums. Bonnie does not play the clarinet. The shortest child plays the piano. Tell who plays each instrument.

2. The place cards tell where Joe, Sue, Emily, Marv, and Mike will sit. Emily will sit between 2 boys. Marv will sit between 2 girls. Tell, in order, whose place card is white, whose is blue, and whose is yellow.

3. There are 4 blue socks and 4 black socks in the drawer. It's too dark to tell the blue ones from the black ones. You take 2 socks out of the drawer. Can you be sure that they are the same color?

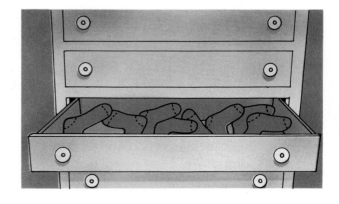

4. Suppose you take 3 socks out of the drawer. Can you be sure that 2 of them are the same color?

5. The teacher is thinking of two animals. These pupils are asked to guess the animals.

Anne guessed only one of the animals correctly. One pupil guessed both animals correctly. Who guessed both animals correctly?

6. The 6-gallon jug is filled with water. The other two jugs are empty. Tell how you could pour water from jug to jug so that you end up with 2 gallons of water in each jug.

7. Tell how you could end up with 5 gallons of water in one jug and 1 gallon of water in another.

8. Al came home after Marge. Marge came home after Carl. Carl came home at 6:00. Gene came home before Carl. Dinner was served at 6:00. Which two people were late for dinner?

125

SKILLS REVIEW

Add.

1.   18
  +40
	2. 57
	  +21
		3. 75
		  +16
			4. 29
			  +63
				5. 38
				  +67

6.   502
  +350
	7. 842
	  + 39
		8. 486
		  +418
			9. 275
			  +685
				10. 807
				  + 93

Subtract and check.

11.   36
  −14
	12. 88
	  −53
		13. 92
		  −66
			14. 45
			  −39
				15. 73
				  − 8

16.   256
  −133
	17. 485
	  −351
		18. 992
		  − 47
			19. 703
			  −242
				20. 500
				  −386

Multiply.

21.   43
  ×2
	22. 28
	  ×3
		23. 19
		  ×5
			24. 57
			  ×2
				25. 68
				  ×4

26.   302
  ×3
	27. 229
	  ×4
		28. 194
		  ×2
			29. 175
			  ×6
				30. 588
				  ×2

Divide and check.

31. $8\overline{)72}$	32. $1\overline{)9}$	33. $7\overline{)0}$	34. $9\overline{)58}$
35. $2\overline{)40}$	36. $6\overline{)84}$	37. $3\overline{)74}$	38. $8\overline{)99}$
39. $4\overline{)248}$	40. $3\overline{)675}$	41. $5\overline{)354}$	42. $7\overline{)623}$

Puzzle Problems

1. Lay 6 coins like this.　Move 2 coins to get this.

2. Lay 10 coins like this.　Move 3 coins to get this.

3. Make 12 strips the same length. Lay them to form 4 small squares like this. Move 3 strips so there will be only 3 squares.

4. Draw a figure like that at the right. Write the numerals 1, 2, 3, 4, 7, 8, and 9 in the other squares so the sum for each row, for each column, and from corner to corner is always 15.

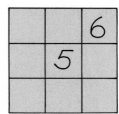

5. All 6 faces of a block like this were painted red. Then the block was cut into 27 small blocks as shown. How many of the small blocks have only this many red faces?

0   1   2   3

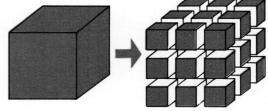

6. You have 35¢. What is the greatest number of coins you could have? What is the least number of coins you could have?

7. Tom had 7 coins whose value was 35¢. The coins are not all the same. What coins did he have?

CHAPTER REVIEW

Solve each problem.

1. 3 pencils cost 54¢. How much does 1 pencil cost?

2. 14 jars are in a paint set. How many jars are in 6 paint sets?

3. An elephant can live 84 years. A tiger can live 25 years. How much longer can an elephant live?

4. There are 136 toys. Each pupil will get 4 toys. How many pupils will get toys?

5. A radio costs $49. A TV costs $258 more than that. How much does the TV cost?

6. It takes 500 points to win. You had 126 points. Then you scored 89 more points. How many points do you still need to win?

Write what else you need to know to solve these problems.

7. How many beans are there?

8. How much less do the marbles cost?

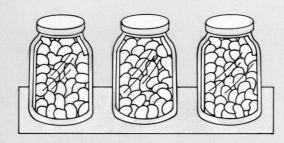

Use the picture. Make up a problem in which you must do this.

9. Add

10. Subtract.

11. Multiply.

12. Divide.

128

6 Geometry

Photri

Geometric Shapes

Here are some shapes we see and use.

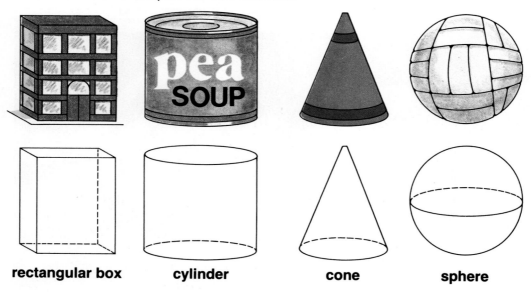

rectangular box   **cylinder**   **cone**   **sphere**

Exercises

Use the shapes above. Tell which have the following:

1. only flat surfaces

2. straight edges

3. only curved surfaces

4. curved edges

5. some flat and some curved surfaces

6. no edges

Name the shape of each object.

7.

8.

9.
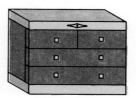

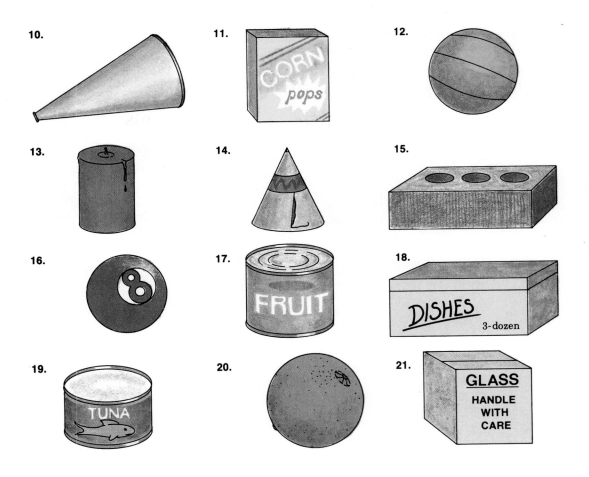

10.   11.   12.

13.   14.   15.

16.   17.   18.

19.   20.   21.

List examples in the room of each shape.

22. box   23. cylinder   24. cone   25. sphere

Which shape can you make from these?

26.   27.   28.

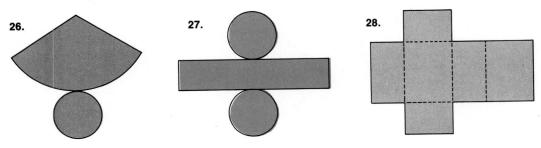

Geometric Shapes

Find objects in the picture that have these shapes.

triangle
(3 sides)

quadrilateral
(4 sides)

pentagon
(5 sides)

Exercises

Count the sides. Name each shape.

1.

2.

3.
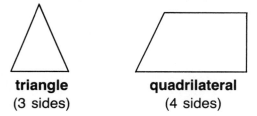

4.

5.

6.

132

7.

8.

9.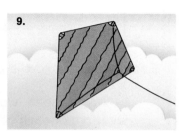

10.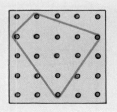

11.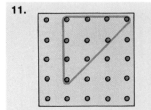

12.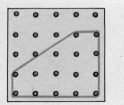

13.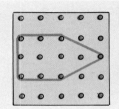

14.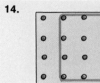

15.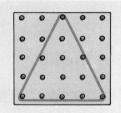

More Sides

A **hexagon** has 6 sides. An **octagon** has 8 sides.

Count the sides. Name each shape.

1.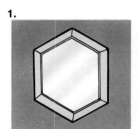

2.

3.

4.

Kinds of Lines

Each edge of a box is part of a line.

Would these two lines
ever cross each other?

Do these two lines
cross each other?

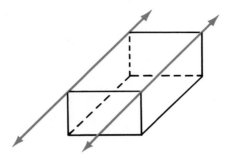

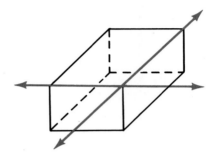

parallel lines

intersecting lines

Exercises

Write *P* for parallel lines.
Write *I* for intersecting lines.

1.

2.

3.

4.

5.

6.

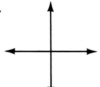

7.

8.

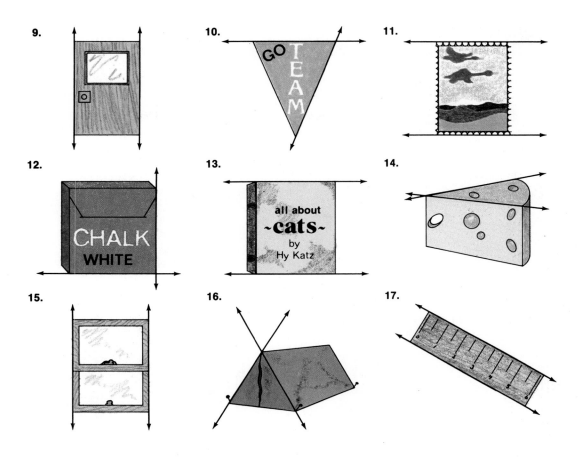

List examples in the room that show these.

18. parallel lines   **19.** intersecting lines

What Kind of Lines?

1. Could these two lines ever cross? Use a box to find out.

2. Are they parallel lines?

3. The lines are called **skew lines.** Find examples of skew lines in the classroom.

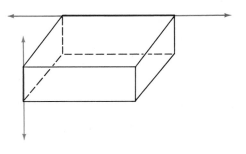

Extra Practice—Set A, page 329

Angles

These pictures show **angles.**

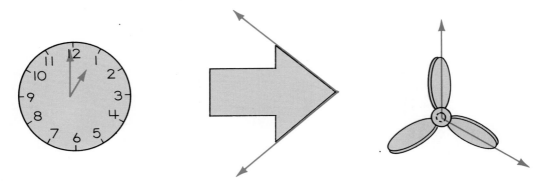

These pictures show **right angles.**

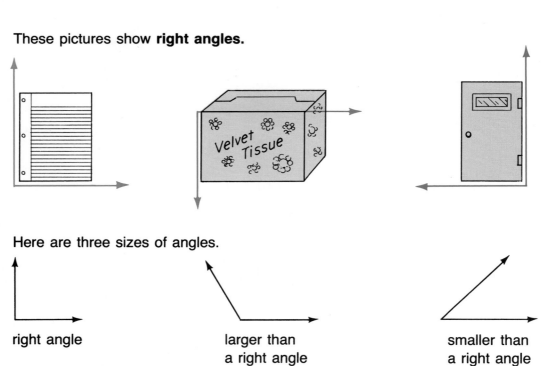

Here are three sizes of angles.

right angle

larger than
a right angle

smaller than
a right angle

Name things in the room that show right angles.

Name things in the room that show other angles.

Exercises

Write *R* if it is a *right angle.*
Write *L* if it is *larger.* Write *S* if it is *smaller.*

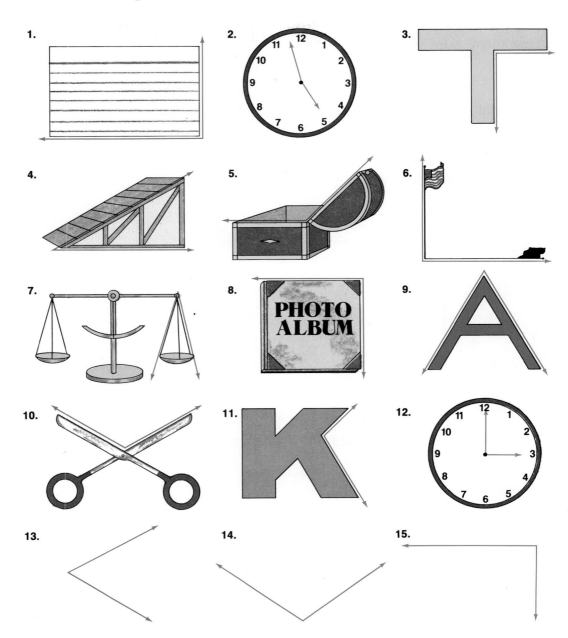

1.

2.

3.

4.

5.

6.

7.

8.

9.

10.

11.

12.

13.

14.

15.

137

Rectangles

If you trace around the bottom of this box, you get a **rectangle.**

How many sides?

How many right angles?

A special kind of rectangle is shown below.

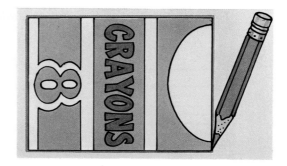

Lay a strip of paper along one side of the rectangle. Mark the length of that side as shown.

Now lay the strip along the other sides to compare their lengths.

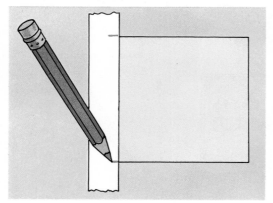

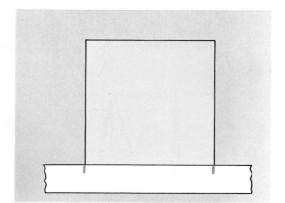

What did you discover about the four sides?

This rectangle is called a **square** because all four sides have the same length.

Exercises

1. Name some things that look like rectangles.

2. Name some things that look like squares.

138

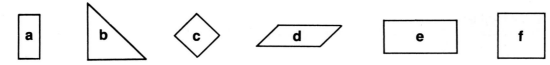

a   b   c   d   e   f

3. Write the letter of each figure that is a rectangle.

4. Write the letter of each figure that is a square.

5.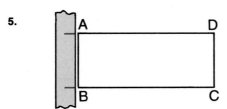

Mark the length of side AB on a strip of paper. Find another side of the rectangle that has the same length.

6.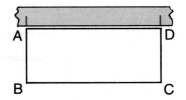

Mark the length of side AD on a strip of paper. Find another side that has the same length.

Answer these questions without measuring.

7. How long is side MN?

8. How long is side MR?

9. Which side looks parallel to side MN?

10. Which side looks parallel to side MR?

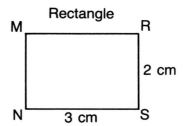

11. Draw a 4-sided figure with opposite sides the same length that is not a rectangle.

12. Draw a figure with 4 sides the same length that is not a square.

Can You Find Them?

1. How many squares are shown in the figure?

2. How many rectangles are shown in the figure?

Extra Practice—Set B, page 329   **139**

Triangles

Triangles are often used in things we make. You can name triangles as shown below.

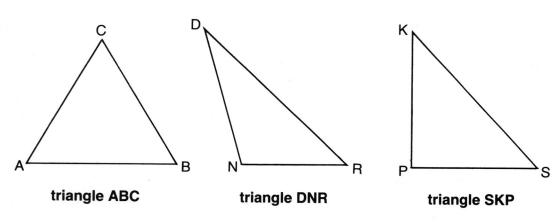

triangle ABC   **triangle DNR**   **triangle SKP**

Which triangle has one right angle?

Triangle SKP is called a **right triangle.**

Exercises

1. Name the figure that is a triangle.

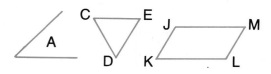

2. Name the triangle that is a right triangle.

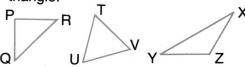

Use the grid pictures.

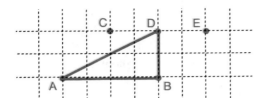

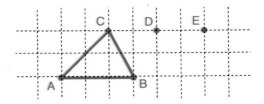

3. Name the triangle that is a right triangle.

4. Name the triangle that has one angle larger than a right angle.

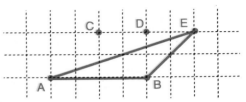

5. Name the triangle that has each angle smaller than a right angle.

6. Which two points of this rectangle could you connect so that two triangles are formed?

7. Name the triangles that are formed.

8. What kind of triangles are they?

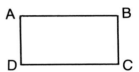

"Equi" Means "Equal"

1. Compare the lengths of the sides of the triangle.

2. What did you discover?

A triangle with all sides the same length is called an **equilateral triangle.**

3. Name the triangle that is an equilateral triangle.

    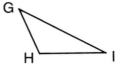 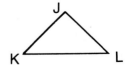

141

Circles

Here are two ways to draw a **circle**.

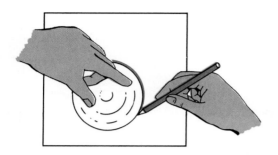

Trace around a lid.

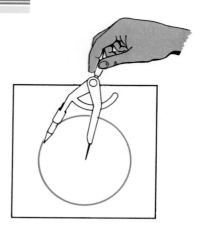

Use a compass.

Point G is *on* the circle. Point C is the **center.** It is inside the circle.

The line segment from C to G is a **radius** (RAYD-ee-uhs). From C to R is another radius.

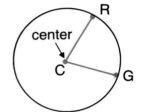

Points A and B are *on* the circle. The line segment from A to B is a **diameter** (dy-AM-uht-ur).

From M to N is another diameter. Notice that a diameter goes through the center.

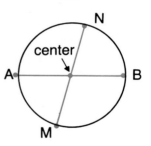

Exercises

Is each figure a circle? Write *Yes* or *No*.

1.

2.

3.

4.

5. Which drawing shows a radius?

a b c

6. Which drawing shows a diameter?

a b c

7. Which point is the center?

8. Name a radius.

9. Name a diameter.

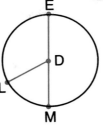

Complete the following for each circle.

10.

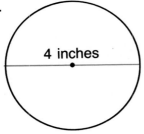

4 inches

diameter: ____ inches

radius: ____ inches

11.

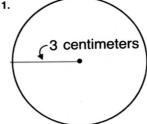

3 centimeters

diameter: ____ centimeters

radius: ____ centimeters

Try These for Size!

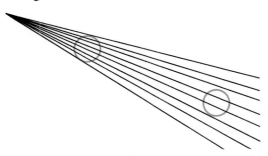

1. Are these circles the same size?

2. Are the inside circles the same size?

Size and Shape

These tubes of toothpaste do not have the same size. But they have the same shape.

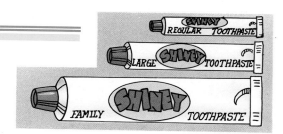

Exercises

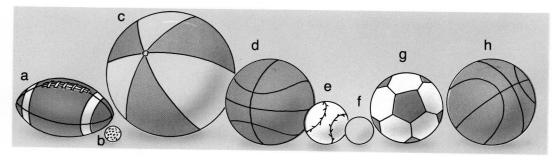

1. Which ball is the largest?

2. Which ball is the smallest?

3. Which balls have the same size?

4. Which balls have the same shape?

5. Which balls have the same size and the same shape?

Do these objects have the same size and shape? Write *Yes* or *No*.

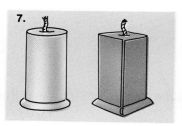

144

Which two objects have the same size and shape?

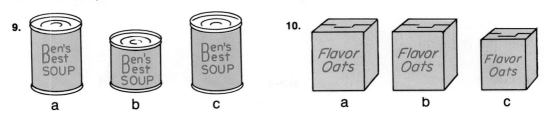

9.
a   b   c

10.
a   b   c

11. Which rectangle has the same size and shape as the blue one?

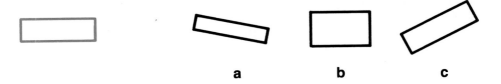

a   b   c

12. Which triangle has the same size and shape as the red one?

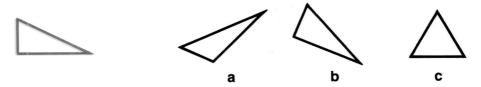

a   b   c

Which figure has the same size and shape as the red one?

13.

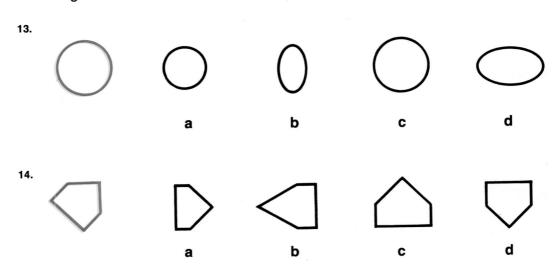

a   b   c   d

14.

a   b   c   d

Extra Practice—Set B, page 330

SKILLS REVIEW

Write the numeral.

1. 600 + 4

2. 2000 + 500 + 80

3. 6000 + 80 + 3

4. 20,000 + 1000 + 9

5. 800,000 + 500 + 50

6. 600,000 + 90,000

Write < or > for each ●.

7. 56 ● 65

8. 81 ● 79

9. 90 ● 89

10. 608 ● 599

11. 429 ● 438

12. 354 ● 345

13. 8904 ● 8877

14. 6898 ● 7100

15. 6569 ● 6570

Complete each number pattern.

16. 14, 16, 18, ___, ___

17. 55, 53, 51, ___, ___

18. 45, 50, 55, ___, ___

19. 86, 76, 66, ___, ___

Round to the nearest ten.

20. 83

21. 8

22. 41

23. 75

24. 97

Round to the nearest hundred.

25. 387

26. 226

27. 150

28. 908

29. 655

30. There are 187 fourth graders and 126 fifth graders. Estimate how many pupils there are.

146

Add or subtract. Watch the signs!

31.	600 +198	32.	47 +899	33.	726 −596	34.	820 − 96	35.	399 + 8

36.	500 − 49	37.	867 − 8	38.	643 +257	39.	900 −123	40.	408 + 96

Multiply.

41.	38 ×4	42.	68 ×6	43.	54 ×9	44.	87 ×8	45.	93 ×7

46.	116 ×7	47.	590 ×6	48.	346 ×8	49.	705 ×7	50.	798 ×9

Divide.

51. $8\overline{)48}$ 52. $7\overline{)63}$ 53. $8\overline{)60}$ 54. $6\overline{)53}$

55. $6\overline{)84}$ 56. $9\overline{)89}$ 57. $2\overline{)90}$ 58. $3\overline{)639}$

59. $5\overline{)843}$ 60. $8\overline{)336}$ 61. $4\overline{)920}$ 62. $7\overline{)624}$

63. Anita is 13 years old. Her mother is 28 years older than that. How old is her mother?

64. Chet found 59 shells. Ava found 4 times that many shells. How many shells did Ava find?

65. 232 chairs were put in 8 rows of the same size. How many chairs were put in each row?

66. A sofa costs $500. Mrs. Berg has only $265. How much more does she need to buy the sofa?

67. Justin bought a newspaper for 45¢ and a pen for 28¢. He gave the clerk 80¢. How much change did he get back?

68. 3 large boxes weigh 46 pounds each. There is also a small box that weighs 25 pounds. Find the total weight of the boxes.

147

Matching Shapes

Tell which piece fits each hole.

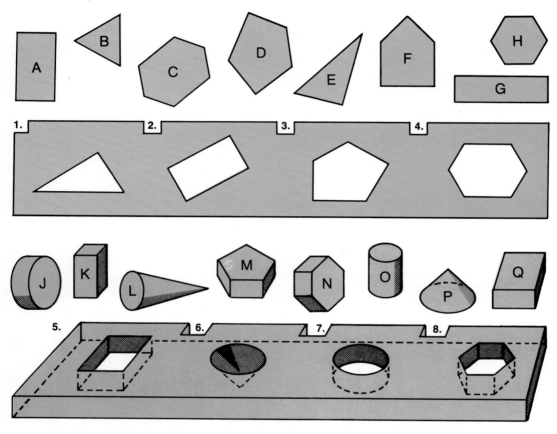

Make 24 paper strips the same length.

9. Lay 17 strips to form 6 squares as shown below. Remove 5 strips and leave 3 squares.

10. Lay 24 strips to form 9 squares. Remove 4 strips and leave 5 squares.

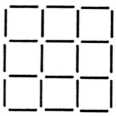

Think of folding on the red line. Will one part fit exactly on the other part? Write *Yes* or *No.*

11.

12.

13.

14.

15.

16.

17.

18.

19.

20.

21.

22.

On which line could you fold so that one part will fit exactly on the other? Write *Red* or *Blue.*

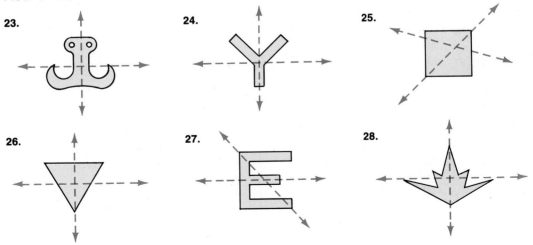

23.

24.

25.

26.

27.

28.

149

CHAPTER REVIEW

Write one of these names for each shape.

box *cylinder* *cone* *sphere*

1.   **2.**   **3.**   **4.**

Write one of these names for each shape.

triangle *quadrilateral* *pentagon*

5.   **6.**   **7.**   **8.**

Look at the figures in exercises 5–8.

9. Which exercise shows a square? **10.** Which exercises show a rectangle?

Write *parallel* or *intersecting* for these lines.

11. 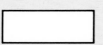 **12.**   **13.**   **14.**

15. Which angle is a right angle?

16. Name the triangle that is a right triangle.

17. Name a diameter. Name a radius.

18. Which two figures have the same size and shape?

a b c

7 Measurement

Centimeter

The thumbtack is **1 centimeter** long. You can also say it is **1 cm** long.

How long is the pencil?

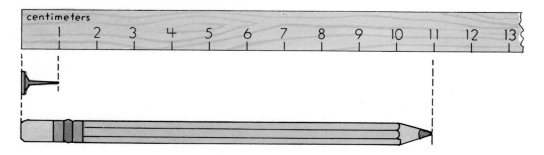

Exercises

Tell the length in centimeters.

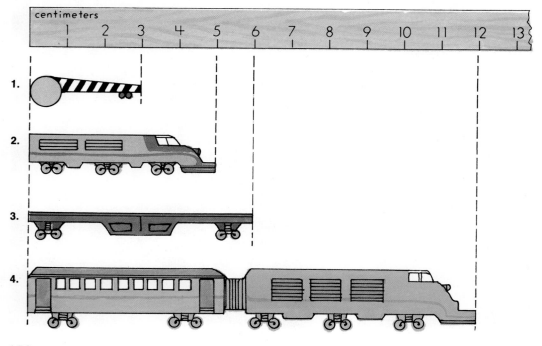

1.

2.

3.

4.

Use a ruler to find the length in centimeters.

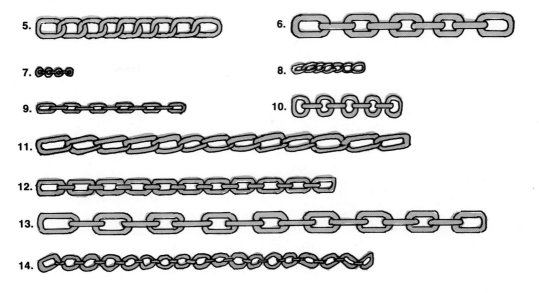

5.

6.

7.

8.

9.

10.

11.

12.

13.

14.

What Is a Millimeter?

The nail is **15 millimeters** long. You can also say it is **15 mm** long.

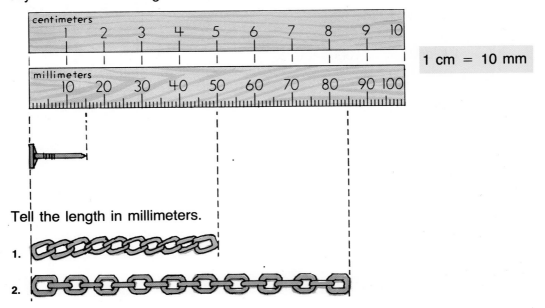

1 cm = 10 mm

Tell the length in millimeters.

1.

2.

Meter and Kilometer

Mabelle's umbrella is about **1 meter** or **1 m** long. Her front door is about 2 meters high.

> 1 meter = 100 centimeters
>
> 1 m = 100 cm

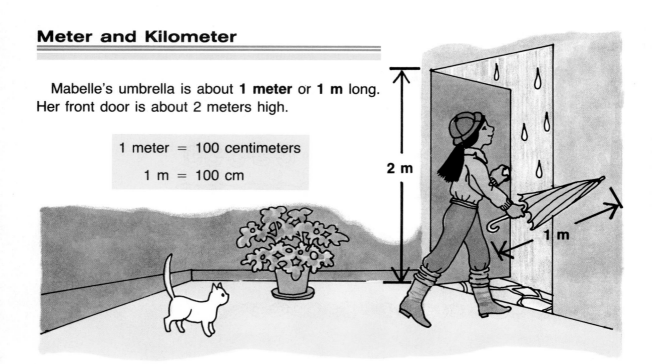

Bonnie jogged around a football field, including end zones, 3 times. She jogged a distance of about **1 kilometer** or **1 km.**

> 1 kilometer = 1000 meters
>
> 1 km = 1000 m

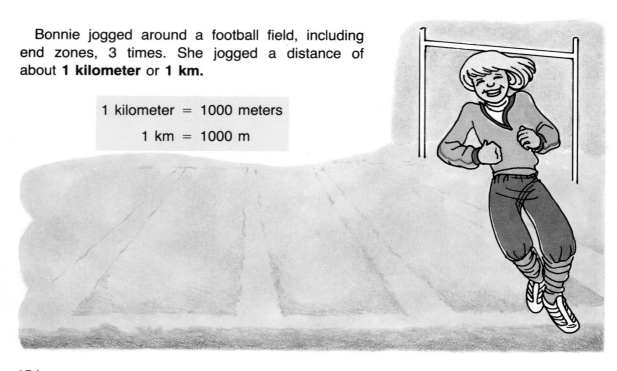

Exercises

Would you use *meters* or *kilometers* to find these?

1. height of a tree

2. distance to the next town

3. distance across the street

4. distance across an ocean

Choose the best answer.

5.

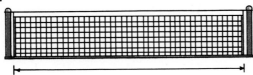

    a. 10 centimeters
    b. 10 meters
    c. 10 kilometers

6.

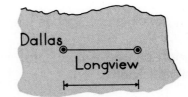

    a. 75 centimeters
    b. 75 meters
    c. 75 kilometers

7.

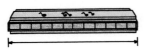

    a. 15 centimeters
    b. 15 meters
    c. 15 kilometers

8.

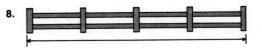

    a. 7 centimeters
    b. 7 meters
    c. 7 kilometers

Complete.

9. 100 cm = ___ m

10. 4 m = ___ cm

11. 1000 m = ___ km

12. 3 km = ___ m

13. 200 cm = ___ m

14. 3 m = ___ cm

15. 600 cm = ___ m

16. 9 m = ___ cm

17. 4000 m = ___ km

18. 7 km = ___ m

19. 3000 m = ___ km

20. 5 km = ___ m

Extra Practice—Set A, page 331

155

Inch and Foot

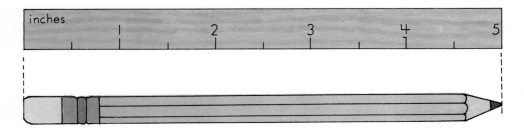

The pencil is ___ inches long.

1 inch can be written **1 in.** A length of *12 inches* is called **1 foot** or **1 ft.**

> 12 inches = 1 foot
>
> 12 in = 1 ft

The drawings below are not actual size. They show things that are measured in feet.

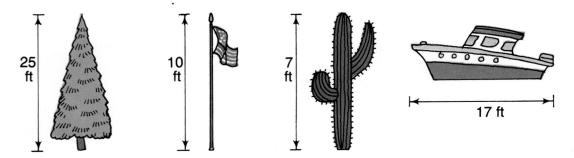

Exercises

Would you use *inches* or *feet* to find the length of

1. a comb

2. a bus

3. a pencil

4. a hallway

5. your finger

6. a ladder

156

Find the length of each drawing in inches.

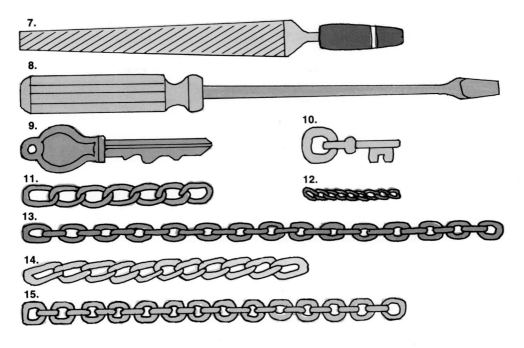

7.

8.

9.

10.

11.

12.

13.

14.

15.

Choose the best answer.

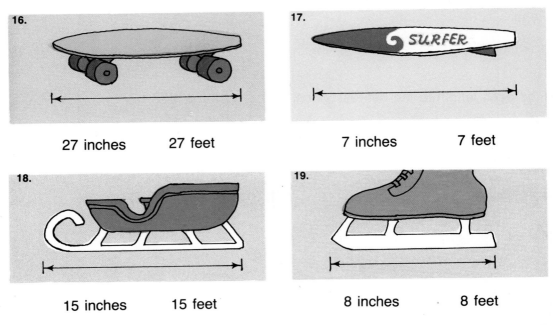

16.

27 inches   27 feet

17.

7 inches   7 feet

18.

15 inches   15 feet

19.

8 inches   8 feet

Half Inch

Sometimes people measure things to the nearest half inch. This ruler is marked in half inches.

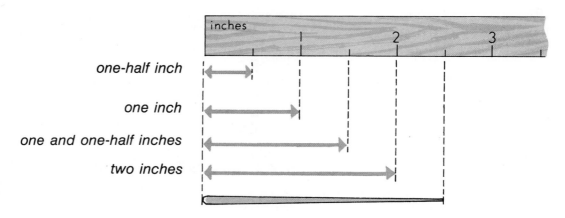

one-half inch

one inch

one and one-half inches

two inches

The toothpick is ____ inches long.

Exercises

Read.

1. $2\frac{1}{2}$ in

2. $5\frac{1}{2}$ in

3. $3\frac{1}{2}$ in

4. $10\frac{1}{2}$ in

Find each length to the nearest $\frac{1}{2}$ inch.

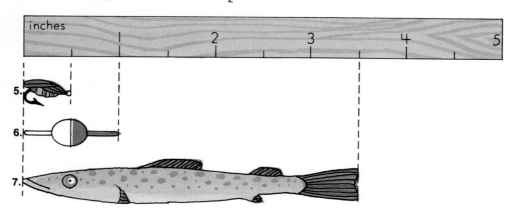

158

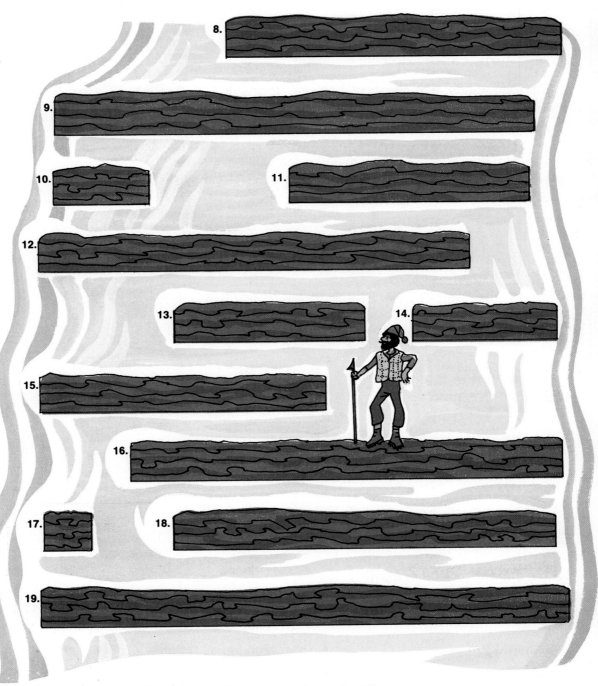

Use a ruler to draw line segments with these lengths.

20. $2\frac{1}{2}$ inches   **21.** $3\frac{1}{2}$ inches   **22.** $5\frac{1}{2}$ inches   **23.** $7\frac{1}{2}$ inches

159

Mile

On road maps the distance between towns is marked in **miles.**

1 mile = 5280 feet
1 mi = 5280 ft

The red numerals tell how many miles are between towns on the map below.

Waterbury is 15 miles from Meriden.

Norwalk is 5 + 8, or 13, miles from Greenwich.

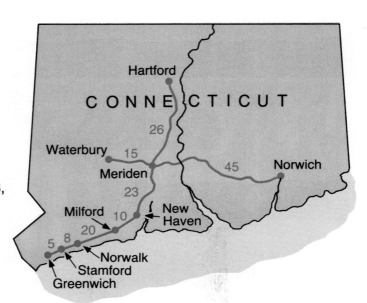

Exercises

Tell how many miles it is from

1. Stamford to Norwalk

2. Hartford to Meriden

3. Stamford to Greenwich

4. Meriden to Hartford

5. Milford to New Haven

6. Norwich to Meriden

7. New Haven to Meriden

8. Waterbury to Meriden

160

Use the map on page 160. Add to find these distances.

9. Stamford to Milford

10. New Haven to Hartford

11. Waterbury to Norwich

12. Hartford to Waterbury

13. Stamford to New Haven

14. Milford to Hartford

15. Norwalk to Meriden

16. Milford to Norwich

17. Waterbury to Norwich and back to Waterbury

18. Hartford to New Haven and back to Hartford

19. Greenwich to Hartford

20. Greenwich to Norwich

Would you use *inches, feet,* or *miles* to find these?

21. length of an airplane

22. distance across an ocean

23. length of a spoon

24. length of a hammer

25. length of a river

26. distance across a room

Choose the best answer.

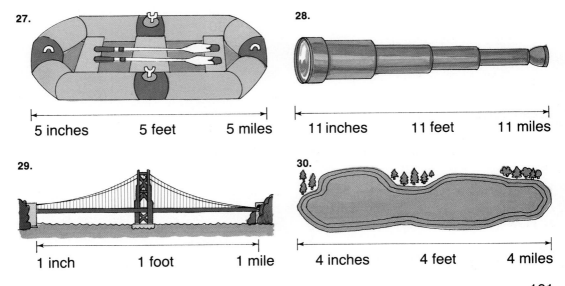

27.
5 inches   5 feet   5 miles

28.
11 inches   11 feet   11 miles

29.
1 inch   1 foot   1 mile

30.
4 inches   4 feet   4 miles

Perimeter

If you walk all the way around this pool, you walk 150 meters.

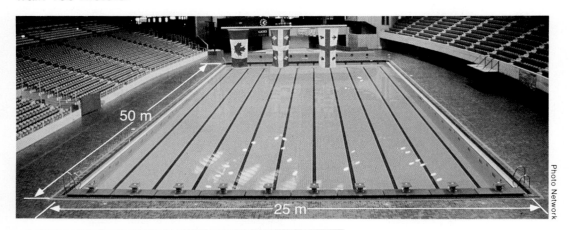

50 m

25 m

The *distance around* a figure is its **perimeter.**

You can find the perimeter of a figure by adding the lengths of its sides.

$$\begin{array}{r} 50 \\ 25 \\ 50 \\ +25 \\ \hline 150 \end{array}$$

The perimeter is 150 meters.

Exercises

1. How many sides does the triangle have?

2. Tell the length of each side.

3. How would you find the perimeter?

4. Find the perimeter.

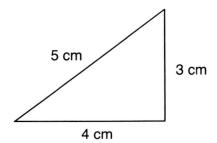

5 cm

3 cm

4 cm

Find each perimeter in the units shown.

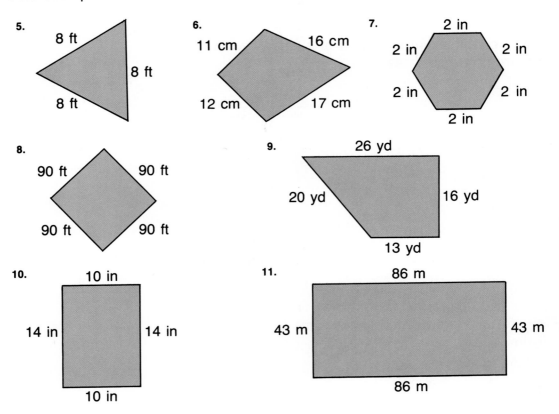

5.
8 ft
8 ft
8 ft

6.
11 cm
16 cm
12 cm
17 cm

7.
2 in
2 in
2 in
2 in
2 in
2 in

8.
90 ft
90 ft
90 ft
90 ft

9.
26 yd
20 yd
16 yd
13 yd

10.
10 in
14 in
14 in
10 in

11.
86 m
43 m
43 m
86 m

Measure the sides of each figure in centimeters. Find each perimeter.

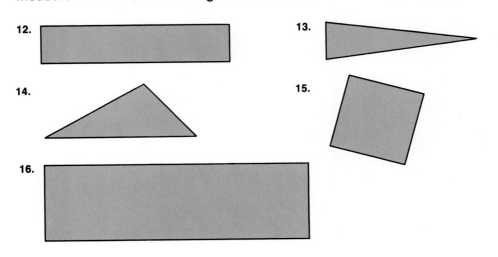

12.

13.

14.

15.

16.

Area

You can measure the inside of a figure by using **square units** like these.

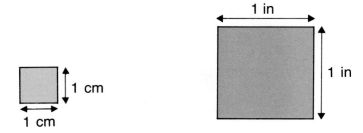

1 square centimeter   **1 square inch**

To find the **area** of a figure, find how many square units are needed to cover the inside of the figure.

Exercises

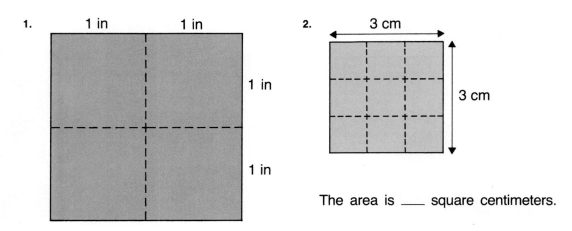

1.

The area is ___ square inches.

2.

The area is ___ square centimeters.

The drawings below are actual size. Find the area of each figure.

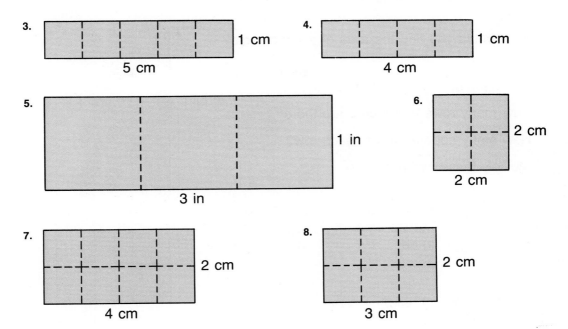

3. 5 cm, 1 cm

4. 4 cm, 1 cm

5. 3 in, 1 in

6. 2 cm, 2 cm

7. 4 cm, 2 cm

8. 3 cm, 2 cm

These drawings are *not* actual size. Find each area in the units shown.

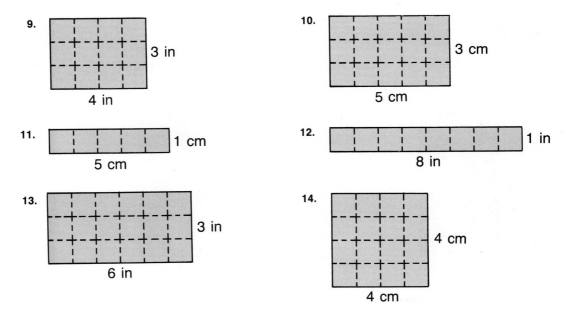

9. 4 in, 3 in

10. 5 cm, 3 cm

11. 5 cm, 1 cm

12. 8 in, 1 in

13. 6 in, 3 in

14. 4 cm, 4 cm

Area of a Rectangle

How would you find the area of the rectangle?

Try this fast way to find the area:

How many rows of squares are there?

How many squares are in each row?

Multiply those two numbers.

number of rows		number of square units in each row		number of square units in the rectangle
9	×	3	=	27
length	×	width	=	area

The area is 27 square centimeters.

1 cm

1 cm

length

width

Exercises

The drawings below are actual size. Find the area of each figure.

1.

2 cm

4 cm

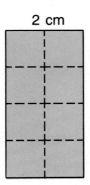

2.

2 cm

5 cm

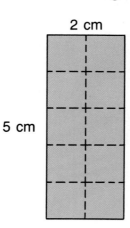

The drawings below are *not* actual size. Find each area in the units shown.

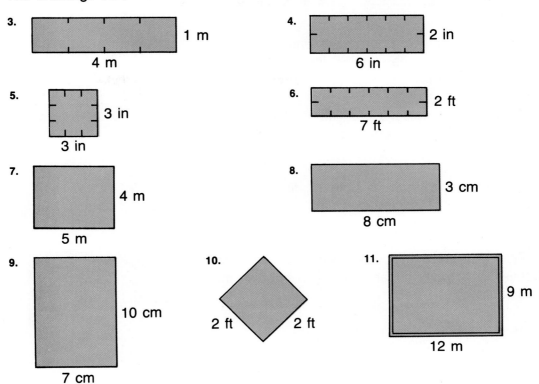

3. 1 m
4 m

4. 2 in
6 in

5. 3 in
3 in

6. 2 ft
7 ft

7. 4 m
5 m

8. 3 cm
8 cm

9. 10 cm
7 cm

10. 2 ft 2 ft

11. 9 m
12 m

Rectangle Challenge

Each figure has been made by putting rectangles together. Find the area of each figure.

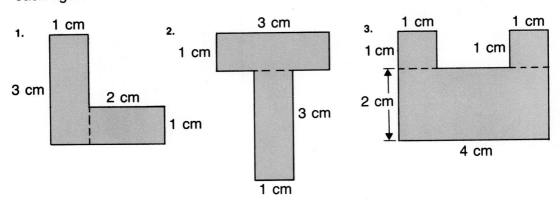

1. 1 cm
3 cm
2 cm
1 cm

2. 3 cm
1 cm
3 cm
1 cm

3. 1 cm 1 cm
1 cm 1 cm
2 cm
4 cm

Extra Practice—Set A, page 332

Volume

Some figures, like a box, have *length, width,* and *height.* You can measure the inside of a box by using **cubic units.**

Suppose you made a box like this. It is called a cube. Its **volume** is **1 cubic centimeter.**

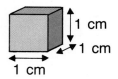

To find the **volume** of a figure, find how many cubic units will fit inside the figure.

Think of stacking cubes like the one shown above. How many cubes would you need to make this figure?

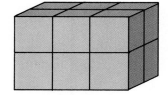

Its volume is ___ cubic centimeters.

Exercises

Think of stacking cubes. What is each volume in cubic centimeters?

1.

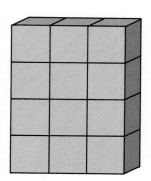

2.

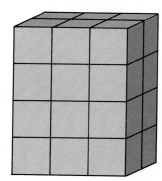

168

3.

4.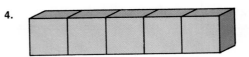

5.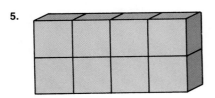

6.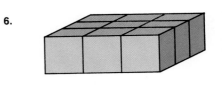

7.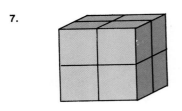

8.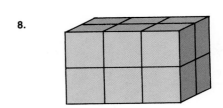

9.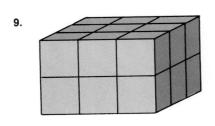

10.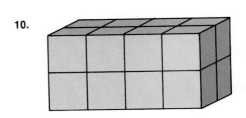

11.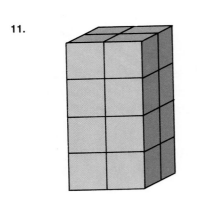

12.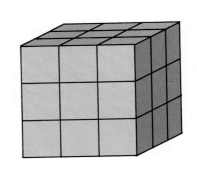

SKILLS REVIEW

Add.

1.	2.	3.	4.	5.
32	78	572	336	898
+46	+12	+119	+492	+ 76

Subtract.

6.	7.	8.	9.	10.
83	584	408	800	910
−51	− 94	−116	−523	−517

Multiply.

11.	12.	13.	14.	15.
21	35	17	29	46
×3	×2	×5	×4	×8

16.	17.	18.	19.	20.
102	439	250	147	265
×4	×7	×8	×9	×8

Divide.

21. $5\overline{)75}$ 22. $6\overline{)88}$ 23. $2\overline{)94}$ 24. $3\overline{)86}$

25. $7\overline{)574}$ 26. $9\overline{)486}$ 27. $2\overline{)825}$ 28. $3\overline{)762}$

29. Clothes need 12 minutes to wash and 31 minutes to dry. How much longer does the drying take?

30. 27 gallons of water are used for 1 load of clothes. How many gallons are needed for 4 loads?

31. 219 shirts were washed today and 167· yesterday. How many shirts were washed in the two days?

32. 760 grams of soap were used for 8 loads of clothes. How many grams were used for 1 load?

Exercises

1. How many quarts does it take to make 1 gallon?

2. How many pints does it take to make 1 quart?

3. How many cups does it take to make 1 pint?

4. How many cups does it take to make 1 gallon?

Which is more?

5. 1 quart or 1 pint

6. 1 pint or 3 cups

7. 1 gallon or 6 pints

8. 1 quart or 6 cups

9. 2 gallons or 6 quarts

10. 3 quarts or 8 pints

11. 2 gallons or 18 pints

12. 2 quarts or 6 cups

Complete.

13. 1 gallon = ___ pints

14. 1 quart = ___ cups

15. 4 cups = ___ pints

16. 8 pints = ___ quarts

17. 3 gallons = ___ quarts

18. 16 cups = ___ quarts

19. 6 quarts = ___ pints

20. 10 pints = ___ cups

21. 8 quarts = ___ cups

22. 8 quarts = ___ gallons

23. 16 pints = ___ gallons

24. 5 gallons = ___ cups

25. Mr. Morales bought 1 gallon of milk. Mrs. Chin bought 3 quarts of milk. Who bought more milk? How much more?

26. Gladys drank 1 pint of milk at breakfast, 1 cup of milk at lunch, and 1 cup of milk at dinner. How much milk did she drink in all?

Gram and Kilogram

The weight of some objects is given in **grams.**

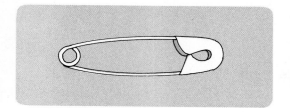

A safety pin weighs
about 1 gram or **1 g.**

A baseball weighs
about 145 grams or 145 g.

Heavier objects are weighed in **kilograms.**

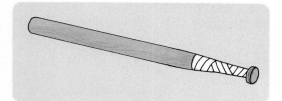

A bat weighs about
1 kilogram or **1 kg.**

A bicycle weighs about
20 kilograms or 20 kg.

$$1 \text{ kilogram } = 1000 \text{ grams}$$
$$1 \text{ kg } = 1000 \text{ g}$$

Exercises

Would you weigh these in *grams* or *kilograms?*

1. crayon

2. desk

3. penny

4. banana

5. horse

6. chair

7. automobile

8. football

9. vitamin pill

174

Choose the best answer.

10.

1 gram   1 kilogram

11.

600 grams   600 kilograms

12.

40 grams   40 kilograms

13.

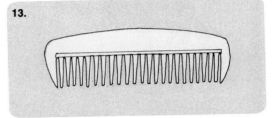

5 grams   5 kilograms

14.

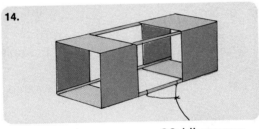

90 grams   90 kilograms

15.

230 grams   230 kilograms

16. A roll of nickels weighs 200 grams. Each nickel weighs 5 grams. How many nickels are in a roll?

17. A man weighs 72 kilograms. His horse weighs 7 times that much. How much does his horse weigh?

18. You and Ida get on a scale. The reading is 66 kilograms. Ida gets off and the reading is 37 kilograms. How much does Ida weigh?

19. A loaf of bread weighs 460 grams. You eat four 20-gram slices. How much does the rest of the loaf weigh?

Ounce, Pound, and Ton

9 pennies weigh about
1 ounce or **1 oz.**

A loaf of bread weighs
about **1 pound** or **1 lb.**

A male bison weighs
about **1 ton.**

1 pound = 16 ounces

1 lb = 16 oz

1 ton = 2000 pounds

Exercises

Would you weigh these in *ounces, pounds,* or *tons?*

1. bag of potatoes

2. airplane

3. apple

4. tennis ball

5. cat

6. ship

Complete.

7. 3 pounds = ___ ounces

8. 5 pounds = ___ ounces

9. 32 ounces = ___ pounds

10. 2 tons = ___ pounds

11. Give the weight of the left side in ounces.

12. How many ounces are needed on the right side to make the scale balance?

2 lb 3 oz   28 oz

Extra Practice—Set A, page 334

Challenge Problems

1. You are to put a fence around a garden like this. How many feet of fence do you need?

2. Find the area of the garden.

3. A tomato plant needs 4 square feet of ground. How many tomato plants could be in the garden?

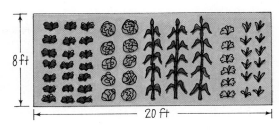

Find the weight of each ball.

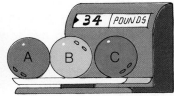

4. Ball A

5. Ball B

6. Ball C

Do the following:

7. Draw a figure like this on heavy paper. Then cut it out. (Each square has sides 10 centimeters long.)

8. Fold on the dashed lines, and tape the pieces to make a box like this.

9. Find the volume of the box.

10. It takes *1 liter* of water to fill such a box. That much water weighs *1 kilogram.*

11. A box like this is filled with water. How much would the water weigh?

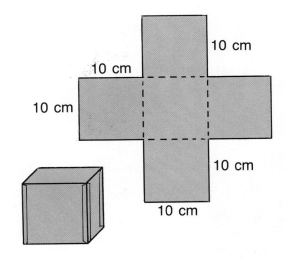

Find the length of the blue line segment

1. in centimeters

2. in inches

3. Find the length of the red line segment to the nearest $\frac{1}{2}$ inch.

4. Would you use *centimeters, meters,* or *kilometers* to find the distance between two towns?

5. Would you use *inches, feet,* or *miles* to find the length of a telephone pole?

6. Find the perimeter.

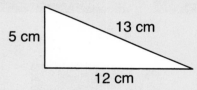

5 cm   13 cm

12 cm

7. Find the area in square inches.

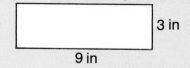

3 in

9 in

8. Find the volume in cubic centimeters.

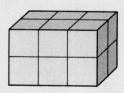

9. Choose the best answer.

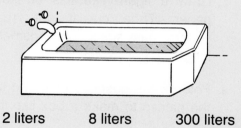

2 liters   8 liters   300 liters

Complete.

10. 1 gallon = ___ quarts

11. 1 pint = ___ cups

12. Would you use *grams* or *kilograms* to find the weight of a nickel?

13. Would you use *ounces, pounds,* or *tons* to find the weight of a large dog?

8 Addition and Subtraction

Frank A. Cezus

Addition (4-digit)

The parachute was invented in 1783. The airplane was invented 120 years later. In what year was the airplane invented?

Add the ones and the tens.	Add the hundreds.	Add the thousands.

Th	H	T	O
		⬚1	
1	7	8	3
+	1	2	0
		0	3

8 T
+ 2 T
⬚1 0 T

Th	H	T	O
	1		
1	7	8	3
+	1	2	0
	9	0	3

1 H
7 H
+1 H
9 H

Th	H	T	O
	1		
1	7	8	3
+	1	2	0
1	9	0	3

The airplane was invented in 1903.

Explain what is done in each step below.

```
   3653        ⬚1           ⬚1 1        1 1
 + 2876  →    3653    →    3653    →    3653
 _____    +2876        +2876        +2876
      9         29          529         6529
```

Exercises

1. 8641
   +1325

2. 3724
   +4106

3. 6431
   + 298

4. 1862
   +1844

5. 1540
   +6813

6. 3575
   +4809

7. 2806
   +3487

8. 6285
   + 994

9. 6320
   +1750

10. 2203
    + 906

11. 8888
    + 22

12. 3643
    +4527

13. 1271
 +8429

14. 7070
 +1982

15. 6438
 + 590

16. 1892
 +5436

17. 8999
 + 64

18. 4828
 +2987

19. 2965
 +5761

20. 4608
 +4608

21. 5475
 +2925

22. 5995
 + 9

23. 6549
 + 678

24. 1978
 +1949

25. 1919
 + 191

26. 6078
 +2948

27. 4567
 +3879

28. 4879
 + 799

29. The sewing machine was invented in 1790. The vacuum cleaner was invented 117 years later. When was the vacuum cleaner invented?

30. The first motion picture was shown in 1895. This was 31 years before TV was invented. When was TV invented?

What Invention?

I was invented by a man named Bell
so that people would not have to yell.

To name the invention, write the letter for the exercise wherever the answer appears below.

P 385
 837
 +794
 2016

N 787
 640
 +899

H 905
 488
 +516

L 1398
 5658
 +1029

T 9895
 430
 + 10

O 827
 18
 +8946

E 1
 1999
 +7090

| 10,335 | 9090 | 8085 | 9090 | P 2016 | 1909 | 9791 | 2326 | 9090 |

Addition (5-digit)

County Fair

Saturday	45,230 people
Sunday	38,465 people

How many people went to the fair these two days?

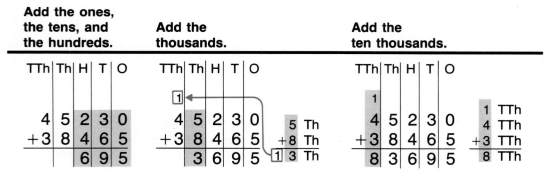

Add the ones, the tens, and the hundreds.

TTh	Th	H	T	O
	4	5	2	3	0
+ 3	8	4	6	5
		6	9	5

Add the thousands.

TTh	Th	H	T	O
1				
	4	5	2	3	0
+ 3	8	4	6	5
	3	6	9	5

  5 Th
+ 8 Th
1 3 Th

Add the ten thousands.

TTh	Th	H	T	O
1				
4	5	2	3	0
+ 3	8	4	6	5
8	3	6	9	5

  1 TTh
  4 TTh
+ 3 TTh
  8 TTh

83,695 people went to the fair.

Exercises

1. 54,072
   +32,624

2. 16,405
   +46,270

3. 24,050
   +28,869

4. 62,285
   + 4,765

5. 10,698
   +84,313

6. 29,614
   + 2,057

7. 41,650
   +29,673

8. 83,592
   + 8,499

9. 72,600 +13,410	**10.** 12,345 +24,065	**11.** 67,092 + 8,148	**12.** 45,017 +34,968
13. 49,897 + 760	**14.** 62,400 +28,700	**15.** 45,527 +30,476	**16.** 37,884 +39,322
17. 60,708 +36,789	**18.** 88,888 + 99	**19.** 54,623 +19,857	**20.** 25,487 + 4,513
21. 62,459 +14,263	**22.** 34,215 +38,695	**23.** 63,246 +18,798	**24.** 99,999 + 1
25. 73,005 14,853 +10,662	**26.** 44,370 3,677 + 215	**27.** 8,045 18,036 + 3,006	**28.** 586 1,694 +89,719

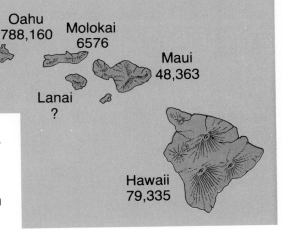

Niihau 296 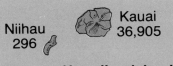 Kauai 36,905   Oahu 788,160   Molokai 6576

Hawaiian Islands
(estimated population)

Lanai ?

Maui 48,363

Hawaii 79,335

29. How many people live on the islands of Maui and Hawaii?

30. What is the combined population of Kauai and Molokai?

31. If all the people on Molokai went to Maui, how many people would be on Maui?

32. How many people live on the islands of Niihau, Molokai, and Maui?

33. 2479 more people live on Lanai than live on Niihau. How many people live on Lanai?

34. What is the total population of the Hawaiian Islands?

Rounding

A youth group collected 5726 pounds of paper. Rounded to the nearest 1000, that is *about 6000* pounds.

Jacqueline Durand

Here is a way to round to the nearest thousand.

Look at the *hundreds digit.*	5 **4** 4 8 ↓ Less than 5, so round down to **5000**	5 **5** 0 0 ↓ Equal to 5, so round up to **6000**	5 **7** 2 6 ↓ More than 5, so round up to **6000**

This is what you are really doing.

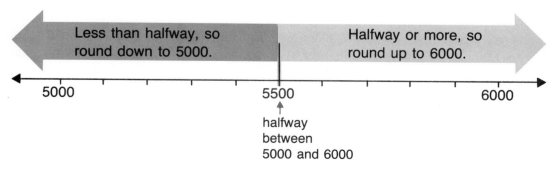

Less than halfway, so round down to 5000.

Halfway or more, so round up to 6000.

5000   5500   6000

↑ halfway between 5000 and 6000

Exercises

What number is halfway between

1. 0 and 1000
2. 3000 and 4000
3. 5000 and 6000

4. 2000 and 3000
5. 8000 and 9000
6. 7000 and 8000

Round to the nearest thousand.

7. 6002
8. 2500
9. 5230
10. 4795

11. 5100
12. 4400
13. 5900
14. 4500

15. 2750
16. 9280
17. 3620
18. 1840

19. 908
20. 6449
21. 6500
22. 6501

23. 7625
24. 3448
25. 8903
26. 2175

27. 6173 people came to the sports show.

28. The community chest collected $7905 this week.

29. 1835 pupils go to the schools in my town.

30. The school library has 4087 books.

Name four numbers you would round to

31. 1000
32. 4000
33. 9000
34. 5000

Looking Ahead

Do not add. Guess each sum to the nearest thousand.

1.   2100
   $+3200$

2.   5900
   $+2050$

3.   1300
   $+6008$

4.   4730
   $+3500$

Estimating Sums

John Colwell/Grant Heilman

The net had 2512 fish in the first catch. There were 4328 fish in the second catch.

You can **estimate** how many fish were caught by doing this.

$$
\begin{array}{l}
2512 \longrightarrow \text{Round to the} \longrightarrow 3000 \\
+4328 \longrightarrow \text{nearest 1000.} \longrightarrow +4000 \\
 \text{Add.} \longrightarrow 7000
\end{array}
$$

About 7000 fish were caught.

Exercises

Estimate each sum to the nearest thousand.

1. $\begin{array}{r} 6732 \\ +948 \end{array} \longrightarrow \begin{array}{r} 7\ 0\ 0\ 0 \\ +1\ 0\ 0\ 0 \\ \hline \blacksquare\ \blacksquare\ \blacksquare\ \blacksquare \end{array}$

2. $\begin{array}{r} 2317 \\ +2098 \end{array}$

3. $\begin{array}{r} 3595 \\ +2405 \end{array}$

4. $\begin{array}{r} 4250 \\ +3180 \end{array}$

5. $\begin{array}{r} 5630 \\ +2810 \end{array}$

6. $\begin{array}{r} 2703 \\ +6098 \end{array}$

7. $\begin{array}{r} 3349 \\ +3902 \end{array}$

Write an estimate. Then find the sum.

8. $\begin{array}{r} 2890 \\ +6005 \\ \hline \end{array}$
9. $\begin{array}{r} 3600 \\ +4800 \\ \hline \end{array}$
10. $\begin{array}{r} 1207 \\ +7706 \\ \hline \end{array}$
11. $\begin{array}{r} 2450 \\ +2569 \\ \hline \end{array}$

12. $\begin{array}{r} 7869 \\ +\ 994 \\ \hline \end{array}$
13. $\begin{array}{r} 3135 \\ +3925 \\ \hline \end{array}$
14. $\begin{array}{r} 1764 \\ +\ 842 \\ \hline \end{array}$
15. $\begin{array}{r} 4196 \\ +4509 \\ \hline \end{array}$

16. $\begin{array}{r} 1049 \\ +1278 \\ \hline \end{array}$
17. $\begin{array}{r} 3492 \\ +\ 508 \\ \hline \end{array}$
18. $\begin{array}{r} 6399 \\ +2049 \\ \hline \end{array}$
19. $\begin{array}{r} 7183 \\ +2266 \\ \hline \end{array}$

20. $\begin{array}{r} 5558 \\ +3247 \\ \hline \end{array}$
21. $\begin{array}{r} 905 \\ +7901 \\ \hline \end{array}$
22. $\begin{array}{r} 2727 \\ +6273 \\ \hline \end{array}$
23. $\begin{array}{r} 3984 \\ +5016 \\ \hline \end{array}$

24. $\begin{array}{r} 2731 \\ +\ 985 \\ \hline \end{array}$
25. $\begin{array}{r} 7196 \\ +1239 \\ \hline \end{array}$
26. $\begin{array}{r} 1055 \\ +2987 \\ \hline \end{array}$
27. $\begin{array}{r} 6744 \\ +\ 256 \\ \hline \end{array}$

Estimate each distance to the nearest thousand miles.

28. from New York to Nairobi and then to Paris

29. from San Francisco to Lima and then to Mexico City

30. from London to New York and then to Rio de Janeiro

31. from New York to Rio de Janeiro and then to Nairobi

32. from New York to Rio de Janeiro to Nairobi and then to New York

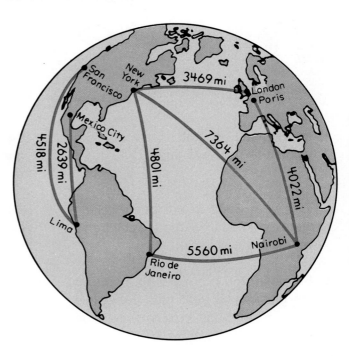

Solving Problems

The village of Homewood holds a picnic each year. Only people who live in Homewood may come.

People at Picnic		Admission	
This Year	1057	Adults	$5
Last Year	893	Children	$2

1. How many people came to the picnic the past two years?

2. 294 adults came to the picnic last year. How many children came to the picnic last year?

3. This year $962 in children's tickets were sold. How many children's tickets were sold?

4. 576 adults came to the picnic this year. How much did they pay for their tickets altogether?

5. Suppose 250 more people come to the picnic next year than came this year. How many people would be at the picnic next year?

6. This year 20,943 people who live in Homewood did not come to the picnic. How many people live in Homewood?

Multiply.

1. 70 ×3	2. 800 ×6	3. 21 ×4	4. 37 ×2	5. 88 ×5
6. 27 ×8	7. 49 ×7	8. 63 ×9	9. 86 ×5	10. 240 ×2
11. 108 ×9	12. 731 ×4	13. 609 ×3	14. 446 ×9	15. 358 ×5

Divide and check.

16. 1)8̅

17. 7)0̅

18. 7)51̅

19. 8)51̅

20. 3)90̅

21. 6)71̅

22. 5)90̅

23. 4)852̅

24. 7)847̅

25. 3)835̅

26. 5)415̅

27. 9)710̅

28. There are 52 weeks in a year. How many weeks are in 5 years?

29. 5 people shared $745 equally. How much money did each person get?

30. A score of 500 wins. Your score is 299. How many more points do you need to win?

31. Lynn has $149. Earl has $151 more than that. How much does Earl have?

32. Write the letter of each figure that is a rectangle.

33. Write the letter of each figure that is a square.

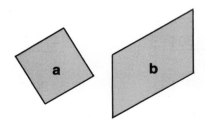
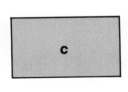
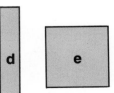
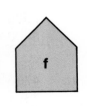

189

Subtraction (4-digit)

You can subtract 4-digit numbers like this.

Subtract the ones and the tens.	Rename.	Subtract the hundreds and the thousands.

Th	H	T	O
5	2	9	8
−4	5	8	6
		1	2

	4	12		
Th	H	T	O
5̸	2	9	8
−4	5	8	6
		1	2

Rename 5 thousands,
2 hundreds as
4 thousands, 12 hundreds.

	4	12		
Th	H	T	O
5̸	2̸	9	8
−4	5	8	6
	7	1	2

Exercises

1. $\begin{array}{r} 3540 \\ -\ 200 \\ \hline \end{array}$

2. $\begin{array}{r} 4763 \\ -1230 \\ \hline \end{array}$

3. $\begin{array}{r} 8945 \\ -4575 \\ \hline \end{array}$

4. $\begin{array}{r} 6263 \\ -3047 \\ \hline \end{array}$

5. $\begin{array}{r} 2062 \\ -\ 203 \\ \hline \end{array}$

6. $\begin{array}{r} 4650 \\ -\ 471 \\ \hline \end{array}$

7. $\begin{array}{r} 2700 \\ -1599 \\ \hline \end{array}$

8. $\begin{array}{r} 4000 \\ -3415 \\ \hline \end{array}$

9. $\begin{array}{r} 4682 \\ -\ 193 \\ \hline \end{array}$

10. $\begin{array}{r} 2170 \\ -1943 \\ \hline \end{array}$

11. $\begin{array}{r} 8276 \\ -4358 \\ \hline \end{array}$

12. $\begin{array}{r} 6731 \\ -5038 \\ \hline \end{array}$

13. $\begin{array}{r} 5980 \\ -3400 \\ \hline \end{array}$

14. $\begin{array}{r} 4990 \\ -\ 950 \\ \hline \end{array}$

15. $\begin{array}{r} 3628 \\ -1304 \\ \hline \end{array}$

16. $\begin{array}{r} 7094 \\ -\ 83 \\ \hline \end{array}$

17. $\begin{array}{r} 4706 \\ -4384 \\ \hline \end{array}$

18. $\begin{array}{r} 3204 \\ -\ 161 \\ \hline \end{array}$

19. $\begin{array}{r} 6044 \\ -2912 \\ \hline \end{array}$

20. $\begin{array}{r} 2093 \\ -\ 545 \\ \hline \end{array}$

21. 7043
   − 85
	22. 3835
	  −3698
		23. 5472
		  −3863
			24. 8183
			  − 195

25. 2376
  −1859
	26. 6028
	  − 78
		27. 4132
		  − 246
			28. 7346
			  −5267

29. 8791
  −3895
	30. 4000
	  −1876
		31. 6000
		  − 647
			32. 5922
			  −4947

33. George Washington was elected President in 1789. How old was he then?

34. How old was George Washington when he died?

35. How old was Benjamin Franklin when he died?

36. How old was Benjamin Franklin when George Washington was born?

37. Delaware became the first state in 1787. Washington became a state in 1889. How many years after Delaware became a state did Washington become a state?

George Washington

Born: 1732

Died: 1799

Benjamin Franklin

Born: 1706

Died: 1790

What Is Missing?

1.   8 2 5 7
  −6 3 4 ▪
  ▪ ▪ ▪ 9

2.   6 8 3 ▪
  −1 9 ▪ 1
  ▪ ▪ 9 9

3.   ▪ 3 ▪ 3
  −7 ▪ 9 ▪
   8 0 6

Subtraction (5-digit)

Mr. Lynch has driven his car 30,670 miles. Dr. Bauer has driven her car 11,750 miles. How much farther has Mr. Lynch driven his car?

Subtract the ones and the tens.	Rename and subtract the hundreds.	Subtract the thousands and the ten thousands.

TTh	Th	H	T	O
3	0	6	7	0
−1	1	7	5	0
			2	0

TTh	Th	H	T	O
	9			
2	10	16		
3	0	6	7	0
−1	1	7	5	0
		9	2	0

TTh	Th	H	T	O
	9			
2	10	16		
3	0	6	7	0
−1	1	7	5	0
1	8	9	2	0

Mr. Lynch has driven his car 18,920 miles farther.

Exercises

1. 72,340
   − 60,130

2. 88,390
   − 46,250

3. 26,407
   − 16,103

4. 50,436
   − 40,206

5. 78,573
   − 54,509

6. 65,828
   − 1,376

7. 92,674
   −   931

8. 43,822
   − 10,619

9. 78,421
   − 35,410

10. 90,407
    −   800

11. 62,300
    − 1,600

12. 26,480
    − 23,290

13. 46,827
    − 13,357

14. 82,500
    − 3,446

15. 39,017
    −   589

16. 50,000
    − 26,328

17.	23,703 − 1,428	18.	52,455 − 369	19.	89,106 − 4,275	20.	61,561 −20,608
21.	55,482 −29,567	22.	54,829 − 7,249	23.	46,300 − 643	24.	75,000 −19,506
25.	20,000 −14,939	26.	30,367 −24,598	27.	60,742 −41,764	28.	40,000 − 2,428

29. How many more miles has Ron's jeep been driven than Pam's car?

30. Pam's car needs an oil change at 10,500 miles. How many miles can she go before that?

31. At 60,000 miles Ron will buy a new jeep. How many more miles will he drive the jeep?

32. Ron had a tune-up on his jeep at 28,757 miles. How many miles has he driven since then?

Guess the number

Clues:

Ones digit: number of coins in an empty purse

Tens digit: number of sides in a pentagon

Hundreds digit: half a dozen

Thousands digit: number of days in a week

Ten Thousands digit: seventeen less than twenty-five

193

Checking Subtraction

You can check the answer of a subtraction by adding.

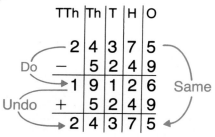

Exercises

Subtract and check.

1.   6 7 0 9
    −   4 3 2
    ▨ ▨ ▨ ▨
    +   4 3 2
    ▨ ▨ ▨ ▨

2.   3 5 4 8
    −1 3 0 1
    ▨ ▨ ▨ ▨
    +1 3 0 1
    ▨ ▨ ▨ ▨

3.   439
    −405

4.   622
    −560

5.   4251
    −   80

6.   96,813
    − 3,407

7.   8200
    − 625

8.   9929
    −6843

9.   50,000
    −   500

10.   706
    −607

11.   2647
    − 392

12.   57,265
    −38,074

13.   9929
    − 989

14.   42,160
    − 8,925

15.   537
    −248

16.   661
    −465

17.   34,414
    − 2,429

18.   8821
    −3476

19.   60,000
    −12,384

20.   7040
    − 432

21.   355
    − 88

22.   87,690
    − 6,240

23.   7346
    − 230

24.   51,130
    − 210

25.   604
    −310

26.   442
    − 60

27.   28,427
    −12,496

28.   4062
    −2846

29.   94,066
    −72,089

30.   848
    −379

31.   5426
    − 148

Extra Practice—Set A, page 336

Treasure Hunt

Follow the directions to find the treasure.
The final answer will tell you the number of gold coins.

START

Add 8443.

Subtract 2165.

Add 80,096.

Subtract 54,720.

POISON WATER

Add 1325.

Subtract 9419.

Subtract 10,000.

Estimating Differences

The *Maria* has 4863 passengers. The *Dianna* has 7128 passengers. About how many more people are on the *Dianna*?

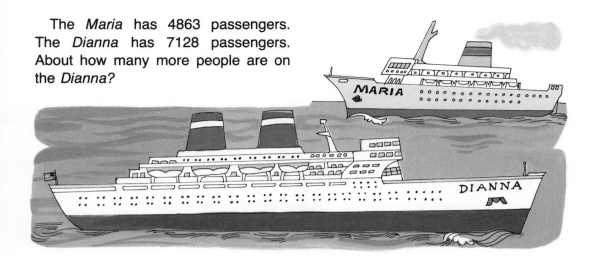

Estimate the difference to find out.

```
7128  ─────── Round to the    ────▶   7000
−4863 ─────── nearest 1000.   ────▶  −5000
                  Subtract.   ────▶   2000
```

There are about 2000 more people on the *Dianna*.

Exercises

Estimate each difference.

1. 2942 ──▶   3 0 0 0
     −1799   −2 0 0 0
                 ▪ ▪ ▪ ▪

2.   5190
    − 924

3.   8722
    −1500

4. 7209
    −3353

5.   8828
    −3047

6.   6148
    −3804

7.   5851
    −2158

Write an estimate. Then find the difference.

8. 4953
  − 1218

9. 8017
  − 940

10. 3530
  − 2511

11. 9432
  − 5102

12. 2508
  − 1579

13. 4204
  − 901

14. 5622
  − 2950

15. 4623
  − 2683

16. 2275
  − 1347

17. 4539
  − 2641

18. 8508
  − 4653

19. 7400
  − 5178

20. 5852
  − 2056

21. 9500
  − 3987

22. 3001
  − 965

23. 6002
  − 2994

24. There were 6950 gallons of fuel. A crew put 2215 gallons in one plane and 3905 gallons in another. About how many gallons of fuel were left?

25. 9124 people live in a town. Ten years ago only 7825 people lived in that town. About how many more people live in the town now?

Photo Researchers

First in History

How long ago were these? Subtract to find out.

1. The first bicycle with 2 wheels the same size was built in 1889.

2. The first skyscraper was built in 1884.

3. The first basketball game was played in 1892.

4. The first math text in China was written about the year 295.

Extra Practice—Set B, page 336

Solving Problems

1. Mount St. Helens was 9677 feet tall. It lost 1079 feet from the top when it erupted in 1980. How tall was it then?

2. Mount St. Helens erupted in 1857. It did not erupt again until 1980. How many years were there between eruptions?

3. In 1669 Mount Etna erupted. Mount Tambora erupted 146 years later. In what year did Mount Tambora erupt?

4. Mauna Loa, a volcano in Hawaii, is 13,677 feet tall. Paricutin, a volcano in Mexico, is 9213 feet tall. How much taller is Mauna Loa?

5. Surtsey, a volcano in the Atlantic Ocean, is 567 feet tall. How many yards is that? (3 feet = 1 yard)

6. Masada, a huge rock in Israel, is 467 yards tall. How many feet is that?

7. Mount Logan is 19,850 feet tall. A plane is flying 4250 feet above it. How high is the plane flying?

8. Mount Rainier is 14,410 feet tall. A climber climbs up 5280 feet. How much farther must the climber go in order to reach the top?

9. Disneyland opened in 1955. Disney World opened 16 years later. In what year did Disney World open?

10. How many years ago did Disneyland open?

11. Donald Duck first appeared in 1934. How old is Donald Duck?

12. Mickey Mouse is 6 years older than Donald Duck. In what year did Mickey Mouse first appear?

13. Pluto rides the train 135 times a week. How many times does he ride the train in 4 weeks?

14. Goofy shook hands with 1725 boys and 1875 girls. How many children did he shake hands with?

15. 544 pupils rode to Disneyland in 8 buses. The same number of pupils rode in each bus. How many pupils rode in each bus?

16. The trip to Disneyland is 1434 miles. They have already driven 578 miles. How many miles are left to go?

17. 38,286 children were at Disney World. There were 75,460 people altogether. How many of them were adults?

18. 8 people go on a ride at a time. There are 96 people ahead of you in line for the ride. How many groups of 8 will go before you?

CHAPTER REVIEW

Add.

1. 1437
    + 268

2. 5243
    +2631

3. 3442
    +4598

4. 6027
    + 786

5. 54,782
    +   367

6. 26,104
    + 9,897

7. 31,094
    +42,059

8. 65,453
    +20,847

Write an estimate. Then find the sum.

9. 4002
    +3900

10. 6540
     +2161

11. 3288
     +5500

12. 1841
     + 992

Subtract.

13. 3412
     - 179

14. 1650
     - 521

15. 7174
     -4508

16. 4209
     -2347

17. 78,613
     -    324

18. 34,721
     -    275

19. 83,400
     - 6,236

20. 22,801
     -15,093

Write an estimate. Then subtract and check.

21. 6100
     -4900

22. 8840
     -5170

23. 7921
     -1285

24. 5019
     - 924

25. A jigsaw puzzle has 1500 pieces. You have 785 pieces put together. How many pieces do you still have to put together?

26. 15,687 fans saw the Sox play yesterday, and 22,816 fans saw them play today. How many fans saw the 2 games?

9 Multiplication

Fredrik D. Bodin

Multiplying 1000's

	2 thousands	→	Th	H	T	O	→	2000
	$\times 4$		2	0	0	0		$\times 4$
	8 thousands		$\times$		4			8000
			8	0	0	0		

	6 thousands	→	TTh	Th	H	T	O	→	6,000
	$\times 5$			6	0	0	0		$\times 5$
	30 thousands			$\times$		5			30,000
			3	0	0	0	0		

	9 thousands	→	TTh	Th	H	T	O	→	9,000
	$\times 6$			9	0	0	0		$\times 6$
	54 thousands			$\times$		6			54,000
			5	4	0	0	0		

Exercises

1.
$$\begin{array}{r} 2 \text{ thousands} \\ \times 3 \\ \hline 6 \text{ thousands} \end{array} \longrightarrow \begin{array}{r} 2000 \\ \times 3 \\ \hline \end{array}$$

2.
$$\begin{array}{r} 8 \text{ thousands} \\ \times 5 \\ \hline 40 \text{ thousands} \end{array} \longrightarrow \begin{array}{r} 8000 \\ \times 5 \\ \hline \end{array}$$

3.
$$\begin{array}{r} 1000 \\ \times 7 \\ \hline \end{array}$$

4.
$$\begin{array}{r} 9000 \\ \times 2 \\ \hline \end{array}$$

5.
$$\begin{array}{r} 7000 \\ \times 4 \\ \hline \end{array}$$

6.
$$\begin{array}{r} 8000 \\ \times 6 \\ \hline \end{array}$$

7.
$$\begin{array}{r} 2000 \\ \times 2 \\ \hline \end{array}$$

8.
$$\begin{array}{r} 5000 \\ \times 1 \\ \hline \end{array}$$

9.
$$\begin{array}{r} 3000 \\ \times 2 \\ \hline \end{array}$$

10.
$$\begin{array}{r} 2000 \\ \times 6 \\ \hline \end{array}$$

11.
$$\begin{array}{r} 3000 \\ \times 4 \\ \hline \end{array}$$

12.
$$\begin{array}{r} 4000 \\ \times 2 \\ \hline \end{array}$$

13.
$$\begin{array}{r} 3000 \\ \times 5 \\ \hline \end{array}$$

14.
$$\begin{array}{r} 6000 \\ \times 3 \\ \hline \end{array}$$

15.
$$\begin{array}{r} 4000 \\ \times 5 \\ \hline \end{array}$$

16.
$$\begin{array}{r} 2000 \\ \times 8 \\ \hline \end{array}$$

17.
$$\begin{array}{r} 8000 \\ \times 3 \\ \hline \end{array}$$

18.
$$\begin{array}{r} 9000 \\ \times 4 \\ \hline \end{array}$$

19.	9000 ×5	20.	3000 ×9	21.	7000 ×5	22.	6000 ×8
23.	6000 ×6	24.	2000 ×5	25.	2000 ×9	26.	8000 ×7
27.	7000 ×7	28.	5000 ×9	29.	5000 ×5	30.	9000 ×7
31.	4000 ×4	32.	8000 ×9	33.	8000 ×8	34.	9000 ×9

35. Pins come in boxes of 1000 each. How many pins are in 7 boxes?

36. A company makes 5000 toys each day. How many toys does it make in 8 days?

37. A theater holds 2000 people. There are 9 shows a day. How many people can see the show in a day?

38. 9 tank trucks are filled with fuel. Each truck holds 6000 gallons. How many gallons are in all the trucks?

Money Math

Complete. Name each amount in two other ways.

	Number of Dollars	Number of Dimes	Number of Pennies
	1	10	100
1.	10		
2.		20	
3.			2000
4.		500	
5.	500		

Multiplication (4-digit by 1-digit)

The largest pizza ever made had an area of 5027 square feet. What would the area of 4 of those pizzas be?

Multiply the ones and the tens by 4.	Multiply the hundreds by 4.	Multiply the thousands by 4.

Th	H	T	O
	1	2	
5	0	2	7
		×	4
		0	8

Th	H	T	O
	1	2	
5	0	2	7
		×	4
1		0	8

$$\begin{array}{r} 0 \text{ H} \\ \times 4 \\ \hline 0 \text{ H} \\ +1 \text{ H} \\ \hline 1 \text{ H} \end{array}$$

TTh	Th	H	T	O
		1	2	
	5	0	2	7
			×	4
2	0	1	0	8

$$\begin{array}{r} 5 \text{ Th} \\ \times 4 \\ \hline 2\,0 \text{ Th} \end{array}$$

The area would be 20,108 square feet.

Exercises

1. 2430
   ×2

2. 3114
   ×2

3. 2067
   ×4

4. 9256
   ×3

5. 4089
   ×5

6. 8365
   ×2

7. 1128
   ×7

8. 8109
   ×7

9. 1029
×6

10. 1104
×9

11. 2475
×2

12. 1098
×8

13. 1173
×5

14. 1064
×7

15. 3286
×3

16. 2185
×4

17. 2065
×8

18. 7349
×2

19. 2079
×9

20. 6458
×2

21. 4136
×6

22. 5087
×7

23. 8259
×3

24. 9165
×5

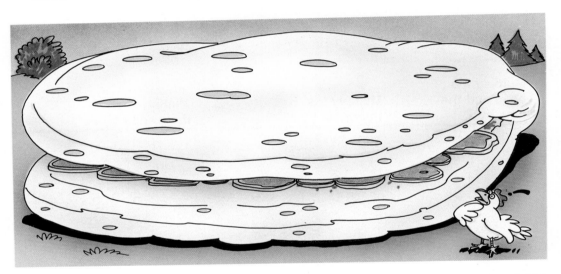

25. The largest omelette ever made weighed 2284 pounds. How much would 3 of those omelettes weigh?

26. Mr. Lucci made a sausage 2122 feet long. The longest sausage ever made was 5 times that long. How long was it?

27. Henny made an omelette with 3110 eggs. There were 4 times that many eggs in the largest omelette ever made. How many eggs were in it?

28. The longest sausage ever made weighed 1245 kilograms. How much would 3 of those sausages weigh?

Multiplication (4-digit by 1-digit)

One person uses about 1505 liters of water each day. How much water is that each week?

Multiply the ones and the tens by 7.	Multiply the hundreds by 7.	Multiply the thousands by 7.

Th	H	T	O
		3	
1	5	0	5
		×	7
		3	5

Th	H	T	O
③		3	
1	5	0	5
		×	7
	5	3	5

    5 H
   ×7
  ③5 H

TTh	Th	H	T	O
	3		3	
	1	5	0	5
			×	7
1	0	5	3	5

    1 Th
   ×7
    7 Th
  +3 Th
  1 0 Th

That is about 10,535 liters each week.

Exercises

1. 2400
   ×4

2. 1730
   ×5

3. 4605
   ×2

4. 2562
   ×3

5. 1801
   ×6

6. 3623
   ×4

7. 2714
   ×7

8. 5264
   ×8

9. 2673
×2

10. 1584
×6

11. 1239
×8

12. 2964
×3

13. 1852
×4

14. 4709
×2

15. 1655
×5

16. 1076
×7

17. 6095
×3

18. 5237
×4

19. 4761
×9

20. 7394
×6

21. 8254
×7

22. 6498
×5

23. 9957
×3

24. 7458
×8

25. Each aircraft carrier has a crew of 4940 persons. How many people are on the crews of 8 aircraft carriers?

26. Each crew member is served 3 meals a day. How many meals are served each day on one aircraft carrier?

Poles Apart

1. How far is it through the earth from the North Pole to the South Pole?

2. How far is it through the earth from point A to point B?

3. How far is it around the earth from the North Pole to the South Pole and back to the North Pole?

4. It is 24,902 miles around the earth at the equator. How much farther is that than around the earth from pole to pole?

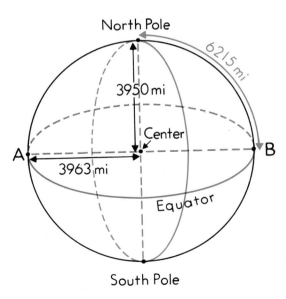

North Pole

6215 mi

3950 mi

Center

A

B

3963 mi

Equator

South Pole

Extra Practice—Set B, page 337

Multiples of 10

Notice the pattern of 0's.

$$\begin{array}{r} 2 \\ \times 3 \\ \hline 6 \end{array}$$

$$\begin{array}{r} 20 \\ \times 3 \\ \hline 60 \end{array}$$
 1 zero
+ no zeros
1 zero

$$\begin{array}{r} 20 \\ \times 30 \\ \hline 600 \end{array}$$
 1 zero
+ 1 zero
2 zeros

$$\begin{array}{r} 200 \\ \times 30 \\ \hline 6000 \end{array}$$
 2 zeros
+ 1 zero
3 zeros

See how the pattern continues.

$$\begin{array}{r} 4 \\ \times 7 \\ \hline 28 \end{array}$$

$$\begin{array}{r} 40 \\ \times 7 \\ \hline 280 \end{array}$$
 1 zero
+ no zeros
1 zero

$$\begin{array}{r} 40 \\ \times 70 \\ \hline 2800 \end{array}$$
 1 zero
+ 1 zero
2 zeros

$$\begin{array}{r} 400 \\ \times 70 \\ \hline 28,000 \end{array}$$
 2 zeros
+ 1 zero
3 zeros

Tell how the pattern is shown below.

$$\begin{array}{r} 6 \\ \times 5 \\ \hline 30 \end{array}$$

$$\begin{array}{r} 60 \\ \times 5 \\ \hline 300 \end{array}$$

$$\begin{array}{r} 60 \\ \times 50 \\ \hline 3000 \end{array}$$

$$\begin{array}{r} 600 \\ \times 50 \\ \hline 30,000 \end{array}$$

Exercises

1. $\begin{array}{r} 10 \\ \times 90 \\ \hline \end{array}$
2. $\begin{array}{r} 100 \\ \times 90 \\ \hline \end{array}$
3. $\begin{array}{r} 40 \\ \times 20 \\ \hline \end{array}$
4. $\begin{array}{r} 400 \\ \times 20 \\ \hline \end{array}$
5. $\begin{array}{r} 30 \\ \times 30 \\ \hline \end{array}$

6. $\begin{array}{r} 30 \\ \times 40 \\ \hline \end{array}$
7. $\begin{array}{r} 300 \\ \times 40 \\ \hline \end{array}$
8. $\begin{array}{r} 80 \\ \times 50 \\ \hline \end{array}$
9. $\begin{array}{r} 800 \\ \times 50 \\ \hline \end{array}$
10. $\begin{array}{r} 500 \\ \times 50 \\ \hline \end{array}$

11. $\begin{array}{r} 30 \\ \times 80 \\ \hline \end{array}$
12. $\begin{array}{r} 50 \\ \times 40 \\ \hline \end{array}$
13. $\begin{array}{r} 700 \\ \times 50 \\ \hline \end{array}$
14. $\begin{array}{r} 60 \\ \times 60 \\ \hline \end{array}$
15. $\begin{array}{r} 900 \\ \times 40 \\ \hline \end{array}$

16. $\begin{array}{r} 800 \\ \times 80 \\ \hline \end{array}$
17. $\begin{array}{r} 90 \\ \times 70 \\ \hline \end{array}$
18. $\begin{array}{r} 700 \\ \times 70 \\ \hline \end{array}$
19. $\begin{array}{r} 800 \\ \times 70 \\ \hline \end{array}$
20. $\begin{array}{r} 90 \\ \times 90 \\ \hline \end{array}$

Extra Practice—Set A, page 338

Multiples of 10

You can use the pattern of 0's to multiply 21 by 40.

$$
\begin{array}{ccc}
21 & 21 & \text{no zeros} \\
\times 4 \longrightarrow \times 40 & & +1 \text{ zero} \\
\hline
84 & 840 & 1 \text{ zero}
\end{array}
$$

Tell how the pattern is used to multiply 56 by 70.

$$
\begin{array}{cc}
\overset{4}{56} & 56 \\
\times 7 \longrightarrow \times 70 \\
\hline
392 & 3920
\end{array}
$$

Exercises

1. $\begin{array}{r}21\\ \times 40\\ \hline\end{array}$	2. $\begin{array}{r}88\\ \times 10\\ \hline\end{array}$	3. $\begin{array}{r}13\\ \times 50\\ \hline\end{array}$	4. $\begin{array}{r}36\\ \times 20\\ \hline\end{array}$	5. $\begin{array}{r}91\\ \times 30\\ \hline\end{array}$	6. $\begin{array}{r}21\\ \times 50\\ \hline\end{array}$
7. $\begin{array}{r}47\\ \times 50\\ \hline\end{array}$	8. $\begin{array}{r}36\\ \times 30\\ \hline\end{array}$	9. $\begin{array}{r}17\\ \times 30\\ \hline\end{array}$	10. $\begin{array}{r}74\\ \times 20\\ \hline\end{array}$	11. $\begin{array}{r}28\\ \times 40\\ \hline\end{array}$	12. $\begin{array}{r}82\\ \times 40\\ \hline\end{array}$
13. $\begin{array}{r}25\\ \times 60\\ \hline\end{array}$	14. $\begin{array}{r}29\\ \times 20\\ \hline\end{array}$	15. $\begin{array}{r}22\\ \times 80\\ \hline\end{array}$	16. $\begin{array}{r}39\\ \times 50\\ \hline\end{array}$	17. $\begin{array}{r}18\\ \times 90\\ \hline\end{array}$	18. $\begin{array}{r}67\\ \times 70\\ \hline\end{array}$
19. $\begin{array}{r}54\\ \times 60\\ \hline\end{array}$	20. $\begin{array}{r}63\\ \times 90\\ \hline\end{array}$	21. $\begin{array}{r}78\\ \times 80\\ \hline\end{array}$	22. $\begin{array}{r}96\\ \times 70\\ \hline\end{array}$	23. $\begin{array}{r}87\\ \times 50\\ \hline\end{array}$	24. $\begin{array}{r}55\\ \times 90\\ \hline\end{array}$
25. $\begin{array}{r}86\\ \times 60\\ \hline\end{array}$	26. $\begin{array}{r}81\\ \times 70\\ \hline\end{array}$	27. $\begin{array}{r}49\\ \times 30\\ \hline\end{array}$	28. $\begin{array}{r}83\\ \times 80\\ \hline\end{array}$	29. $\begin{array}{r}46\\ \times 40\\ \hline\end{array}$	30. $\begin{array}{r}65\\ \times 70\\ \hline\end{array}$

31. A car can go 35 miles on a gallon of gasoline. How far can it go on 20 gallons?

32. A school put 28 desks in each of 50 rooms. How many desks were there altogether?

Multiplication (2-digit by 2-digit)

You have learned how to multiply 21 by 40. Now multiply 21 by 43.

Multiply by 3.	Multiply by 40.	Add the products.

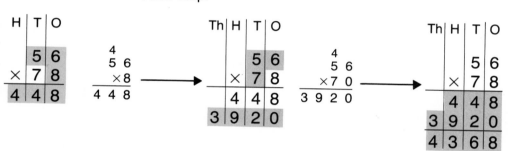

Tell what is done in each step.

Exercises

1. 23 ×32		**2.** 33 ×33		**3.** 16 ×12		**4.** 36 ×21		**5.** 51 ×16		**6.** 25 ×38	
7. 37 ×19		**8.** 43 ×41		**9.** 54 ×25		**10.** 30 ×67		**11.** 98 ×22		**12.** 18 ×13	
13. 85 ×37		**14.** 12 ×15		**15.** 39 ×17		**16.** 34 ×22		**17.** 62 ×19		**18.** 84 ×16	

19.	42 ×21	20.	50 ×24	21.	48 ×39	22.	32 ×51	23.	26 ×86	24.	44 ×44
25.	94 ×36	26.	86 ×47	27.	54 ×78	28.	69 ×63	29.	75 ×84	30.	59 ×15
31.	40 ×76	32.	86 ×87	33.	58 ×61	34.	96 ×83	35.	97 ×92	36.	28 ×36

37. Chu Lin is 12 years old today. How many months is that?

38. A quarter has the same value as 25¢. What is the value of 16 quarters?

39. Some astronauts were in space for 84 days. How many hours were they in space?

40. It took Columbus 36 days to cross the Atlantic Ocean. How many hours did it take?

Order, Please!

Complete.

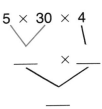

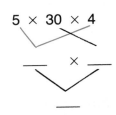

Are the answers the same?

Does it matter which two numbers you multiply first?

Now see if you can do these in your head.

1. $8 \times 70 \times 5 = \square$ 2. $90 \times 5 \times 6 = \square$ 3. $25 \times 9 \times 4 = \square$

Estimating Products

Lee's heart beats about 87 times a minute. Estimate how many times it beats in 33 minutes.

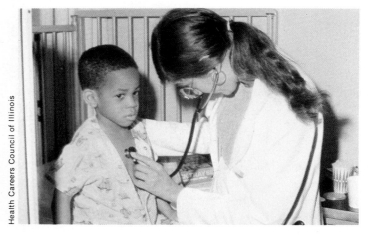

Health Careers Council of Illinois

To estimate the product of 87 and 33, round both numbers. Then multiply the new numbers.

87 —— to the nearest 10 ⟶ 90
×33 —— to the nearest 10 ⟶ ×30
                                    2700

Lee's heart beats about 2700 times.

Exercises

Estimate each product.

1. 35 ⟶ 4 0
   ×41   × 4 0
   ▮ ▮ ▮ ▮

2. 21
   ×19

3. 38
   ×11

4. 51
   ×18

5. 49
   ×48

6. 72
   ×54

7. 65
   ×87

8. 28
   ×71

9. 92
   ×83

10. 31
×24

11. 12
×29

12. 38
×18

13. 64
×11

14. 25
×33

15. 71
×12

16. 24
×26

17. 81
×12

18. 19
×37

19. 85
×93

20. 41
×48

21. 32
×35

22. 53
×59

23. 68
×22

24. 42
×77

25. 92
×36

26. 26
×49

27. 55
×34

28. 88
×18

29. 43
×83

30. 65
×58

31. 84
×62

32. 36
×54

33. 67
×79

34. 97
×14

35. An elephant's heart beats about 34 times a minute. About how many times does it beat in 45 minutes?

36. Each minute a mouse's heart beats about 17 times as often as an elephant's heart. About how many times does a mouse's heart beat each minute?

It's Your Choice

You have been offered a job for 10 days. You may choose one of these two ways to be paid.

Way 1:

$50 a day for 10 days

Way 2:

$1 on day 1, $2 on day 2, $4 on day 3, $8 on day 4, $16 on day 5, and so on

Which way would you choose?

How much more would you earn with your way than with the other way?

Extra Practice—Set A, page 339

213

Multiplication (3-digit by 2-digit)

Farmer Frank planted 113 acres of soybeans. He hopes to get 45 bushels of soybeans from each acre. How many bushels does he hope to get?

Multiply by 5.	Multiply by 40.	Add the products.

Multiply by 5.

H	T	O
1	1	3
×	4	5
5	6	5

```
  1
 113
  ×5
 565
```

Multiply by 40.

Th	H	T	O
	1	1	3
	×	4	5
	5	6	5
4	5	2	0

```
   1
  113
  ×40
 4520
```

no zeros
+ 1 zero
1 zero

Add the products.

Th	H	T	O
	1	1	3
	×	4	5
	5	6	5
4	5	2	0
5	0	8	5

He hopes to get 5085 bushels of soybeans.

Tell what is done in each step.

Th	H	T	O
	7	0	8
	×	6	9
6	3	7	2

```
   7
  708
   ×9
 6372
```

TTh	Th	H	T	O
		7	0	8
		×	6	9
	6	3	7	2
4	2	4	8	0

```
    4
  708
  ×60
 42480
```

TTh	Th	H	T	O
		7	0	8
		×	6	9
	6	3	7	2
4	2	4	8	0
4	8	8	5	2

Exercises

1. 112×42

2. 231×30

3. 100×39

4. 678×11

5. 310×23

6. 350×10

7. 204×34

8. 800×72

9. 512×45

10. 876×12

11. 267×90

12. 246×38

13. 609×17

14. 179×48

15. 900×50

16. 460×46

17. 399×70

18. 187×68

19. 807×79

20. 500×89

21. 351×69

22. 578×84

23. 904×97

24. 999×90

25. 750×75

26. Farmer Frank bought 105 bags of corn seed. Each bag cost $60. How much did he pay for corn seed?

27. Farmer Frank planted 425 acres of corn. He hopes to get 95 bushels of corn from each acre. How many bushels does he hope to get?

28. A bushel of corn weighs 56 pounds. How much do 875 bushels weigh?

Extra Practice—Set B, page 339

Multiplication Practice

1. $\begin{array}{r} 7000 \\ \times\ 8 \\ \hline \end{array}$

2. $\begin{array}{r} 3204 \\ \times\ 2 \\ \hline \end{array}$

3. $\begin{array}{r} 50 \\ \times\ 50 \\ \hline \end{array}$

4. $\begin{array}{r} 62 \\ \times\ 40 \\ \hline \end{array}$

5. $\begin{array}{r} 41 \\ \times\ 21 \\ \hline \end{array}$

6. $\begin{array}{r} 7720 \\ \times\ 3 \\ \hline \end{array}$

7. $\begin{array}{r} 6409 \\ \times\ 4 \\ \hline \end{array}$

8. $\begin{array}{r} 800 \\ \times\ 40 \\ \hline \end{array}$

9. $\begin{array}{r} 39 \\ \times\ 60 \\ \hline \end{array}$

10. $\begin{array}{r} 600 \\ \times\ 50 \\ \hline \end{array}$

11. $\begin{array}{r} 2168 \\ \times\ 5 \\ \hline \end{array}$

12. $\begin{array}{r} 8084 \\ \times\ 7 \\ \hline \end{array}$

13. $\begin{array}{r} 57 \\ \times\ 50 \\ \hline \end{array}$

14. $\begin{array}{r} 163 \\ \times\ 10 \\ \hline \end{array}$

15. $\begin{array}{r} 46 \\ \times\ 36 \\ \hline \end{array}$

16. $\begin{array}{r} 6008 \\ \times\ 9 \\ \hline \end{array}$

17. $\begin{array}{r} 4440 \\ \times\ 5 \\ \hline \end{array}$

18. $\begin{array}{r} 98 \\ \times\ 18 \\ \hline \end{array}$

19. $\begin{array}{r} 375 \\ \times\ 61 \\ \hline \end{array}$

20. $\begin{array}{r} 83 \\ \times\ 27 \\ \hline \end{array}$

21. $\begin{array}{r} 4321 \\ \times\ 8 \\ \hline \end{array}$

22. $\begin{array}{r} 9000 \\ \times\ 9 \\ \hline \end{array}$

23. $\begin{array}{r} 26 \\ \times\ 26 \\ \hline \end{array}$

24. $\begin{array}{r} 37 \\ \times\ 80 \\ \hline \end{array}$

25. $\begin{array}{r} 250 \\ \times\ 37 \\ \hline \end{array}$

26. $\begin{array}{r} 1607 \\ \times\ 3 \\ \hline \end{array}$

27. $\begin{array}{r} 4090 \\ \times\ 2 \\ \hline \end{array}$

28. $\begin{array}{r} 91 \\ \times\ 19 \\ \hline \end{array}$

29. $\begin{array}{r} 670 \\ \times\ 70 \\ \hline \end{array}$

30. $\begin{array}{r} 66 \\ \times\ 84 \\ \hline \end{array}$

31. $\begin{array}{r} 5794 \\ \times\ 6 \\ \hline \end{array}$

32. $\begin{array}{r} 8379 \\ \times\ 9 \\ \hline \end{array}$

33. $\begin{array}{r} 65 \\ \times\ 48 \\ \hline \end{array}$

34. $\begin{array}{r} 64 \\ \times\ 80 \\ \hline \end{array}$

35. $\begin{array}{r} 777 \\ \times\ 90 \\ \hline \end{array}$

36. $\begin{array}{r} 3004 \\ \times\ 7 \\ \hline \end{array}$

37. $\begin{array}{r} 7140 \\ \times\ 5 \\ \hline \end{array}$

38. $\begin{array}{r} 54 \\ \times\ 45 \\ \hline \end{array}$

39. $\begin{array}{r} 589 \\ \times\ 76 \\ \hline \end{array}$

40. $\begin{array}{r} 68 \\ \times\ 37 \\ \hline \end{array}$

41. $\begin{array}{r} 9074 \\ \times\ 8 \\ \hline \end{array}$

42. $\begin{array}{r} 5555 \\ \times\ 8 \\ \hline \end{array}$

43. $\begin{array}{r} 617 \\ \times\ 59 \\ \hline \end{array}$

44. $\begin{array}{r} 44 \\ \times\ 99 \\ \hline \end{array}$

45. $\begin{array}{r} 880 \\ \times\ 64 \\ \hline \end{array}$

Divide and check.

1. 6)48   2. 9)63   3. 6)0   4. 1)9

5. 8)50   6. 6)59   7. 7)43   8. 2)60

9. 4)68   10. 2)95   11. 7)89   12. 5)84

13. 8)520   14. 5)244   15. 6)900   16. 4)587

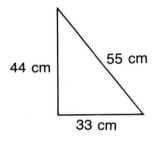

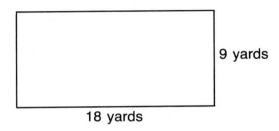

17. Find the perimeter.

18. Find the area in square yards.

Add or subtract. Watch the signs!

19.
```
  30,500
− 29,640
```

20.
```
  80,999
+    111
```

21.
```
  40,000
−  3,899
```

22.
```
  48,763
+ 48,989
```

23. There is enough lead in one pencil to draw a line 35 miles long. How long a line could you draw with 8 pencils?

24. Peggy worked 5 weeks and earned $895. She earned the same amount each week. How much did she earn each week?

25. There are 2625 chickens on one farm and 3585 chickens on another farm. How many chickens are on both farms?

26. The adding machine was invented in 1642. The electronic computer was invented in 1946. How many years apart were those inventions?

Solving Problems

1. The store ordered 36 boxes of baseball gloves. How many gloves were ordered?

2. The store ordered 8 cartons of referee whistles. How many whistles was that?

3. The Little League spent $375 on baseballs. How many baseballs did it buy?

4. 117 schools each bought a box of basketball uniforms. How many uniforms did they buy?

5. Each basketball uniform costs $19. How much does a box of basketball uniforms cost?

6. A customer bought 685 whistles from the carton. How many whistles were left?

7. You buy a baseball glove for $16, a bat for $9, and 2 baseballs. How much do you spend?

8. The storekeeper decides to put the baseballs in packs of 3 each. At most, how many baseballs could be left over?

9. Each rack car can carry 12 automobiles. How many automobiles can 15 rack cars carry?

10. How many piggyback flatcars are needed to carry 86 truck trailers?

11. A train was made up of a 74-foot engine, 26 piggyback flatcars, 18 rack cars, and a 50-foot caboose. How long was the train?

12. It takes 3000 ties to build 1 mile of railroad track. How many ties are needed to build 9 miles of track?

13. 8 spikes are needed for each tie. How many spikes are needed to build 1 mile of track?

14. A railroad track is 9 miles long. How many feet is that?
(1 mile = 5280 feet)

15. 432 people rode in 8 cars. The same number of people rode in each car. How many people rode in each car?

16. One of the fastest trains goes about 125 miles per hour. How far can it go in 19 hours?

17. An empty car weighs 52,265 pounds. Loaded with people and luggage, the car weighs 62,455 pounds. Find the weight of the people and luggage.

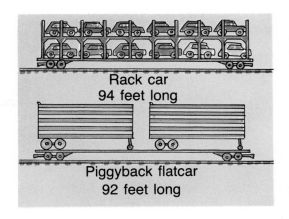

Rack car
94 feet long

Piggyback flatcar
92 feet long

CHAPTER REVIEW

1. 8000
   ×2

2. 6000
   ×9

3. 3185
   ×3

4. 3709
   ×7

5. 7498
   ×9

6. 7008
   ×8

7. 60
   ×70

8. 50
   ×80

9. 800
   ×90

10. 73
    ×50

11. 65
    ×90

12. 42
    ×13

13. 81
    ×62

14. 49
    ×75

15. 80
    ×19

16. 37
    ×37

17. 310
    ×23

18. 394
    ×60

19. 687
    ×49

20. 709
    ×58

Write an estimate for exercises 21-24.

21. 36
    ×17

22. 48
    ×21

23. 65
    ×79

24. 84
    ×52

25. 6000 balloons were given away each day. How many balloons were given away in 7 days?

26. There are 5280 feet in 1 mile. How many feet are in 8 miles?

27. There are 40 balloons in a bag. How many balloons are in 80 bags?

28. There are 12 eggs in 1 dozen. How many eggs are in 40 dozen?

29. A water softener uses 35 pounds of salt each week. How many pounds does it use in 52 weeks?

30. Ralph weighs 106 pounds. Find his weight in ounces.
    (1 pound = 16 ounces)

220

10 Division

Don Walkoe

Division (0's in the quotient)

A robot company made 807 arms. That is enough for how many robots? How many arms would be left over?

You can find the answers by dividing 807 by 2.

Estimate the hundreds digit.	Multiply and subtract.	Estimate the tens digit. Multiply and subtract.	Estimate the ones digit. Multiply and subtract.
2)807 2)8 is 4. Use 4 as the hundreds digit.	H T O 4 2)8 0 7 −8 0	H T O 4 0 2)8 0 7 −8 0 − 0 0 2)0 is 0. Use 0 as the tens digit.	H T O 4 0 3 R1 2)8 0 7 −8 0 − 0 7 − 6 1

There are enough arms for 403 robots. There would be 1 arm left over.

Exercises

Estimate the digit for each ▬.

1. 3)7 4 4

2. 4)5 6 2

3. 4)8 0 3

4. 7)6 3 5

222

5.
$$
\begin{array}{r}
1\ \blacksquare \\
4\overline{)705} \\
-4\downarrow \\
\overline{30}
\end{array}
$$

6.
$$
\begin{array}{r}
3\ \blacksquare \\
3\overline{)927} \\
-9\downarrow \\
\overline{02}
\end{array}
$$

7.
$$
\begin{array}{r}
1\ \blacksquare \\
5\overline{)502} \\
-5\downarrow \\
\overline{00}
\end{array}
$$

8.
$$
\begin{array}{r}
8\ \blacksquare \\
8\overline{)647} \\
-64\downarrow \\
\overline{07}
\end{array}
$$

Divide.

9. $4\overline{)407}$ 10. $2\overline{)815}$ 11. $3\overline{)811}$ 12. $8\overline{)966}$

13. $3\overline{)603}$ 14. $9\overline{)978}$ 15. $6\overline{)365}$ 16. $2\overline{)800}$

17. $2\overline{)781}$ 18. $3\overline{)913}$ 19. $4\overline{)803}$ 20. $7\overline{)285}$

21. $3\overline{)902}$ 22. $7\overline{)845}$ 23. $8\overline{)726}$ 24. $2\overline{)818}$

25. $4\overline{)435}$ 26. $4\overline{)901}$ 27. $7\overline{)840}$ 28. $9\overline{)725}$

29. A company packed 615 tennis balls into cans of 3 each. How many cans were there?

30. 605 eggs were put into cartons of 6 each. How many cartons were used? How many eggs were left over?

31. Tickets sold for $4 each. How many tickets were sold if $560 was collected?

32. 454 pounds of sugar was put into bags of 5 pounds each. How many bags were filled? How many pounds were left over?

Can You Tell?

How can you tell that each division is wrong?

1.
$$
\begin{array}{r}
367 \\
2\overline{)534}
\end{array}
$$

2.
$$
\begin{array}{r}
156\ \text{R}6 \\
4\overline{)630}
\end{array}
$$

3.
$$
\begin{array}{r}
16 \\
2\overline{)212}
\end{array}
$$

4.
$$
\begin{array}{r}
9\ \text{R}3 \\
6\overline{)543}
\end{array}
$$

Average

Bowling Score Sheet

Name	Game 1	Game 2	Game 3
Les	88	115	91
Maureen	97	113	120

Les found his **average** score was 98. Here is how he found the average.

Step 1:

He added the scores of all his games.

```
    88
   115
 +  91
   294
```

Step 2:

He divided that sum by the number of games.

```
      98
  3)294
   -27
    24
   -24
     0
```

Which game did Les bowl above his average?

How would you find Maureen's average bowling score?

Exercises

1. What is the sum of the scores?

2. How many scores are there?

3. By what number would you divide the sum?

4. What is the average score?

Math Scores

```
   8 9
   9 5
   7 8
 + 8 2
 ▦ ▦ ▦
```

```
     ▦ ▦
 4)3 4 4
  -3 2
    2 4
   -2 4
      0
```

224

Find the average of each group of numbers.

5. 85, 55

6. 100, 260, 390

7. 26, 47, 39, 56

8. 152, 264, 215, 189

9. 11, 13, 8, 23, 17, 0

10. 21, 21, 36, 28, 34, 52

11. 113, 84, 109, 89, 80

12. 8, 17, 9, 11, 7, 15, 10, 19

13. A sports shop sold 282 bicycles in 6 weeks. Find the average number of bicycles sold each week.

14. The Sterns drove 938 miles in 2 days. Find the average number of miles driven each day.

15. Find the average height.

16. Whose height is above the average?

17. How many inches below the average is Cathy's height?

Name	Height (inches)
Cathy	42
Kareem	50
Joyce	45
Rusty	43

18. Joseph kept this record of how many minutes he practiced piano. Find the average number of minutes practiced each day.

19. On which days did he practice less than the average?

20. On which days did he practice more than the average?

Sunday	45 minutes
Monday	35 minutes
Tuesday	60 minutes
Wednesday	50 minutes
Thursday	45 minutes
Friday	30 minutes
Saturday	50 minutes

21. Find Tim's average score.

22. Suppose Tim's teacher does not count the 30. Find the average of Tim's 3 other scores.

Pupil	Scores			
Tim	80	100	90	30

Division Patterns

Think	Write

$4 \times 2 = 8$ $8 \div 2 = 4$

$40 \times 2 = 80$ $80 \div 2 = 40 \longrightarrow$ $\dfrac{40}{2)80}$

$400 \times 2 = 800$ $800 \div 2 = 400 \longrightarrow$ $\dfrac{400}{2)800}$

$4000 \times 2 = 8000$ $8000 \div 2 = 4000 \longrightarrow$ $\dfrac{4000}{2)8000}$

$3 \times 8 = 24$ $24 \div 8 = 3$

$30 \times 8 = 240$ $240 \div 8 = 30 \longrightarrow$ $\dfrac{30}{8)240}$

$300 \times 8 = 2400$ $2400 \div 8 = 300 \longrightarrow$ $\dfrac{300}{8)2400}$

$2 \times 5 = 10$ $10 \div 5 = 2$

$20 \times 5 = 100$ $100 \div 5 = 20 \longrightarrow$ $\dfrac{20}{5)100}$

$200 \times 5 = 1000$ $1000 \div 5 = 200 \longrightarrow$ $\dfrac{200}{5)1000}$

Exercises

Write a digit for each ■.

1. $\dfrac{■\ 0}{2)4\ 0}$ 2. $\dfrac{■\ 0\ 0}{2)4\ 0\ 0}$ 3. $\dfrac{■\ 0\ 0\ 0}{2)4\ 0\ 0\ 0}$ 4. $\dfrac{■}{5)3\ 0}$

5. $\dfrac{■\ 0}{5)3\ 0\ 0}$ 6. $\dfrac{■\ 0\ 0}{5)3\ 0\ 0\ 0}$ 7. $\dfrac{■\ 0}{6)3\ 6\ 0}$ 8. $\dfrac{■\ 0\ 0}{6)3\ 6\ 0\ 0}$

Divide.

9. $3\overline{)6000}$ 10. $2\overline{)6000}$ 11. $3\overline{)9000}$ 12. $5\overline{)1000}$

13. $4\overline{)1200}$ 14. $3\overline{)1800}$ 15. $7\overline{)2100}$ 16. $4\overline{)3200}$

17. $5\overline{)2000}$ 18. $6\overline{)2400}$ 19. $9\overline{)2700}$ 20. $7\overline{)3500}$

21. $4\overline{)3600}$ 22. $8\overline{)4800}$ 23. $3\overline{)2100}$ 24. $7\overline{)4900}$

25. $6\overline{)3000}$ 26. $5\overline{)4000}$ 27. $8\overline{)5600}$ 28. $9\overline{)4500}$

29. $7\overline{)6300}$ 30. $8\overline{)6400}$ 31. $6\overline{)5400}$ 32. $9\overline{)8100}$

33. 3200 bottles were packed into cartons of 8 bottles each. How many cartons were there?

34. There are 9 seats in each row. How many rows are needed for 6300 people?

35. 6000 pounds of salt was loaded on 3 trucks. Each truck had the same amount. How much salt was on each truck?

36. 3500 pounds of flour was put into bags of 5 pounds each. How many bags were needed?

37. If each flashlight needs 2 batteries, how many flashlights could you fill with the box of batteries?

38. If each flashlight needs 3 batteries, how many flashlights could you fill with the box of batteries?

Division (4-digit by 1-digit)

You are to find the average number of pupils in each school.

The numbers have already been added, so all you have to do is divide 1876 by 4.

School	Number of pupils
Adams	482
Benny	501
Lincoln	398
Manor	495

TOTAL 1876

Estimate the hundreds digit.

$$4\overline{)1876}$$

$4\overline{)18}$ is about 4.
Try 4 as the hundreds digit.

Multiply and subtract.

Th	H	T	O
	4		
4)1	8	7	6
−1	6		
	2		

Estimate the tens digit. Multiply and subtract.

Th	H	T	O
	4	6	
4)1	8	7	6
−1	6		
	2	7	
−	2	4	
		3	

Estimate the ones digit. Multiply and subtract.

Th	H	T	O
	4	6	9
4)1	8	7	6
−1	6		
	2	7	
−	2	4	
		3	6
−		3	6
			0

The average number of pupils is 469.

Exercises

Estimate the digit for each ▨.

1. $2\overline{)1\ 4\ 3\ 6}$

2. $3\overline{)1\ 7\ 4\ 0}$

3. $7\overline{)3\ 2\ 4\ 1}$

4. $6\overline{)3\ 0\ 1\ 2}$

5.
```
    6 ▢
4)2 5 6 4
 -2 4
    1 6
```

6.
```
    8 ▢
5)4 0 7 5
 -4 0
    0 7
```

7.
```
    6 ▢
6)3 6 5 4
 -3 6
    0 5
```

8.
```
    6 ▢
8)4 8 0 8
 -4 8
    0 0
```

Divide.

9. 3)1299 **10.** 2)1642 **11.** 4)2064 **12.** 7)1491

13. 6)2112 **14.** 8)2976 **15.** 5)3255 **16.** 9)5787

17. 2)1950 **18.** 5)4380 **19.** 3)2871 **20.** 7)4753

Watch out for zeros in the quotient!

21. 4)3280 **22.** 8)6480 **23.** 6)5226 **24.** 9)6759

25. 8)2520 **26.** 5)1520 **27.** 2)1308 **28.** 7)5950

29. 3)8400 **30.** 4)3880 **31.** 7)2863 **32.** 6)5784

33. 9)7254 **34.** 2)1016 **35.** 3)1218 **36.** 5)3015

37. A machine filled 2472 bottles and put them into cartons of 8 each. How many cartons were there?

38. Another machine filled 2472 bottles and put them into cartons of 6 each. How many cartons were there?

39. On Sunday, the same number of people entered the zoo at each of 3 gates. How many people came through each gate?

40. Find the average number of people at the zoo each day on Saturday and Sunday.

Day	Number of people at the zoo
Saturday	764
Sunday	1152

Division (4-digit by 1-digit)

You can divide 7824 by 3 as shown below.

Estimate the thousands digit. Multiply and subtract.	Estimate the hundreds digit. Multiply and subtract.	Estimate the tens digit. Multiply and subtract.	Estimate the ones digit. Multiply and subtract.

```
     Th H T O        Th H T O         Th H T  O         Th H T  O

      2                2 6              2 6 0             2 6 0 8
   3)7 8 2 4        3)7 8 2 4        3)7 8 2 4         3)7 8 2 4
    -6               -6               -6                -6
     1                  1 8              1 8               1 8
                      -1 8             -1 8              -1 8
                         0                    2                 2
                                          -   0             -   0
                                              2                 2 4
                                                            -   2 4
                                                                0
```

Here is how you can divide 6018 by 6.

Estimate the thousands digit.	Estimate the hundreds digit.	Estimate the tens digit.	Estimate the ones digit.

```
      ▓                1 ▓             1 0 ▓            1 0 0 ▓
   6)6 0 1 8        6)6 0 1 8        6)6 0 1 8        6)6 0 1 8
                     -6               -6               -6
                        0                0                0
                                       -0               -0
                                         1                1
                                                        -0
                                                          1 8
```

Exercises

Estimate the thousands digit.

1. $7\overline{)8\ 0\ 5\ 7}$ 2. $5\overline{)9\ 8\ 0\ 0}$ 3. $2\overline{)9\ 4\ 1\ 2}$ 4. $3\overline{)8\ 2\ 7\ 4}$

Divide.

5. $3\overline{)9633}$ 6. $4\overline{)8484}$ 7. $2\overline{)4864}$ 8. $1\overline{)6742}$

9. $7\overline{)7861}$ 10. $5\overline{)8095}$ 11. $9\overline{)9900}$ 12. $6\overline{)7638}$

13. $8\overline{)9248}$ 14. $1\overline{)9358}$ 15. $4\overline{)9540}$ 16. $2\overline{)5146}$

17. $5\overline{)7435}$ 18. $3\overline{)8274}$ 19. $6\overline{)9768}$ 20. $8\overline{)9384}$

Watch out for zeros in the quotient!

21. $7\overline{)7007}$ 22. $1\overline{)1090}$ 23. $4\overline{)4036}$ 24. $2\overline{)2058}$

25. $6\overline{)8946}$ 26. $3\overline{)3012}$ 27. $7\overline{)9086}$ 28. $5\overline{)2515}$

29. $8\overline{)9632}$ 30. $7\overline{)9569}$ 31. $6\overline{)9000}$ 32. $4\overline{)5628}$

33. A patch factory makes 7632 patches in 4 days. What is the average number of patches made each day?

34. 6 kinds of patches were made. There was the same number of each kind in the 7632 patches. How many of each kind were there?

35. A dimestore sold 8784 patches in 8 days. What was the average number of patches sold each day?

36. 9600 patches were put into boxes of 8 patches each. How many boxes were there?

Extra Practice—Set B, page 341

Remainders

Aaron and Jodi each divided 3851 by 7. Who got the correct answer?

Mary Elenz Tranter

Why did Jodi write 0 as the ones digit of the quotient?

Aaron got a remainder of 8. Is that correct?

When you divide by 7, what do you know about the remainder?

Exercises

Find the mistakes in each division below.
Show how you would correct each division.

$$\begin{array}{r} 235 \text{ R5} \\ 1.\ 4\overline{)945} \\ -8 \\ \hline 14 \\ -12 \\ \hline 25 \\ -20 \\ \hline 5 \end{array}$$

$$\begin{array}{r} 82 \\ 2.\ 9\overline{)7386} \\ -72 \\ \hline 18 \\ -18 \\ \hline 0 \end{array}$$

$$\begin{array}{r} 28 \text{ R1} \\ 3.\ 3\overline{)6025} \\ -6 \\ \hline 25 \\ -24 \\ \hline 1 \end{array}$$

$$\begin{array}{r} 750 \text{ R4} \\ 4.\ 9\overline{)6349} \\ -63 \\ \hline 49 \\ -45 \\ \hline 4 \\ -0 \\ \hline 4 \end{array}$$

Divide.

5. 8)1712   6. 3)6515   7. 2)9753   8. 9)1334

9. 4)2041   10. 7)2479   11. 5)6451   12. 4)2956

13. 5)1304   14. 2)6043   15. 6)6875   16. 7)6239

17. 8)8220   18. 2)1603   19. 6)4854   20. 5)5929

21. 4)3401   22. 8)9263   23. 9)2000   24. 3)6270

25. 7)8879   26. 3)9014   27. 9)9638   28. 6)5904

29. 8)8007   30. 4)8278   31. 7)9595   32. 8)6478

33. 2)5815   34. 9)1111   35. 4)7700   36. 7)7565

37. You trade 2203 pennies for nickels. How many nickels should you get? How many pennies will be left over?

38. 3365 birthday candles are put into boxes of 8 each. How many boxes are there? How many candles are left over?

What Is Missing?

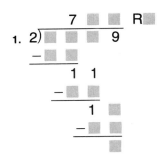

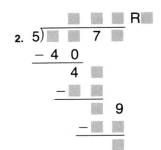

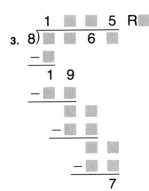

233

Checking Division

To check division, multiply the quotient by the divisor, and then add the remainder.

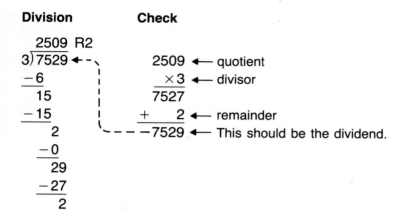

Division

```
    2509 R2
3)7529
  -6
   15
  -15
    2
   -0
   29
  -27
    2
```

Check

```
   2509  ← quotient
    ×3   ← divisor
   7527
 +    2  ← remainder
  -7529  ← This should be the dividend.
```

When the remainder is 0, just multiply the quotient by the divisor.

Division

```
    817
6)4902
  -48
   10
   -6
   42
  -42
    0
```

Check

```
  817  ← quotient
   ×6  ← divisor
 4902  ← This should be the dividend.
```

Exercises

Check each division. Is the answer correct?
Write *Yes* or *No* for each exercise.

1.
```
   136
 6)804
```

2.
```
   80 R7
 9)727
```

3.
```
   106
 9)954
```

4.
```
   86 R2
 7)600
```

234

Correct the mistakes in each division.

```
        85                                    24
  5. 5)475  ◄---¬        85          6. 4)960  ◄----¬        24
     -45          |      ×5             -8           |       ×4
      25          └---425              16           └---96
     -25                              -16
       0                                0
```

```
        83  R1                              1038  R12
  7. 2)1607  ◄--¬        83          8. 7)7278  ◄--¬         1038
     -16         |       ×2             -7          |         ×7
       7         |      166              2          |       7266
      -6         |    +   1             -0          |      +  12
       1         └---167               27          └----7278
                                      -21
                                       68
                                      -56
                                       12
```

Divide and check.

9. 3)609   10. 5)354   11. 2)811   12. 9)700

13. 2)541   14. 4)792   15. 7)923   16. 6)900

17. 4)2982   18. 3)1416   19. 7)5855   20. 5)1804

21. 7)1796   22. 6)3870   23. 8)3709   24. 9)4894

25. 3)4050   26. 2)6337   27. 7)9975   28. 4)6024

29. 1340 trees will be planted in rows of 9 each. How many rows can be planted? How many trees will be left over?

30. 6 stores will sell 2450 TVs. Each store will get the same number of TVs. How many will each store get? How many will be left over?

Name the shape of each figure.

1.

2. [rectangle]

3. [square]

4.

Complete.

5. 3 meters = ____ centimeters

6. 200 centimeters = ____ meters

7. 1 gallon = ____ quarts

8. 1 pint = ____ cups

Find each volume in cubic centimeters.

9.

10.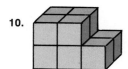

Add or subtract. Watch the signs!

11.	12.	13.	14.
30,020 − 29,200	45,899 + 101	36,784 + 5,928	75,046 − 5,158

Multiply.

15.	16.	17.	18.	19.
10 × 90	60 × 30	20 × 50	100 × 90	600 × 80

20.	21.	22.	23.	24.
47 × 60	79 × 86	300 × 42	704 × 59	472 × 17

25. There are 55 dominoes in a set. How many dominoes are in 72 sets?

26. Kim has $409. Ny has $291 more than that. How much does Ny have?

Dividing by 10's

90 pupils will share 450 carnival tickets equally. To find how many tickets each pupil will get, divide 450 by 90.

$$\frac{?}{90)4\ 5\ 0}$$

Could each pupil get 100 tickets?
There will be no hundreds digit.

$100 \times 90 = 9000$

$$\frac{?}{90)4\ 5\ 0}$$

Could each pupil get 10 tickets?
There will be no tens digit.

$10 \times 90 = 900$

$$\frac{?}{90)4\ 5\ 0}$$

Could each pupil get 1 ticket?
The first digit will be in the ones place.

$1 \times 90 = 90$

Estimate the ones digit.	Multiply and subtract.
90)450	H T O
9)45 is 5. Use 5 as the ones digit.	5
	90)4 5 0
	−4 5 0
	0

Each pupil will get 5 tickets.

Exercises

1. 30)270 2. 50)150 3. 40)320 4. 60)240

5. 20)180 6. 70)490 7. 50)400 8. 60)420

9. 70)560 10. 80)720 11. 90)720 12. 60)540

Extra Practice—Set B, page 342   **237**

Dividing by 10's

600 chairs will be put into rows of 20 chairs each. How many rows will there be?

$$\frac{?}{20)6\ 0\ 0}$$ Could there be 100 rows? $100 \times 20 = 2000$
There will be no hundreds digit.

$$\frac{?}{20)6\ 0\ 0}$$ Could there be 10 rows? $10 \times 20 = 200$
The first digit will be in the tens place.

Estimate the tens digit.	Multiply and subtract.	Estimate the ones digit.	Multiply and subtract.

20)600
 	
2)6 is 3.
Use 3 as the tens digit.
 	
There will be 30 rows.
	H T O
	   3
	20)6 0 0
	 −6 0
	   0
		H T O
		   3
		20)6 0 0
		 −6 0
		       0
		
		20)0 is 0. Use 0 as the ones digit.
			H T O
			   3 0
			20)6 0 0
			 −6 0
			       0
			   − 0
			       0

You can use what you know to divide 510 by 30.
In which place will the first digit of the quotient be?

Estimate the tens digit.	Multiply and subtract.	Estimate the ones digit.	Multiply and subtract.

30)510
 	
3)5 is about 1.
Try 1 as the tens digit.
	H T O
	   1
	30)5 1 0
	 −3 0
	   2 1
		H T O
		   1
		30)5 1 0
		 −3 0
		   2 1 0
		
		3)21 is 7. Use 7 as the ones digit.
			H T O
			   1 7
			30)5 1 0
			 −3 0
			   2 1 0
			  −2 1 0
			       0

238

Exercises

1. $20\overline{)800}$

2. $30\overline{)900}$

3. $10\overline{)800}$

4. $50\overline{)500}$

5. $40\overline{)800}$

6. $10\overline{)900}$

7. $60\overline{)600}$

8. $30\overline{)600}$

9. $30\overline{)360}$

10. $20\overline{)260}$

11. $10\overline{)170}$

12. $40\overline{)280}$

13. $10\overline{)470}$

14. $30\overline{)630}$

15. $20\overline{)520}$

16. $10\overline{)770}$

17. $40\overline{)720}$

18. $70\overline{)700}$

19. $50\overline{)850}$

20. $30\overline{)840}$

21. $80\overline{)880}$

22. $60\overline{)900}$

23. $20\overline{)980}$

24. $50\overline{)700}$

25. $40\overline{)960}$

26. $90\overline{)990}$

27. $30\overline{)960}$

28. $80\overline{)800}$

29. $50\overline{)900}$

30. $70\overline{)910}$

31. $60\overline{)840}$

32. $30\overline{)750}$

33. 240 pupils ride bicycles to school. Each bicycle rack can hold 20 bicycles. How many bicycle racks are needed?

34. 40 bicycles can go through the safety-check line each hour. How long will it take to check 400 bicycles?

35. 600 spokes are used to make 20 bicycle wheels. All the wheels are the same size. How many spokes are used in each wheel?

36. 870 bicycle tires were sold. There were 30 tires in each box sold. How many boxes were sold?

37. A store ordered 800 bicycle locks. The locks were in boxes of 50 each. How many boxes were ordered?

Bohdan Hrynewych/Picture Group

Extra Practice—Set A, page 343

Division Practice

Divide.

1. $3\overline{)906}$ 2. $4\overline{)828}$ 3. $5\overline{)254}$ 4. $8\overline{)400}$

5. $8\overline{)4000}$ 6. $2\overline{)6000}$ 7. $3\overline{)2438}$ 8. $4\overline{)1636}$

9. $3\overline{)4835}$ 10. $2\overline{)2796}$ 11. $5\overline{)6102}$ 12. $7\overline{)7035}$

13. $40\overline{)280}$ 14. $60\overline{)480}$ 15. $10\overline{)700}$ 16. $50\overline{)650}$

17. $6\overline{)720}$ 18. $7\overline{)750}$ 19. $40\overline{)440}$ 20. $7\overline{)2171}$

21. $10\overline{)890}$ 22. $7\overline{)5600}$ 23. $8\overline{)9146}$ 24. $9\overline{)9279}$

25. $20\overline{)800}$ 26. $8\overline{)645}$ 27. $5\overline{)2004}$ 28. $60\overline{)420}$

29. $4\overline{)9043}$ 30. $40\overline{)920}$ 31. $7\overline{)6300}$ 32. $9\overline{)540}$

33. $90\overline{)540}$ 34. $8\overline{)5616}$ 35. $2\overline{)8011}$ 36. $5\overline{)7285}$

37. $9\overline{)8100}$ 38. $4\overline{)700}$ 39. $30\overline{)810}$ 40. $90\overline{)810}$

41. $8\overline{)9176}$ 42. $60\overline{)960}$ 43. $9\overline{)6389}$ 44. $7\overline{)748}$

Find the average of each group of numbers.

45. 8, 15, 29, 28

46. 75, 79, 96, 98, 57

47. 5, 12, 0, 15, 8, 8

48. 102, 220, 179, 499

240

Solving Problems

1. Mrs. Lucky won the grand prize. She paid $19,806 of the prize in taxes. How much money was left after taxes?

2. Joe won the second prize. He will get the same amount of money each month for 8 months. How much will he get each month?

3. The third prize will be paid in $20 bills. How many $20 bills is that?

4. The fourth prize will be paid in $10 bills. How many $10 bills is that?

The Super-Duper Contest

Grand Prize	$50,000
First Prize	$675 a month for 36 months
Second Prize	$4800
Third Prize	$380
Fourth Prize	$180

5. Sara won the first prize. How much money will she get in all?

6. It takes about 9 pounds of milk to make 1 pound of cheese. How many pounds of cheese can be made from 7875 pounds of milk?

7. A town has 5 schools. There are 5200 pupils in those schools. What is the average number of pupils in each school?

8. Jon's birthday will be in 285 days. His birthday will be in ___ weeks and ___ days.

9. Ruby took some tests. Her scores were 100, 98, 98, 67, and 87. Find her average score.

John Colwell/Grant Heilman

241

CHAPTER REVIEW

Divide.

1. 3)905

2. 7)422

3. 6)840

4. 4)832

5. 3)9000

6. 8)5600

7. 8)4000

8. 2)1254

9. 4)1046

10. 5)3025

11. 9)8647

12. 8)6240

13. 3)6074

14. 2)8015

15. 6)6990

16. 7)9042

17. 50)250

18. 70)490

19. 40)800

20. 30)900

21. 20)320

22. 10)890

23. 50)600

24. 70)840

Divide and check.

25. 6)6017

26. 8)879

27. 7)9805

28. 60)960

Find the average of each group of numbers.

29. 6, 12, 5, 12, 10

30. 99, 100, 0, 81

31. An airplane flew 960 miles in 3 hours. What is the average number of miles flown each hour?

32. 4851 oranges are put into cartons of 8 oranges each. How many cartons are filled? How many oranges are left over?

33. How many hours are there in 480 minutes? (1 hour = 60 minutes)

34. How many minutes are there in 840 seconds? (1 minute = 60 seconds)

11 Fractions and Decimals

Runk/Schoenberger/Grant Heilman

Fractions

All figures in this lesson are separated into parts of the same size.

3 ⟵ number of parts colored

$\overline{4}$ ⟵ number of parts in all

$\frac{3}{4}$ or *three fourths* of the figure is colored.

$\frac{3}{4}$ is called a **fraction.**

What would you write here?

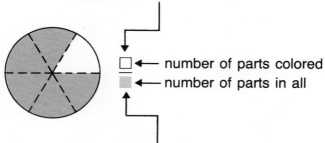

☐ ⟵ number of parts colored

▨ ⟵ number of parts in all

What would you write here?

How much of the figure is colored?

How much of the figure is not colored?

Exercises

Write as a fraction.

1. two thirds

2. four eighths

3. one half

4. five sixths

5. four fourths

6. eight tenths

Write a fraction to tell how much is colored.
Then write a fraction to tell how much is not colored.

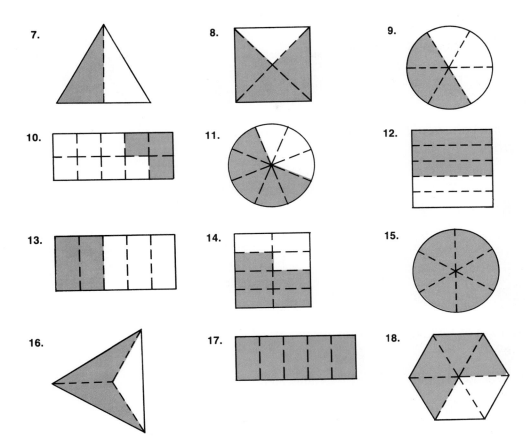

7.

8.

9.

10.

11.

12.

13.

14.

15.

16.

17.

18.

Half and Half

You want $\frac{1}{2}$ of the money and $\frac{1}{2}$ of the coins. Which coins should you take?

Extra Practice—Set B, page 343

Fractions

2 ⟵ number of yellow bats
―
5 ⟵ number of bats in all

$\frac{2}{5}$ or *two fifths* of the bats are yellow.

What fraction would you write for the bats that are green?

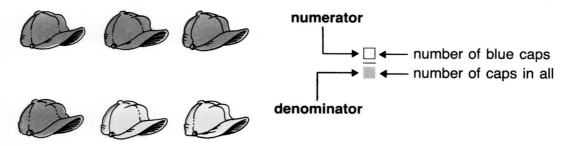

numerator

⟶ ☐ ⟵ number of blue caps
⟶ ▨ ⟵ number of caps in all

denominator

What fraction would you write for the caps that are blue?

What fraction would you write for the caps that are yellow?

Exercises

Write a fraction for the objects that are blue.
Then write a fraction for the objects that are not blue.

1.

2.

3.

4.

Write a fraction for the objects that are orange.
Then write a fraction for the objects that are not orange.

5.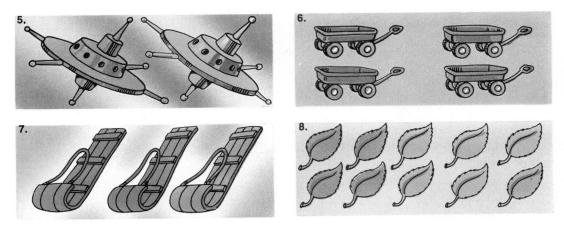

6.

7.

8.

Write a fraction to complete each sentence.

9. ____ of the bottles are empty.

10. ____ of the balls are yellow.

11. ____ of the kites are blue.

12. ____ of the vegetables are carrots.

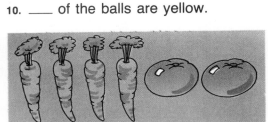

13. ____ of the ribbons say *1st Place.*

14. ____ of the chairs are upside down.

247

Equivalent Fractions

$\frac{1}{2}$ of the rectangle is red.

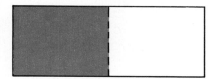

You can show the red part of the rectangle in other ways.

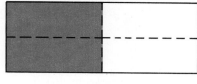

$\frac{2}{4}$ is red.

$\frac{4}{8}$ is red.

$\frac{1}{2}$, $\frac{2}{4}$, and $\frac{4}{8}$ all name the same part of the rectangle.

$$\frac{1}{2} = \frac{2}{4} = \frac{4}{8}$$

Fractions can also name whole numbers.

How many $\frac{1}{2}$'s are in 1?

Two halves are equal to 1.

$$\frac{2}{2} = 1$$

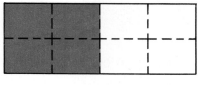

How many $\frac{1}{2}$'s are in 2?

$\frac{4}{2}$ names which whole number?

248

Exercises

1. Write two fractions for the red part of the rectangle.

2. Write two fractions for the white part of the rectangle.

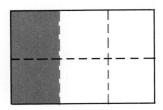

Complete.

3.

$$\frac{1}{2} = \frac{\blacksquare}{6}$$

4.

$$\frac{2}{3} = \frac{\blacksquare}{6}$$

5.

$$\frac{1}{2} = \frac{\blacksquare}{8}$$

6.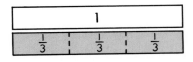

$$\frac{\blacksquare}{3} = 1$$

7.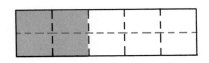

$$\frac{2}{5} = \frac{\blacksquare}{10}$$

8.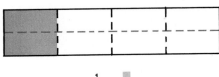

$$\frac{1}{4} = \frac{\blacksquare}{8}$$

9.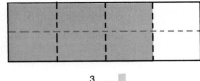

$$\frac{3}{4} = \frac{\blacksquare}{8}$$

10.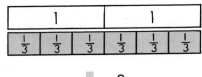

$$\frac{1}{2} = \frac{\blacksquare}{10}$$

11.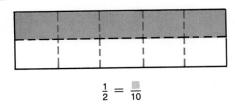

$$\frac{\blacksquare}{3} = 2$$

249

Comparing Fractions

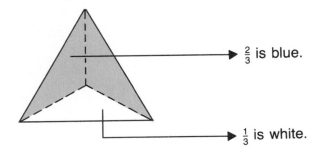

$\frac{2}{3}$ is blue.

$\frac{1}{3}$ is white.

Is there more blue or more white?

$\frac{2}{3}$ is greater than $\frac{1}{3}$.

$$\frac{2}{3} > \frac{1}{3}$$

Is there less blue or less white?

$\frac{1}{3}$ is less than $\frac{2}{3}$.

$$\frac{1}{3} < \frac{2}{3}$$

Exercises

Write $<$, $>$, or $=$ for each ●.

1. $\frac{3}{10}$ ● $\frac{5}{10}$

2. $\frac{5}{10}$ ● $\frac{3}{10}$

3. $\frac{1}{2}$ ● $\frac{5}{10}$

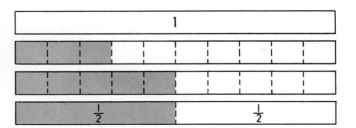

4.

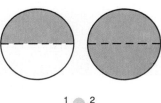

$\frac{1}{2}$ ● $\frac{2}{2}$

5.

$\frac{3}{4}$ ● $\frac{2}{4}$

250

6.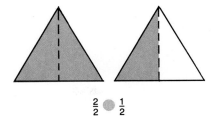

$\frac{2}{2}$ $\frac{1}{2}$

7.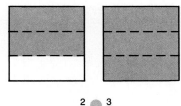

$\frac{2}{3}$ ⬤ $\frac{3}{3}$

8.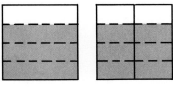

$\frac{3}{4}$ ⬤ $\frac{6}{8}$

9.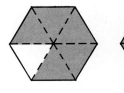

$\frac{5}{6}$ ⬤ $\frac{6}{6}$

10.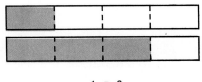

$\frac{4}{5}$ ⬤ $\frac{1}{5}$

11.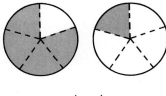

$\frac{2}{4}$ ⬤ $\frac{4}{8}$

12.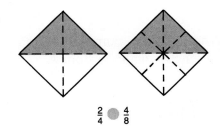

$\frac{1}{4}$ ⬤ $\frac{3}{4}$

13.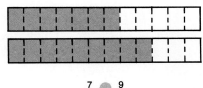

$\frac{7}{12}$ ⬤ $\frac{9}{12}$

14.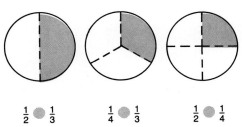

$\frac{1}{2}$ ⬤ $\frac{1}{3}$ $\frac{1}{4}$ ⬤ $\frac{1}{3}$ $\frac{1}{2}$ ⬤ $\frac{1}{4}$

15.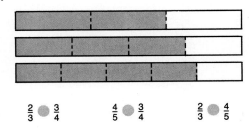

$\frac{2}{3}$ ⬤ $\frac{3}{4}$ $\frac{4}{5}$ ⬤ $\frac{3}{4}$ $\frac{2}{3}$ ⬤ $\frac{4}{5}$

Extra Practice—Set A, page 344   **251**

Mixed Numerals

two and one-third cups

$2 + \frac{1}{3}$ cups

$2\frac{1}{3}$ cups

$2\frac{1}{3}$ is a **mixed numeral.**

What mixed numeral would you write for the distance from A to B?

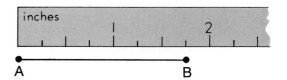

Exercises

Complete the mixed numeral to tell how much is colored.

1.

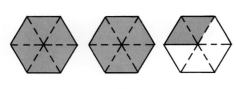

$2\frac{\square}{6}$

2.

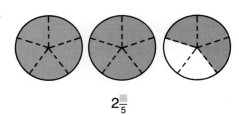

$2\frac{\square}{5}$

3.

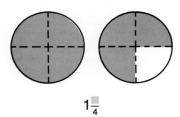

$1\frac{\square}{4}$

4.

$2\frac{\square}{2}$

Write a mixed numeral for each ___.

5.

___ quarts

6.

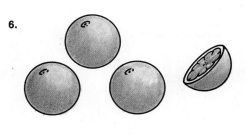

___ oranges

7.

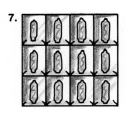

___ dozen

8.

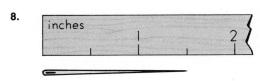

___ inches

9.

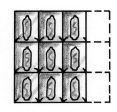

___ inches

10.

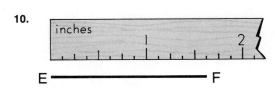

___ inches

11.

___ apples

12.

___ pounds

Tenths

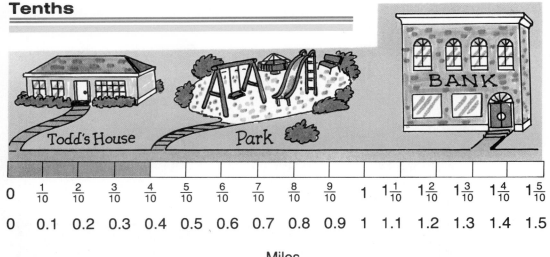

| 0 | $\frac{1}{10}$ | $\frac{2}{10}$ | $\frac{3}{10}$ | $\frac{4}{10}$ | $\frac{5}{10}$ | $\frac{6}{10}$ | $\frac{7}{10}$ | $\frac{8}{10}$ | $\frac{9}{10}$ | 1 | $1\frac{1}{10}$ | $1\frac{2}{10}$ | $1\frac{3}{10}$ | $1\frac{4}{10}$ | $1\frac{5}{10}$ |

| 0 | 0.1 | 0.2 | 0.3 | 0.4 | 0.5 | 0.6 | 0.7 | 0.8 | 0.9 | 1 | 1.1 | 1.2 | 1.3 | 1.4 | 1.5 |

Miles

The distance from Todd's house to the park is $\frac{4}{10}$ mile.

$\frac{4}{10}$ can be written as 0.4. $\frac{4}{10} = 0.4$ 0.4 is called a **decimal.**

decimal point ———→

Both $\frac{4}{10}$ and 0.4 are read "four tenths."

In the picture above, which mixed numeral tells how far it is from Todd's house to the bank?

$1\frac{3}{10}$ can be written as 1.3. $1\frac{3}{10} = 1.3$ 1.3 is read "one and three tenths."

Exercises

Write a decimal to tell how much is colored.

1.

2.

3.

4.

254

5.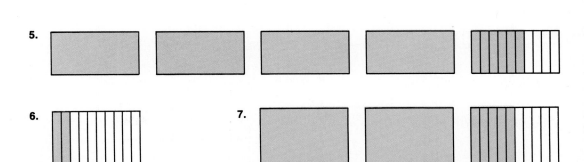

6. 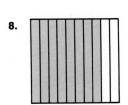   **7.**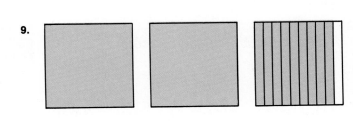

8.   **9.**

Write a decimal for each fraction and mixed numeral.

10. $\dfrac{4}{10}$ **11.** $\dfrac{8}{10}$ **12.** $2\frac{5}{10}$ **13.** $23\frac{3}{10}$

14. $\dfrac{2}{10}$ **15.** $\dfrac{9}{10}$ **16.** $1\frac{1}{10}$ **17.** $18\frac{6}{10}$

Write a fraction or mixed numeral for each decimal.

18. 0.1   **19.** 0.6   **20.** 2.3   **21.** 24.9

22. 0.9   **23.** 1.1   **24.** 5.2   **25.** 36.7

26. A baseball weighs about $\frac{5}{10}$ pound. Write a decimal for the weight of a baseball.

27. A pencil is $7\frac{2}{10}$ inches long. Write a decimal for the length of a pencil.

28. One city block is about $\frac{1}{10}$ mile long. Write a decimal for the length of a block.

29. A car's gasoline tank can hold $20\frac{9}{10}$ gallons. Write a decimal for how much gasoline the tank can hold.

255

Hundredths

$\frac{1}{100}$ of the square is blue.

$\frac{1}{100}$ can be written as 0.01.

$$\frac{1}{100} = 0.01$$

Both $\frac{1}{100}$ and 0.01 are read "one hundredth."

$\frac{17}{100}$ or 0.17 of the square is red.

$$\frac{17}{100} = 0.17$$

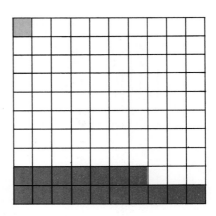

$1\frac{32}{100}$ can be written as 1.32.

$$1\frac{32}{100} = 1.32$$

How would you read $1\frac{32}{100}$ or 1.32?

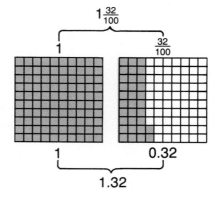

Exercises

Write a decimal to tell how much is colored.

1.

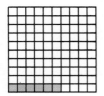

2.

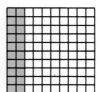

256

3.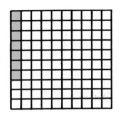

4.

5.

6.

7.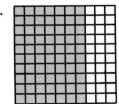

8.

Write a decimal for each fraction and mixed numeral.

9. $\dfrac{2}{100}$

10. $\dfrac{5}{100}$

11. $\dfrac{28}{100}$

12. $\dfrac{80}{100}$

13. $\dfrac{13}{100}$

14. $\dfrac{50}{100}$

15. $1\frac{12}{100}$

16. $5\frac{60}{100}$

17. $1\frac{1}{100}$

18. $3\frac{49}{100}$

19. $17\frac{6}{100}$

20. $63\frac{20}{100}$

Write a fraction or mixed numeral for each decimal.

21. 0.09

22. 0.05

23. 0.10

24. 0.84

25. 4.01

26. 25.30

27. 46.18

28. 59.09

Money and Decimals

You know that 100 cents = 1 dollar.

So 1 cent = $\frac{1}{100}$ dollar, or 1 cent = 0.01 dollar.

1 and 0.04 dollars

$1.04

one dollar and four cents

1 and 0.20 dollars

$1.20

one dollar and twenty cents

10¢ + 5¢ ⟶

15¢ = $0.15

$0.10 + $0.05 ⟶

How do you read 15¢?

How do you read $0.15?

Exercises

Use a $ and a decimal point to name each amount of money.

1. 14¢   2. 50¢   3. 61¢   4. 8¢   5. 9¢   6. 99¢

258

7.

8.

9.

10.

11.

12.

13. 3 dollars, 2 dimes, 5 pennies

14. 2 dollars, 8 pennies

15. 15 dollars, 9 dimes, 1 penny

16. 10 dollars, 6 dimes

17. seventeen cents

18. two cents

19. four dollars and ten cents

20. one dollar

21. ten dollars and ten cents

22. six dollars and one cent

23. twenty-three dollars and eighty-nine cents

24. thirteen dollars and seven cents

Money and Place Value

	Hundreds	Tens	Ones	Tenths	Hundredths
$			1 .	2	3
$	1	2	1 .	3	2

Exercises

Use a $ and a decimal point to name each amount of money.

1.

2.

	$100 bills	$10 bills	$1 bills	Dimes	Pennies		$100 bills	$10 bills	$1 bills	Dimes	Pennies
3.		4	7	3	5	**4.**	3	0	9	2	5
5.	1	0	3	7	0	**6.**	1	0	0	1	5
7.	5	8	1	0	6	**8.**		9	2	4	8
9.		5	0	0	8	**10.**	7	1	2	9	5

Extra Practice—Set B, page 345

SKILLS REVIEW

Add or subtract.

1. 66,891 +18,999	2. 40,500 − 1,826	3. 3,095 +86,948	4. 54,213 −53,814

Multiply.

5. 7000
 ×9

6. 4687
 ×6

7. 80
 ×90

8. 600
 ×50

9. 47
 ×40

10. 67
 ×76

11. 689
 ×52

12. 408
 ×79

Divide.

13. 2)803

14. 6)4200

15. 7)3581

16. 5)6545

17. 2)8061

18. 40)320

19. 10)700

20. 80)960

Choose the best answer.

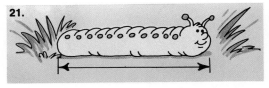

21.

4 meters   4 centimeters
          4 kilometers

22.

1 meter   1 centimeter
          1 kilometer

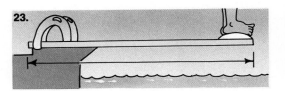

23.

2 meters   2 centimeters
          2 kilometers

24.

16 meters   16 centimeters
          16 kilometers

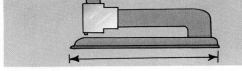

CHAPTER REVIEW

1. Write a fraction for the part that is colored.

2. Write a fraction for the part that is not colored.

3. Write a fraction for the red umbrellas.

4. Write a mixed numeral for the distance from A to B.

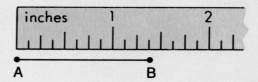

Complete.

5.

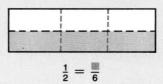

$\frac{1}{2} = \frac{\blacksquare}{6}$

6.

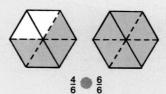

$\frac{\blacksquare}{2} = 2$

Write < or > for each ●.

7.

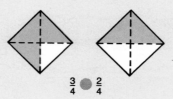

$\frac{3}{4}$ ● $\frac{2}{4}$

8.

$\frac{4}{6}$ ● $\frac{6}{6}$

Write as a decimal.

9. $\frac{4}{10}$

10. $4\frac{3}{10}$

11. $\frac{7}{100}$

12. $6\frac{80}{100}$

Use a $ and a decimal point to name each amount of money.

13. 7¢

14. fifty-one cents

15. twelve dollars and five cents

262

12 Fractions and Decimals (+, –)

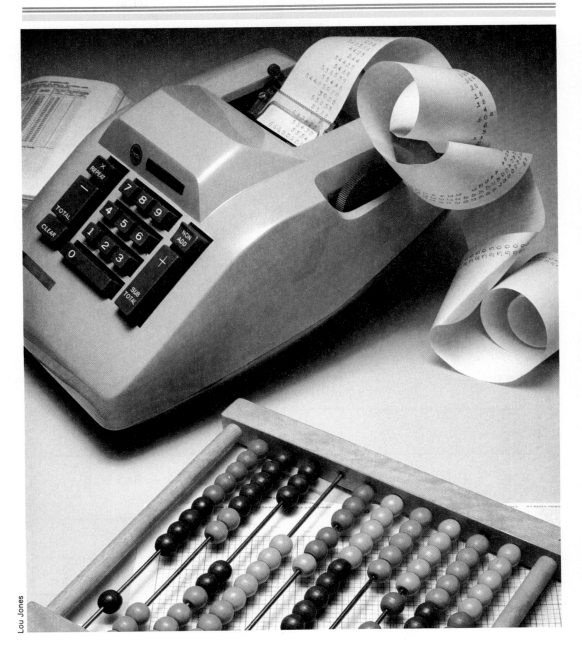

Lou Jones

Adding Fractions

$\frac{2}{6}$ of the page has color photos.

$\frac{3}{6}$ of the page has black-and-white photos.

$\frac{5}{6}$ of the page is filled.

$$\frac{2}{6} + \frac{3}{6} = \frac{5}{6}$$

You can add fractions this way.

Add the numerators.

$$\frac{2}{6} + \frac{3}{6} = \frac{2 + 3}{6} = \frac{5}{6}$$

Use the same denominator.

Exercises

Add the fractions.

1.

$$\frac{2}{4} + \frac{1}{4} = \frac{2+1}{4} = \blacksquare$$

2.

$$\frac{3}{7} + \frac{1}{7} = \frac{3+1}{7} = \blacksquare$$

3.

$$\frac{1}{3} + \frac{1}{3}$$

4.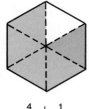

$$\frac{4}{6} + \frac{1}{6}$$

5.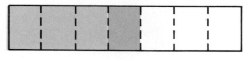

$$\frac{3}{10} + \frac{4}{10}$$

6. $\frac{1}{3} + \frac{1}{3}$ **7.** $\frac{1}{6} + \frac{3}{6}$ **8.** $\frac{2}{5} + \frac{2}{5}$ **9.** $\frac{6}{10} + \frac{2}{10}$

10. $\frac{3}{5} + \frac{1}{5}$ **11.** $\frac{5}{8} + \frac{2}{8}$ **12.** $\frac{2}{8} + \frac{3}{8}$ **13.** $\frac{1}{4} + \frac{2}{4}$

14. $\frac{3}{8} + \frac{4}{8}$ **15.** $\frac{2}{10} + \frac{7}{10}$ **16.** $\frac{4}{10} + \frac{4}{10}$ **17.** $\frac{3}{10} + \frac{5}{10}$

18. $\frac{4}{6} + \frac{1}{6}$ **19.** $\frac{1}{10} + \frac{5}{10}$ **20.** $\frac{4}{10} + \frac{5}{10}$ **21.** $\frac{2}{8} + \frac{5}{8}$

22. You glue a board $\frac{1}{8}$ inch thick to a board $\frac{5}{8}$ inch thick. What is the thickness of the boards together?

23. Jan ate $\frac{1}{6}$ of an apple pie. Beryl also ate $\frac{1}{6}$ of the pie. Write a fraction for how much pie they ate.

24. Tony read $\frac{2}{5}$ of a book today and $\frac{1}{5}$ of the book yesterday. How much of the book has he read?

25. How tall is the stack of two checkers? 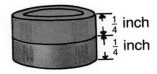 $\frac{1}{4}$ inch $\frac{1}{4}$ inch

26. Mother planted beans in $\frac{3}{8}$ of the garden and carrots in $\frac{2}{8}$ of it. How much of the garden is planted?

27. Mike spent $\frac{3}{10}$ of his money for paint and $\frac{2}{10}$ of his money for decals. How much of his money did he spend?

∩et Results

Find the total time for each pupil. Then tell who played the longest.

Time (in hours)

Name	Morning	Afternoon	Total
Camille	$\frac{4}{10}$	$\frac{3}{10}$	
Mark	$\frac{3}{10}$	$\frac{5}{10}$	
Willie	$\frac{5}{10}$	$\frac{4}{10}$	

Simplest Form

These circles show different names for *one half.*

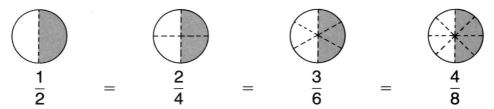

$$\frac{1}{2} \;=\; \frac{2}{4} \;=\; \frac{3}{6} \;=\; \frac{4}{8}$$

Of the fractions, only $\frac{1}{2}$ is in **simplest form.**

To change a fraction to simplest form, divide both the numerator and the denominator by the largest whole number you can. *But the remainders must be 0.*

Here is how to change $\frac{4}{8}$ to simplest form.

Every number can be divided by 1. There is no need to try 1.

Try 2.
4 ÷ 2 = 2

8 ÷ 2 = 4

Try 3.
When you divide 4 by 3, the remainder is not 0.

Try 4.
4 ÷ 4 = 1

8 ÷ 4 = 2

Would any number greater than 4 work?

$$\frac{4}{8} = \frac{4 \div 4}{8 \div 4} = \frac{1}{2} \longleftarrow \text{simplest form}$$

Change $\frac{8}{12}$ to simplest form.

Both 8 and 12 are even, so 2 will work.

$$\frac{8}{12} = \frac{8 \div 2}{12 \div 2} = \frac{4}{6}$$

But both 4 and 6 are even, so 2 will work again.

$$\frac{4}{6} = \frac{4 \div 2}{6 \div 2} = \frac{2}{3} \longleftarrow \begin{array}{l}\text{Is this in}\\ \text{simplest form?}\end{array}$$

How can you change $\frac{8}{12}$ to simplest form in only one step?

Exercises

Change each fraction to simplest form.

1. $\dfrac{3}{6}$ $\dfrac{3 \div 3}{6 \div 3}$

2. $\dfrac{5}{10}$ $\dfrac{5 \div 5}{10 \div 5}$

3. $\dfrac{2}{6}$

4. $\dfrac{2}{4}$

5. $\dfrac{2}{8}$

6. $\dfrac{4}{12}$

7. $\dfrac{2}{10}$

8. $\dfrac{6}{8}$

9. $\dfrac{3}{12}$

10. $\dfrac{4}{6}$

11. $\dfrac{2}{12}$

12. $\dfrac{4}{10}$

13. $\dfrac{6}{12}$

14. $\dfrac{6}{10}$

15. $\dfrac{9}{12}$

16. $\dfrac{8}{10}$

17. $\dfrac{4}{8}$

18. $\dfrac{10}{12}$

Add. Write each answer in simplest form.

19. $\frac{1}{4} + \frac{1}{4}$

20. $\frac{3}{10} + \frac{3}{10}$

21. $\frac{1}{6} + \frac{1}{6}$

22. $\frac{5}{12} + \frac{1}{12}$

23. $\frac{1}{3} + \frac{1}{3}$

24. $\frac{1}{8} + \frac{3}{8}$

25. $\frac{1}{12} + \frac{1}{12}$

26. $\frac{1}{10} + \frac{1}{10}$

27. $\frac{1}{8} + \frac{1}{8}$

28. $\frac{3}{10} + \frac{1}{10}$

29. $\frac{2}{5} + \frac{1}{5}$

30. $\frac{1}{10} + \frac{7}{10}$

31. $\frac{3}{12} + \frac{5}{12}$

32. $\frac{1}{8} + \frac{5}{8}$

33. $\frac{5}{12} + \frac{5}{12}$

34. $\frac{7}{12} + \frac{1}{12}$

35. A recipe calls for $\frac{1}{4}$ cup white sugar and $\frac{1}{4}$ cup brown sugar. How much sugar does it call for?

36. You rode $\frac{3}{10}$ mile to the park and $\frac{5}{10}$ mile to the library. How far did you ride?

37. You live $\frac{3}{10}$ mile from school. You walk to school and back home. How far do you walk?

38. Tim tried to use a bolt that was $\frac{5}{8}$ inch long. It was $\frac{1}{8}$ inch too short. How long should it be?

39. Beth did $\frac{3}{6}$ of an assignment in class and $\frac{1}{6}$ of it after school. How much of the assignment did she do?

40. You have a paintbrush that is $\frac{3}{8}$ inch wide. You need one that is $\frac{1}{8}$ inch wider. How wide a paintbrush do you need?

Subtracting Fractions

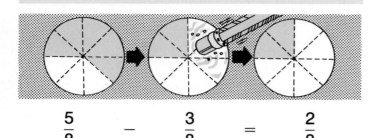

$$\frac{5}{8} \quad - \quad \frac{3}{8} \quad = \quad \frac{2}{8}$$

You can subtract fractions this way.

Subtract the
numerators.

$$\frac{5}{8} - \frac{3}{8} = \frac{5 - 3}{8} = \frac{2}{8}$$

Use the same
denominator.

Change $\frac{2}{8}$ to simplest form. $\qquad \frac{2}{8} = \frac{2 \div 2}{8 \div 2} = \frac{1}{4}$

So, $\frac{5}{8} - \frac{3}{8} = \frac{2}{8}$ or $\frac{1}{4}$.

Exercises

Subtract. Write each answer in simplest form.

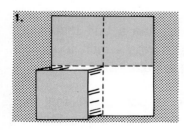

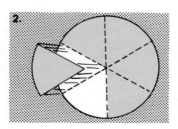

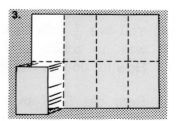

1. $\frac{3}{4} - \frac{1}{4} = \frac{3 - 1}{4} = \frac{2}{4} = \blacksquare$

2. $\frac{5}{6} - \frac{1}{6}$

3. $\frac{7}{8} - \frac{1}{8}$

268

4.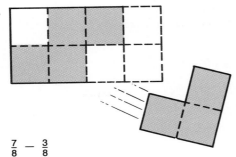

$$\frac{7}{8} - \frac{3}{8}$$

5.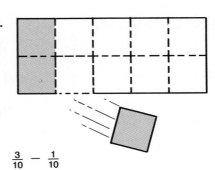

$$\frac{3}{10} - \frac{1}{10}$$

6. $\frac{4}{5} - \frac{1}{5}$ **7.** $\frac{2}{3} - \frac{1}{3}$ **8.** $\frac{7}{9} - \frac{4}{9}$ **9.** $\frac{8}{9} - \frac{2}{9}$

10. $\frac{3}{8} - \frac{1}{8}$ **11.** $\frac{9}{10} - \frac{7}{10}$ **12.** $\frac{7}{12} - \frac{1}{12}$ **13.** $\frac{7}{8} - \frac{5}{8}$

14. $\frac{5}{12} - \frac{1}{12}$ **15.** $\frac{7}{10} - \frac{3}{10}$ **16.** $\frac{5}{8} - \frac{1}{8}$ **17.** $\frac{11}{12} - \frac{5}{12}$

18. $\frac{7}{10} - \frac{1}{10}$ **19.** $\frac{11}{12} - \frac{1}{12}$ **20.** $\frac{5}{8} - \frac{0}{8}$ **21.** $\frac{9}{10} - \frac{1}{10}$

22. $\frac{7}{12} - \frac{5}{12}$ **23.** $\frac{9}{10} - \frac{3}{10}$ **24.** $\frac{3}{5} - \frac{0}{5}$ **25.** $\frac{11}{12} - \frac{7}{12}$

26. $\frac{5}{8}$ gallon of milk was in a bottle before lunch. After lunch there was $\frac{3}{8}$ gallon left. How much was used for lunch?

27. You had $\frac{3}{4}$ pound of wax. You used $\frac{1}{4}$ pound for candles. How much wax do you have left?

Here's 1

Study this.

$$1 - \frac{2}{8} = \frac{8}{8} - \frac{2}{8}$$

$$= \frac{8 - 2}{8}$$

$$= \frac{6}{8} \text{ or } \frac{3}{4}$$

Subtract. Write each answer in simplest form.

1. $1 - \frac{5}{8}$ **2.** $1 - \frac{2}{6}$ **3.** $1 - \frac{6}{8}$

4. $1 - \frac{6}{10}$ **5.** $1 - \frac{4}{10}$ **6.** $1 - \frac{3}{12}$

7. $1 - \frac{5}{5}$ **8.** $1 - \frac{0}{8}$ **9.** $\frac{10}{10} - 1$

SKILLS REVIEW

Which figure has the same size and shape as the red one?

1.

   a   b   c

2.

   a   b   c

3.

   a   b   c

Add or subtract.

4.	5.	6.	7.
41,908 + 9,092	80,000 − 15,607	41,050 − 870	56,271 +28,099

Multiply.

8.	9.	10.	11.
78 × 60	94 × 87	786 × 19	805 × 67

Divide.

12. $4\overline{)809}$ 13. $9\overline{)6300}$ 14. $6\overline{)5490}$ 15. $3\overline{)7518}$

16. $7\overline{)7054}$ 17. $80\overline{)640}$ 18. $30\overline{)600}$ 19. $70\overline{)980}$

Write as a decimal.

20. $\dfrac{2}{10}$ 21. $1\frac{7}{10}$ 22. $\dfrac{5}{100}$ 23. $1\frac{20}{100}$

Use a $ and a decimal point to name each amount of money.

24. 4¢   25. eighty-one cents   26. ten dollars and eight cents

Mixed Numerals

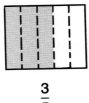

$\dfrac{3}{5}$

$+$

$\dfrac{4}{5}$

$=$

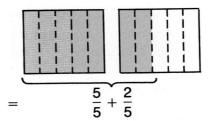

$\dfrac{5}{5} + \dfrac{2}{5}$

The sum can be changed to a mixed numeral.

$\dfrac{5 + 2}{5}$ or $\dfrac{7}{5}$

You know that $\frac{5}{5} = 1$. So,

$\frac{7}{5} = \frac{5}{5} + \frac{2}{5} = 1 + \frac{2}{5} = 1\frac{2}{5}.$

Exercises

Change each fraction to a whole number or a mixed numeral.

1. $\dfrac{4}{3}$ 2. $\dfrac{8}{5}$ 3. $\dfrac{3}{3}$ 4. $\dfrac{3}{2}$ 5. $\dfrac{7}{4}$ 6. $\dfrac{5}{3}$

7. $\dfrac{6}{5}$ 8. $\dfrac{6}{6}$ 9. $\dfrac{11}{8}$ 10. $\dfrac{9}{5}$ 11. $\dfrac{13}{10}$ 12. $\dfrac{9}{8}$

Add. Change each sum to a whole number or a mixed numeral.

13. $\frac{2}{3} + \frac{1}{3}$ 14. $\frac{1}{4} + \frac{3}{4}$ 15. $\frac{5}{6} + \frac{5}{6}$ 16. $\frac{3}{5} + \frac{3}{5}$

17. $\frac{5}{8} + \frac{3}{8}$ 18. $\frac{1}{5} + \frac{4}{5}$ 19. $\frac{5}{8} + \frac{5}{8}$ 20. $\frac{4}{5} + \frac{4}{5}$

21. $\frac{3}{10} + \frac{7}{10}$ 22. $\frac{7}{12} + \frac{7}{12}$ 23. $\frac{5}{12} + \frac{11}{12}$ 24. $\frac{7}{10} + \frac{7}{10}$

25. $\frac{5}{12} + \frac{7}{12}$ 26. $\frac{7}{8} + \frac{7}{8}$ 27. $\frac{3}{10} + \frac{9}{10}$ 28. $\frac{1}{8} + \frac{7}{8}$

29. $\frac{7}{10} + \frac{9}{10}$ 30. $\frac{7}{12} + \frac{11}{12}$ 31. $\frac{9}{10} + \frac{1}{10}$ 32. $\frac{11}{12} + \frac{11}{12}$

Mixed Numerals in Addition

You can add $1\frac{1}{3}$ and $2\frac{1}{3}$ like this.

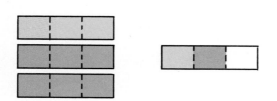

$1\frac{1}{3}$

$+2\frac{1}{3}$

$3\frac{2}{3}$

— Add the fractions.
— Add the whole numbers.

Explain each addition below. Tell how the sum is changed.

$2\frac{5}{8}$
$+3\frac{1}{8}$
$5\frac{6}{8}$ or $5\frac{3}{4}$

$\frac{6}{8} = \frac{6 \div 2}{8 \div 2} = \frac{3}{4}$

$2\frac{2}{3}$
$+4\frac{2}{3}$
$6\frac{4}{3}$ or $7\frac{1}{3}$

$6\frac{4}{3} = 6 + \frac{3}{3} + \frac{1}{3}$
$= 6 + 1 + \frac{1}{3}$
$= 7\frac{1}{3}$

Change the mixed numeral so the fraction is less than 1 and is in simplest form.

Exercises

Add. Write each answer in simplest form.

1. $2\frac{1}{4}$
   $+1\frac{1}{4}$

2. $3\frac{1}{3}$
   $+5\frac{2}{3}$

3. $1\frac{1}{6}$
   $+2\frac{1}{6}$

4. $4\frac{3}{8}$
   $+3\frac{3}{8}$

5. $7\frac{1}{2}$
$+2\frac{1}{2}$

6. $3\frac{1}{10}$
$+1\frac{9}{10}$

7. $8\frac{1}{12}$
$+2\frac{1}{12}$

8. $5\frac{1}{5}$
$+9\frac{3}{5}$

9. $4\frac{1}{3}$
$+6$

10. 8
$+3\frac{3}{4}$

11. $4\frac{3}{8}$
$+4\frac{5}{8}$

12. $7\frac{7}{10}$
$+6\frac{3}{10}$

13. $3\frac{5}{12}$
$+3\frac{5}{12}$

14. $9\frac{3}{4}$
$+4\frac{3}{4}$

15. $8\frac{5}{6}$
$+5\frac{5}{6}$

16. $8\frac{5}{12}$
$+9\frac{7}{12}$

17. $6\frac{7}{8}$
$+5\frac{5}{8}$

18. $7\frac{5}{12}$
$+7\frac{11}{12}$

19. $6\frac{9}{10}$
$+8\frac{7}{10}$

20. $9\frac{11}{12}$
$+9\frac{11}{12}$

Use the time chart.

21. How much time was spent sleeping and eating?

22. How much time was spent studying and playing?

23. How much time was spent resting and working?

Activity	Number of hours
Sleeping	$9\frac{1}{2}$
Studying	$5\frac{3}{4}$
Eating	$1\frac{1}{2}$
Resting	$1\frac{1}{3}$
Working	$1\frac{2}{3}$
Playing	$4\frac{1}{4}$

24. How long is the nail?

$\frac{3}{8}$ inch

$\frac{7}{8}$ inch

25. You live $2\frac{7}{10}$ miles from the park. How far is it from home to the park and back home?

Extra Practice—Set B, page 346   **273**

Mixed Numerals in Subtraction

Bert ran the race in $8\frac{7}{10}$ seconds. Mandy ran it in $7\frac{4}{10}$ seconds. How much longer did it take Bert?

To find the answer, subtract this way.

$$8\frac{7}{10}$$
$$-7\frac{4}{10}$$
$$1\frac{3}{10}$$

Subtract the fractions.
Subtract the whole numbers.

It took Bert $1\frac{3}{10}$ seconds longer.

Explain the subtraction below. Tell how the answer is changed.

$$10\frac{11}{12}$$
$$-\ 6\frac{5}{12}$$
$$4\frac{6}{12} \quad \text{or} \quad 4\frac{1}{2}$$

$\frac{6}{12} = \frac{6 \div 6}{12 \div 6} = \frac{1}{2}$ Change the mixed numeral so the fraction is in simplest form.

Exercises

Subtract. Write each answer in simplest form.

1. $6\frac{3}{8}$
   $-2\frac{1}{8}$

2. $8\frac{5}{12}$
   -3

3. $12\frac{7}{10}$
   $-\ 5\frac{3}{10}$

4. $18\frac{5}{6}$
   $-11\frac{1}{6}$

5. $14\frac{7}{8}$
   $-\ 8\frac{1}{8}$

6. $4\frac{5}{8}$
   $-3\frac{3}{8}$

7. $7\frac{3}{4}$
   $-5\frac{1}{4}$

8. $5\frac{4}{5}$
   -2

9. $9\frac{2}{5}$
  $-6\frac{1}{5}$

10. $8\frac{3}{10}$
  $-2\frac{1}{10}$

11. $6\frac{7}{12}$
  $-1\frac{5}{12}$

12. $7\frac{5}{8}$
  $-4\frac{1}{8}$

13. $8\frac{7}{10}$
  $-5\frac{3}{10}$

14. $12\frac{7}{8}$
  $-\ 9$

15. $15\frac{11}{12}$
  $-\ 7\frac{7}{12}$

16. $10\frac{9}{10}$
  $-\ 6\frac{3}{10}$

17. $11\frac{11}{12}$
  $-\ 6\frac{5}{12}$

18. $18\frac{9}{10}$
  $-\ 9\frac{1}{10}$

19. $2\frac{2}{3}$
  $-1\frac{2}{3}$

20. $13\frac{11}{12}$
  $-\ 4\frac{1}{12}$

21. The school record for the long jump is $5\frac{3}{4}$ feet. Jean jumped $5\frac{1}{4}$ feet. By how much did she miss the record?

22. Ida ran a race in $17\frac{7}{10}$ seconds. Bev beat Ida by $1\frac{3}{10}$ seconds. What was Bev's time?

Holt Confer/Grant Heilman

Barton Silverman/Leo de Wys Inc.

23. You jumped $5\frac{1}{2}$ feet. Your friend jumped 4 feet. How much farther did you jump?

24. Last week Lindy ran the 50-yard dash in $7\frac{3}{10}$ seconds. This week he ran it $\frac{3}{10}$ second faster. What was his time this week?

Extra Practice—Set A, page 347

Adding Tenths

Jamie rode $\frac{4}{10}$ mile to the dime store and then $\frac{9}{10}$ mile to the library. How far did he ride altogether?

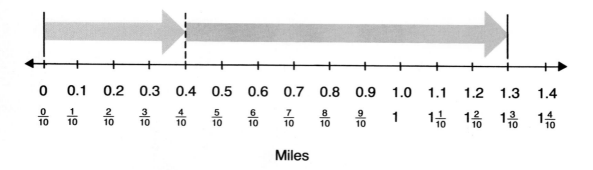

0	0.1	0.2	0.3	0.4	0.5	0.6	0.7	0.8	0.9	1.0	1.1	1.2	1.3	1.4
$\frac{0}{10}$	$\frac{1}{10}$	$\frac{2}{10}$	$\frac{3}{10}$	$\frac{4}{10}$	$\frac{5}{10}$	$\frac{6}{10}$	$\frac{7}{10}$	$\frac{8}{10}$	$\frac{9}{10}$	1	$1\frac{1}{10}$	$1\frac{2}{10}$	$1\frac{3}{10}$	$1\frac{4}{10}$

Miles

You can add fractions or decimals to find the answer.

	Line up the decimal points.	**Add. Put the decimal point in the sum.**

$$\frac{4}{10}$$
$$+\frac{9}{10}$$
$$\frac{13}{10} = 1\frac{3}{10}$$

Ones | Tenths

$$0.4$$
$$+0.9$$

O | Ts

$$\boxed{1}$$
$$0.4 \qquad \text{4 tenths}$$
$$+0.9 \qquad +\ \text{9 tenths}$$
$$1.3 \qquad \boxed{1}\ \text{3 tenths}$$

Jamie rode 1.3 miles.

Tell what is done in each step to add 18.8 and 2.6.

276

Exercises

1. 0.6
    +0.7

    └─ Add tenths.
    └── Add ones.

2. 2.4
    +1.4

    └─ Add tenths.
    └── Add ones.

3. 16.9
    +27.6

    └─ Add tenths.
    └── Add ones.
    └─── Add tens.

4. 0.2
    +0.3

5. 0.5
    +0.3

6. 0.4
    +0.8

7. 0.5
    +0.6

8. 0.8
    +0.2

9. 1.5
    +2.6

10. 3.4
    +4.8

11. 2.3
    +6.0

12. 5.9
    +0.4

13. 4.2
    +0.8

14. 4.7
    +7.6

15. 6.5
    +6.5

16. 9.4
    +5.6

17. 9.0
    +0.9

18. 7.8
    +2.8

19. 10.2
    + 8.3

20. 14.6
    +19.0

21. 22.5
    +18.4

22. 36.7
    +57.7

23. 64.9
    +15.8

24. A jar holds 2.5 liters of juice. A jug holds 4.8 liters of juice. How many liters is that in all?

25. Daisy ran a race in 47.6 seconds. That was 5.8 seconds faster than Nick. How long did it take Nick to run the race?

26. How far is it across 2 pennies?

27. How far is it across 2 nickels?

What Is Missing?

1. 0.6
    +0.▪
    ─────
    1.0

2. ▪.5
    + 0.7
    ─────
    3.▪

3.   1 4.▪
    + 3 ▪.3
    ───────
     ▪8.2

4.   ▪▪.7
    + 6.8
    ───────
     5 0.▪

Extra Practice—Set B, page 347

277

Adding Hundredths

To find the cost of a paint set and an airplane kit, add the prices.

Line up the decimal points.	Add. Put in the decimal point and the $.

	O	Ts	Hs				O	Ts	Hs
							1	1	
$5	.	2	9			$5	.	2	9
+0	.	9	8			+0	.	9	8
						$6	.	2	7

The cost is $6.27.

Tell what is done in each step to find the cost of the dollhouse, the sewing kit, and the model car.

T	O	Ts	Hs		T	O	Ts	Hs
							1	1	
$1	2	.	4	5		$1	2	.	4	5
	1	.	8	4			1	.	8	4
+	3	.	2	5		+	3	.	2	5
						$1	7	.	5	4

Exercises

1.	Juice	$0.82
	Milk	0.99
	Ice cream	+1.29
	Total	

2.	Glue	$ 0.80
	Model car	2.98
	Roller skates	+29.57
	Total	

3. $2.35
   +0.62

4. $1.98
   +4.07

5. $ 7.33
   +10.84

6. $12.86
   + 9.27

7. $4.28
   +5.31

8. $17.05
   + 0.90

9. $30.85
   +69.41

10. $46.07
   +18.53

11. $21.97
     6.39
   +15.42

12. $13.66
     40.50
   + 2.19

13. $2.30
     5.40
   +0.75

14. $1.63
     8.02
   +4.29

15. $16.00
     9.98
   + 0.47

16. $20.55
     18.34
   + 5.95

17. $72.41
     2.78
   +33.04

18. $51.23
     19.80
   +22.85

Use the picture on page 278. Find the cost of these items.

19. model car and paint set

20. sewing kit and airplane kit

21. model ship and model car

22. dollhouse and sewing kit

23. model car, model ship, and airplane kit

24. paint set, sewing kit, and dollhouse

25. dollhouse, model ship, and two paint sets

26. airplane kit, two dollhouses, and model car

Subtracting Tenths

Before a ride through the park, the odometer on Ginny's bicycle looked like this.

tenths

 miles

After the ride, it looked like this.

 miles

To find how far she rode, subtract the decimals.

Line up the decimal points.	Subtract. Put in the decimal point.
O|Ts 8.9 −4.7	O|Ts 8.9 −4.7 4.2

She rode 4.2 miles.

Dr. E. R. Degginger

Here is how to subtract 5.6 from 16.3.

Line up the decimal points.	Rename 16 and 3 tenths as 15 and 13 tenths.	Subtract. Put in the decimal point.
T|O|Ts 1|6.3 − |5.6	T|O|Ts 5|13 1|6.3 − |5.6	T|O|Ts 5|13 1|6.3 − |5.6 1|0.7

Renaming decimals is like renaming whole numbers.

280

Exercises

1. 0.8
   −0.3
   └ Subtract tenths.
   └ Subtract ones.

2. 3.9
   −2.5
   └ Subtract tenths.
   └ Subtract ones.

3. 23.0
   −12.1
   └ Subtract tenths.
   └ Subtract ones.
   └ Subtract tens.

4. 0.8
   −0.1

5. 9.9
   −6.5

6. 5.2
   −1.0

7. 12.8
   − 1.5

8. 10.5
   − 2.3

9. 6.2
   −2.7

10. 4.5
    −1.9

11. 1.1
    −0.8

12. 3.4
    −2.5

13. 9.7
    −8.9

14. 13.5
    − 6.8

15. 16.2
    − 9.3

16. 17.1
    − 8.3

17. 28.3
    −14.5

18. 34.5
    −12.7

19. 41.0
    −15.2

20. 37.2
    −27.6

21. 65.1
    −18.5

22. 20.0
    −13.9

23. 30.0
    − 8.7

Find the distance each pupil rode.

	Before	After
24. Wade		
25. Dara		
26. Betsy		
27. Jack		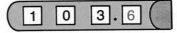
28. Dave		

24. Wade — Before: 72.5, After: 96.2
25. Dara — Before: 36.4, After: 51.0
26. Betsy — Before: 45.8, After: 60.5
27. Jack — Before: 87.1, After: 103.6
28. Dave — Before: 109.3, After: 124.0

Extra Practice—Set B, page 348

281

Subtracting Hundredths

A joke book costs $1.24. If you give the clerk a $5 bill, how much change should you get back?

To find how much change, you can subtract decimals.

Line up the decimal points.	Rename 5 as 4 and 10 tenths. Then rename 10 tenths as 9 tenths and 10 hundredths.	Subtract. Put in the decimal point and the $.
O | Ts | Hs $5. 0 | 0 −1. 2 | 4	O | Ts | Hs 9 4 | 10 | 10 $5. 0 | 0 −1. 2 | 4	O | Ts | Hs 9 4 | 10 | 10 $5. 0 | 0 −1. 2 | 4 $3. 7 | 6

You should get back $3.76.

Tell what is done in each step.

T | O | Ts | Hs	T | O | Ts | Hs	T | O | Ts | Hs
$2 | 6. 2 | 5 −1 | 9. 5 | 0	5 | 12 $2 | 6. 2 | 5 −1 | 9. 5 | 0 . 7 | 5	15 1 | 5 | 12 $2 | 6. 2 | 5 −1 | 9. 5 | 0 $ | 6. 7 | 5

Exercises

1. $0.48
 −0.13

2. $0.76
 −0.29

3. $1.54
 −1.19

4. $2.82
 −1.66

5. $6.46
 −2.03

6. $8.70
 −7.45

7. $4.50
 −1.99

8. $9.19
 −5.67

9. $1.25
 −1.07

10. $5.00
 −2.39

11. $6.15
 −4.08

12. $18.42
 − 7.65

13. $1.00
 −0.92

14. $7.00
 −3.46

15. $1.00
 −0.75

16. $5.00
 −0.63

17. $3.50
 −3.32

18. $1.00
 −0.85

19. $4.25
 −1.18

20. $2.00
 −1.25

21. $11.25
 −10.95

22. $15.75
 −13.87

23. $16.00
 − 4.12

24. $12.00
 − 9.84

25. A pair of jeans cost $15.50. They are put on sale for $9.96. How much less is the sale price of the jeans?

26. You buy the jeans for $9.96. You pay with a $20 bill. How much change should you get back?

27. You buy one pair of jeans for $9.96 and another pair for $8.75. You pay with a $20 bill. How much change should you get?

28. You bought a shirt for $7.49. You also bought a pair of jeans. You got $2.86 in change from $20. How much did the jeans cost?

Do It With a Calculator!

You can use a calculator to add or subtract decimals. Here is how to tell the calculator to subtract 0.67 from 12.05.

Push the keys in this order.	The display will show this.
[C]	*0*
[1] [2] [·] [0] [5]	*12.05*
[−]	*12.05*
[·] [6] [7]	*0.67*
[=]	*11.38*

Ed Hoppe Photography

Use a calculator to find each sum or difference.

1. 0.89
   +1.45

2. 0.09
   +0.91

3. 0.75
   −0.68

4. 43.21
   − 6.99

5. 7.00
   −0.67

6. 38.88
   +47.79

7. 14.60
   −13.72

8. 87.56
   + 0.89

Use a calculator to do each problem.

9. A man bought a snake for $25.15 and a tank for $29.99. How much did the man spend? Now turn the calculator upside down to find out what the snake said when it learned that it was being sold.

10. Yesterday Ida bought some stock for $12.75. Today the stock is worth $90.10. How much did the stock's value go up? Now turn the calculator upside down to see what she should do with the stock.

Fraction-Decimal Practice

Add or subtract. Write each answer in simplest form.

1. $\frac{1}{6} + \frac{2}{6}$ **2.** $\frac{3}{8} + \frac{1}{8}$ **3.** $\frac{3}{4} - \frac{2}{4}$ **4.** $\frac{7}{10} - \frac{1}{10}$

5. $\frac{11}{12} - \frac{3}{12}$ **6.** $\frac{3}{10} + \frac{3}{10}$ **7.** $\frac{5}{8} - \frac{3}{8}$ **8.** $\frac{1}{12} + \frac{8}{12}$

9. $\frac{5}{6} - \frac{1}{6}$ **10.** $\frac{5}{10} + \frac{4}{10}$ **11.** $\frac{5}{12} + \frac{5}{12}$ **12.** $\frac{7}{10} - \frac{0}{10}$

13. $\begin{array}{r} 3\frac{5}{10} \\ + 4\frac{3}{10} \\ \hline \end{array}$ **14.** $\begin{array}{r} 16\frac{7}{10} \\ - 9 \\ \hline \end{array}$ **15.** $\begin{array}{r} 5\frac{1}{6} \\ + 2\frac{2}{6} \\ \hline \end{array}$ **16.** $\begin{array}{r} 10\frac{5}{8} \\ - 7\frac{3}{8} \\ \hline \end{array}$

17. $\begin{array}{r} 5\frac{5}{8} \\ + 1\frac{5}{8} \\ \hline \end{array}$ **18.** $\begin{array}{r} 4\frac{6}{10} \\ + 8\frac{8}{10} \\ \hline \end{array}$ **19.** $\begin{array}{r} 7\frac{3}{4} \\ - 5\frac{3}{4} \\ \hline \end{array}$ **20.** $\begin{array}{r} 6\frac{9}{12} \\ + 5\frac{7}{12} \\ \hline \end{array}$

Add or subtract.

21. $\begin{array}{r} 0.5 \\ + 0.1 \\ \hline \end{array}$ **22.** $\begin{array}{r} 0.8 \\ + 0.9 \\ \hline \end{array}$ **23.** $\begin{array}{r} 0.9 \\ - 0.8 \\ \hline \end{array}$ **24.** $\begin{array}{r} 9.6 \\ - 8.1 \\ \hline \end{array}$

25. $\begin{array}{r} 3.5 \\ - 1.8 \\ \hline \end{array}$ **26.** $\begin{array}{r} 5.6 \\ + 6.5 \\ \hline \end{array}$ **27.** $\begin{array}{r} 35.8 \\ + 4.2 \\ \hline \end{array}$ **28.** $\begin{array}{r} 23.0 \\ - 17.2 \\ \hline \end{array}$

29. $\begin{array}{r} 20.06 \\ + 0.07 \\ \hline \end{array}$ **30.** $\begin{array}{r} 47.55 \\ - 36.99 \\ \hline \end{array}$ **31.** $\begin{array}{r} 58.27 \\ + 39.84 \\ \hline \end{array}$ **32.** $\begin{array}{r} 61.03 \\ - 2.15 \\ \hline \end{array}$

33. $\begin{array}{r} \$89.00 \\ - 0.77 \\ \hline \end{array}$ **34.** $\begin{array}{r} \$34.00 \\ - 19.06 \\ \hline \end{array}$ **35.** $\begin{array}{r} \$43.90 \\ - 7.87 \\ \hline \end{array}$ **36.** $\begin{array}{r} \$92.88 \\ + 7.99 \\ \hline \end{array}$

37. $\begin{array}{r} 46.32 \\ 1.06 \\ + 0.01 \\ \hline \end{array}$ **38.** $\begin{array}{r} 28.06 \\ 12.95 \\ + 30.08 \\ \hline \end{array}$ **39.** $\begin{array}{r} 19.50 \\ 0.87 \\ + 68.09 \\ \hline \end{array}$ **40.** $\begin{array}{r} 0.74 \\ 39.89 \\ + 56.26 \\ \hline \end{array}$

Solving Problems

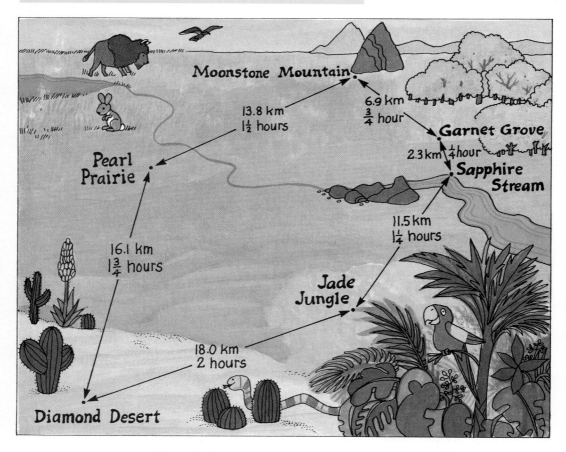

Moonstone Mountain

13.8 km
1½ hours

6.9 km
¾ hour

Garnet Grove

2.3 km ¼ hour

Sapphire Stream

Pearl Prairie

16.1 km
1¾ hours

11.5 km
1¼ hours

Jade Jungle

18.0 km
2 hours

Diamond Desert

1. How long does it take to go from Moonstone Mountain to Garnet Grove and to Sapphire Stream?

2. How far is it from Sapphire Stream to Moonstone Mountain if you go through Garnet Grove?

3. Start at Garnet Grove. How much longer does it take to go to Moonstone Mountain than to Sapphire Stream?

4. You are at Jade Jungle. How much farther are you from Diamond Desert than from Sapphire Stream?

5. How long does it take to go from Diamond Desert to Sapphire Stream if you go through Jade Jungle?

6. You are at Pearl Prairie. How much closer are you to Moonstone Mountain than to Diamond Desert?

286

You are to make this sign.

7. How far is it from the top of the sign to the bottom of the letters?

8. How far is it from the bottom of the letters to the bottom of the sign?

9. How much taller is the "G" than the "o"?

10. The sign is how much taller than it is wide?

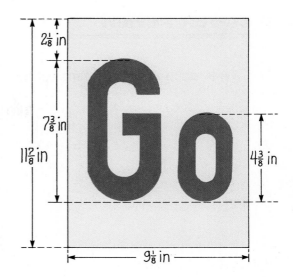

11. How much does it cost to buy the table-tennis paddles and a box of balls?

12. You want to buy 1 pair of socks and 2 T-shirts. Find the total cost.

13. You buy 2 boxes of balls and give the clerk $5.00. How much change should you get back?

14. You have $6.50. How much more do you need to buy a T-shirt and the table-tennis paddles?

15. You have $10.00. How much more do you need to buy all of the things shown above?

16. Suppose T-shirts go on sale for $2.98 each. How much could you save by buying 2 of them on sale?

287

CHAPTER REVIEW

Add. Write each answer in simplest form.

1. $\frac{1}{3} + \frac{1}{3}$

2. $\frac{1}{6} + \frac{1}{6}$

3. $\frac{1}{8} + \frac{5}{8}$

4. $\frac{5}{12} + \frac{5}{12}$

5. $\frac{1}{4} + \frac{3}{4}$

6. $\frac{3}{10} + \frac{7}{10}$

7. $\frac{3}{5} + \frac{4}{5}$

8. $\frac{1}{2} + \frac{1}{2}$

9. $1\frac{1}{4}$
   $+2\frac{1}{4}$

10. $3\frac{1}{2}$
    $+8\frac{1}{2}$

11. $5\frac{3}{8}$
    $+4\frac{1}{8}$

12. $11\frac{7}{12}$
    $+18\frac{7}{12}$

Subtract. Write each answer in simplest form.

13. $\frac{2}{5} - \frac{1}{5}$

14. $\frac{5}{6} - \frac{1}{6}$

15. $\frac{7}{12} - \frac{5}{12}$

16. $\frac{9}{10} - \frac{3}{10}$

17. $2\frac{3}{4}$
    $-1\frac{1}{4}$

18. $6\frac{5}{6}$
    $-4\frac{1}{6}$

19. $12\frac{7}{8}$
    $-5\frac{1}{8}$

20. $15\frac{11}{12}$
    $-11\frac{1}{12}$

21. Some children sold $3\frac{3}{4}$ quarts of lemonade and $2\frac{1}{4}$ quarts of grape juice. How many quarts were sold altogether?

22. Bernard is $55\frac{3}{4}$ inches tall. Martine is $52\frac{1}{4}$ inches tall. How much taller is Bernard?

Add or subtract.

23. 0.6
    $+0.9$

24. 14.4
    $+9.8$

25. $\$1.68$
    $+8.27$

26. $\$25.98$
    $+16.73$

27. 5.0
    -3.4

28. 18.1
    -2.9

29. $\$1.00$
    -0.88

30. $\$16.35$
    -12.97

31. Tim weighs 33.8 kilograms. Sue weighs 29.4 kilograms. They both get on a scale. What should the reading be?

32. A game you want sells for $12.50. You have only $9.15. How much more money do you need for the game?

288

13 Graphs and Probability

Ed Hoppe Photography

Pairs

Each building has 4 apartments. The pupils made the chart below to show where each of them lives.

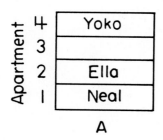

Apartment	A	B	C	D
4	Yoko	Dawn	Otis	Molly
3		Tod	Katie	Hope
2	Ella	Nicole	Scott	Henry
1	Neal	Dessa		Kerry

Building

Scott lives in Building C, Apartment 2.
You can write C2 to tell where he lives.

building ─┘ └─ apartment

Who lives at B1?

Exercises

Name the pupil who lives at

1. A2   2. D1   3. B3   4. C4

5. B2   6. D4   7. A1   8. C3

9. A4   10. B4   11. D3   12. D2

Use the picture on page 290. Tell where each pupil lives.

13. Tod   **14.** Dawn   **15.** Ella   **16.** Dessa

17. Katie   **18.** Neal   **19.** Molly   **20.** Kerry

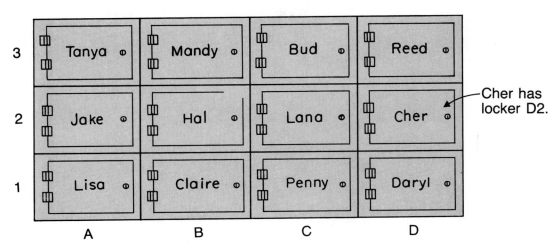

Cher has locker D2.

Who has each of these lockers?

21. B1   **22.** A2   **23.** D3   **24.** C1

25. D1   **26.** C3   **27.** B2   **28.** B3

How would each of these pupils name their locker?

29. Lana   **30.** Tanya   **31.** Daryl   **32.** Lisa

33. Hal   **34.** Mandy   **35.** Jake   **36.** Bud

37. You have ticket S2. Which prize do you win?

38. Which prize will T3 win?

39. You win ⚾. What ticket did you have?

Using a Grid

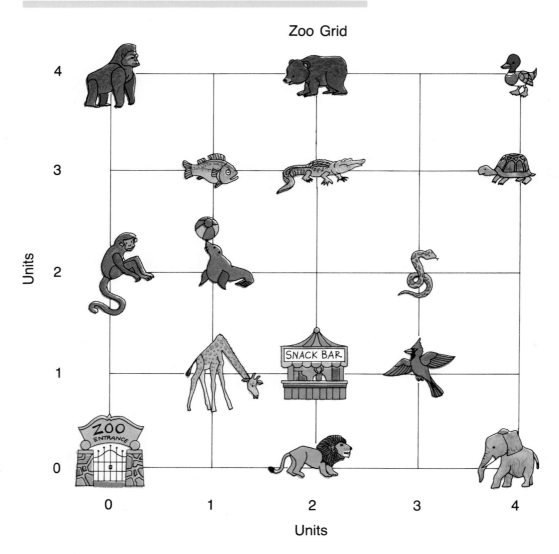

Zoo Grid

Start at the main gate.
The birds are 3 units → and 1 unit ↑.

A short way to write this is 3̲, 1↑.
→

How would you get from the main gate to the monkeys?

292

Exercises

Start at the main gate. Tell where these moves take you.

1. $\underset{\rightarrow}{2}, 1\uparrow$

2. $\underset{\rightarrow}{4}, 0\uparrow$

3. $\underset{\rightarrow}{1}, 3\uparrow$

4. $\underset{\rightarrow}{2}, 4\uparrow$

5. $\underset{\rightarrow}{2}, 0\uparrow$

6. $\underset{\rightarrow}{1}, 2\uparrow$

7. $\underset{\rightarrow}{4}, 4\uparrow$

8. $\underset{\rightarrow}{0}, 4\uparrow$

9. $\underset{\rightarrow}{1}, 1\uparrow$

10. $\underset{\rightarrow}{2}, 3\uparrow$

11. $\underset{\rightarrow}{3}, 2\uparrow$

12. $\underset{\rightarrow}{4}, 3\uparrow$

Tell how to get from the main gate to the

13. seals

14. snack bar

15. ducks

16. snakes

17. alligators

18. giraffes

19. lions

20. bears

21. elephants

22. gorillas

23. fish

24. turtles

Grid Code

Each pair of moves takes you to a letter.

Chen-Chu used this grid code to name her favorite sport.

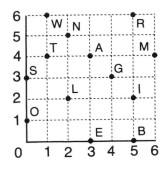

1. What is her favorite sport?

$\underset{\rightarrow}{1}, 4\uparrow$ $\quad\underset{\rightarrow}{3}, 0\uparrow$ $\quad\underset{\rightarrow}{2}, 5\uparrow$ $\quad\underset{\rightarrow}{2}, 5\uparrow$ $\quad\underset{\rightarrow}{5}, 2\uparrow$ $\quad\underset{\rightarrow}{0}, 3\uparrow$

2. What is Mark's favorite sport?

$\underset{\rightarrow}{5}, 0\uparrow$ $\quad\underset{\rightarrow}{3}, 4\uparrow$ $\quad\underset{\rightarrow}{0}, 3\uparrow$ $\quad\underset{\rightarrow}{3}, 0\uparrow$ $\quad\underset{\rightarrow}{5}, 0\uparrow$ $\quad\underset{\rightarrow}{3}, 4\uparrow$ $\quad\underset{\rightarrow}{2}, 2\uparrow$ $\quad\underset{\rightarrow}{2}, 2\uparrow$

3. What is Kathy's favorite sport?

$\underset{\rightarrow}{5}, 0\uparrow$ $\quad\underset{\rightarrow}{0}, 1\uparrow$ $\quad\underset{\rightarrow}{1}, 6\uparrow$ $\quad\underset{\rightarrow}{2}, 2\uparrow$ $\quad\underset{\rightarrow}{5}, 2\uparrow$ $\quad\underset{\rightarrow}{2}, 5\uparrow$ $\quad\underset{\rightarrow}{4}, 3\uparrow$

Ordered Pairs

Start at 0. You can get to point E by these moves.

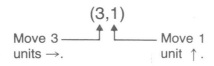

If you always give the number of the → move first, you need not draw the arrow.

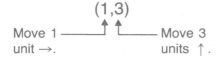

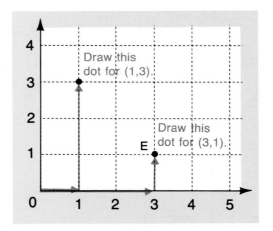

(3,1) and (1,3) are called **ordered pairs.**

Exercises

Write the letter for each of these ordered pairs.

1. (4,0)

2. (0,4)

3. (1,1)

4. (3,3)

5. (3,4)

6. (4,3)

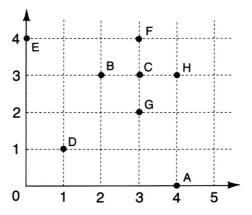

Write the ordered pair for each of these dots on the grid.

7. B   8. G   9. A   10. E

Write the letter for each of these ordered pairs.

11. (4,2)

12. (2,1)

13. (3,6)

14. (6,3)

15. (2,4)

16. (4,4)

17. (5,6)

18. (3,0)

19. (0,3)

20. (6,5)

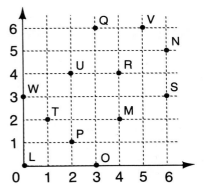

Write the ordered pair for each dot on this grid.

21. L

22. R

23. T

24. P

25. U

26. M

27. O

28. W

Secret Messages

1. A club uses this grid to send secret messages. You get this message. What does it say?

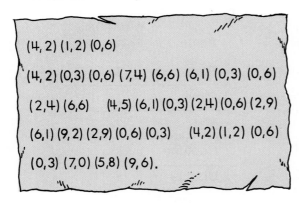

(4,2) (1,2) (0,6)

(4,2) (0,3) (0,6) (7,4) (6,6) (6,1) (0,3) (0,6)

(2,4) (6,6)   (4,5) (6,1) (0,3) (2,4) (0,6) (2,9)

(6,1) (9,2) (2,9) (0,6) (0,3)   (4,2) (1,2) (0,6)

(0,3) (7,0) (5,8) (9,6).

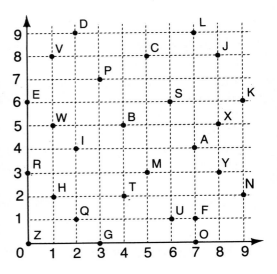

2. Make a secret message of your own.

Extra Practice—Set B, page 349

295

Making Tables

Those planets that have moons are shown below.

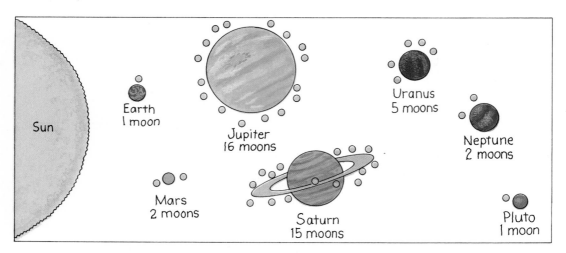

Which planet has the most moons?

Which planets have more than 2 moons?

Which planets have the same number of moons?

To make it easier to answer such questions, you can make a table.

How many more moons does Jupiter have than Earth?

Which planet has 10 fewer moons than Saturn?

How many planets have more than 1 moon?

How many moons are there in all?

Planet	Number of moons
Earth	1
Pluto	1
Mars	2
Neptune	2
Uranus	5
Saturn	15
Jupiter	16

Exercises

Use the drawing of buttons to complete the table.

	Kind of button	Number of buttons
1.		
2.		
3.		
4.		

5. How many more are there than ?

6. How many fewer are there than ?

7. How many buttons are there altogether?

Use the heights of the apple tree. Copy and complete the table.

	Age (years)	Height (feet)
8.	1	
9.	2	
10.	3	
11.	4	

1 year
1 ft tall

2 years
3 ft tall

3 years
6 ft tall

4 years
9 ft tall

12. How much taller is the apple tree at 4 years than at 2 years?

297

Making a Line Graph

The table below shows the growth of an apple tree. The table is really a list of ordered pairs.

Age (years)	Height (feet)	Ordered pairs
0	0	(0,0)
1	1	(1,1)
2	3	(2,3)
3	6	(3,6)
4	9	(4,9)

You can show the growth by making a **line graph.**

Step 1:

Draw this on grid paper.

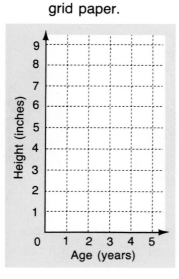

Step 2:

Draw a dot for each ordered pair.

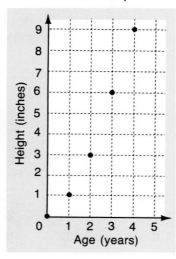

Step 3:

Connect the dots from left to right.

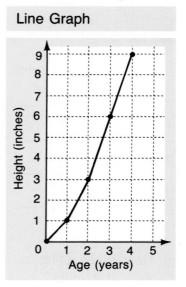

Exercises

The table below shows the growth of a malamute puppy for 8 weeks.

1. Make this on grid paper.

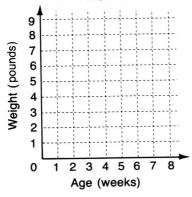

2. Make a line graph from this table.

Age (weeks)	Weight (pounds)
0 (birth)	1
2	3
4	6
6	8
8	9

Make a line graph from each table.

3.

Time (hours)	Snowfall (inches)
1	3
2	6
3	10
4	14
5	17
6	18

4.

Time (hours)	Distance (miles)
0	0
2	3
4	6
6	9
8	12

5.

Time (months)	Weight (pounds)
0 (birth)	1
1	5
2	11
3	14

6.

Time (minutes)	Distance (miles)
0	0
6	1
12	2
18	3

Reading a Line Graph

This line graph shows the growth of an apple tree.

When was
the tree
3 feet tall? --

It was
3 feet tall
at the end
of 2 years.

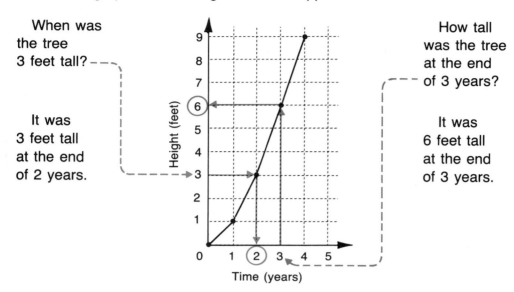

How tall
was the tree
at the end
of 3 years?

It was
6 feet tall
at the end
of 3 years.

Exercises

How tall was the tree at these times?

1. end of 1 year

2. end of 4 years

When was the tree this tall?

3. 9 feet

4. 1 foot

Answer these questions.

5. During which year did the tree grow the least?

6. During which two years did it grow the same amount?

7. When was the tree about 2 feet tall?

300

This line graph shows how far a car traveled.

How far did the car go in

8. 2 minutes   **9.** 6 minutes

10. 10 minutes   **11.** 3 minutes

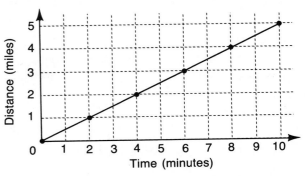

How long did it take the car to go

12. 2 miles   **13.** 3 miles   **14.** 4 miles   **15.** $2\frac{1}{2}$ miles

16. How long do you think it would take the car to go 6 miles?

17. How far do you think the car would go in 20 minutes?

This line graph shows the growth of a sunflower.

How tall was the sunflower at the end of

18. 1 week   **19.** 2 weeks

20. 4 weeks   **21.** $4\frac{1}{2}$ weeks

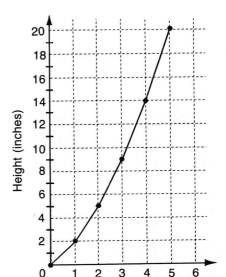

When did the sunflower reach a height of

22. 9 inches   **23.** 20 inches

24. 7 inches   **25.** 5 inches

26. During which week did it grow the least?

27. During which week did it grow the most?

28. How tall do you think it will be at the end of 6 weeks?

Bar Graphs

This table shows how many pupils play each instrument.

Instrument	Number of pupils
Piano	4
Flute	2
Guitar	5
Violin	3

You can show the same thing by making a **bar graph.**

Step 1:
Copy this on grid paper.

Step 2:
In each column, color one square for each pupil who plays that instrument.

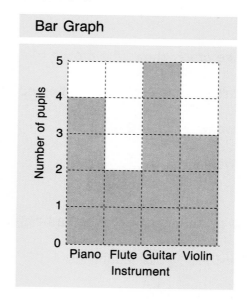

Bar Graph

Exercises

Use the bar graph above. Tell how many more pupils play guitar than play

1. violin

2. piano

3. flute

4. Which instrument is played by the most pupils?

5. Which instrument is played by the fewest pupils?

302

How many moons
does each of
these planets have?

6. Earth   7. Jupiter

8. Mars   9. Neptune

10. Saturn   11. Uranus

12. Which planet has the
    most moons?

13. Which planets have
    the same number of
    moons?

14. How many planets
    have more than 2
    moons?

15. Which planet has 14
    more moons than
    Neptune?

16. Which planet has 3
    times as many moons
    as Uranus?

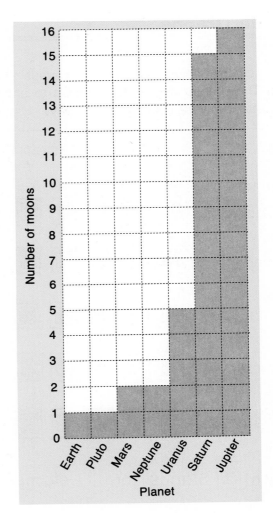

Make a bar graph from each table.

17.

Favorite sport	Number of pupils
Baseball	8
Football	6
Hockey	5
Basketball	7
Tennis	4

18.

Hair color	Number of pupils
Blond	6
Red	9
Brown	15
Black	4

Picture Graphs

The class decided to collect stamps for one week. They made this **picture graph** to show how many stamps were collected each day.

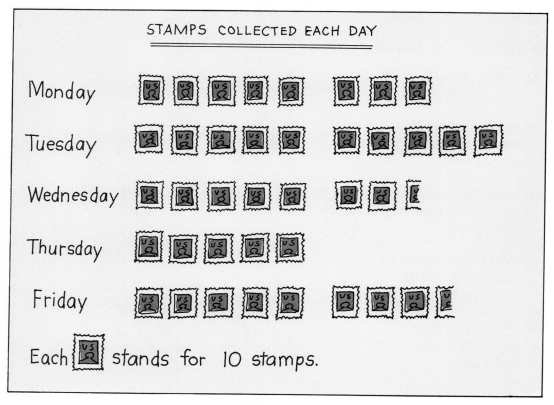

STAMPS COLLECTED EACH DAY

Monday

Tuesday

Wednesday

Thursday

Friday

Each stands for 10 stamps.

How many stamps does each stand for?

How many stamps does a stand for?

Exercises

1. On which day were the fewest stamps collected?

2. On which day were the most stamps collected?

3. How many stamps were collected on Monday?

4. How many stamps were collected on Tuesday?

5. How many stamps were collected on Wednesday?

6. How many more stamps were collected on Friday than on Thursday?

7. How many stamps were collected during the week?

The principal put this graph on the bulletin board.

8. What does each  stand for?

9. In which month did the most pupils have perfect attendance?

10. In which month did the fewest pupils have perfect attendance?

11. How many pupils had perfect attendance in September?

12. How many pupils had perfect attendance in February?

13. In which month did twice as many pupils have perfect attendance as in February?

14. In which two months did the same number of pupils have perfect attendance?

15. Which month was second for perfect attendance?

16. Which month was next to last in perfect attendance?

17. How many more pupils had perfect attendance in April than in March?

18. How many fewer pupils had perfect attendance in February than in January?

305

Most Likely—Least Likely

These marbles are put into an empty bowl.

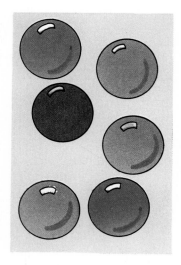

Without looking, you reach in and pick one marble.

The marble you pick might be blue, red, or black.

Guess which color you are *most likely* to pick? Why did you choose that color?

Guess which color you are *least likely* to pick? Why did you choose that color?

Exercises

You are to pick one marble without looking. Tell which color you are *most likely* to pick. Then tell which color you are *least likely* to pick.

1.

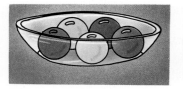

2.

3.

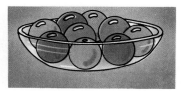

You win if you choose the color on which the pointer stops. Spin the pointer. Which color would you guess?

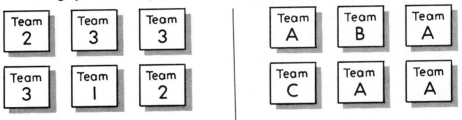

Without looking, you are to pick one card. You will play on that team.

Team 2	Team 3	Team 3
Team 3	Team 1	Team 2

Team A	Team B	Team A
Team C	Team A	Team A

10. On which team are you most likely to play?

11. On which team are you least likely to play?

12. On which team are you most likely to play?

13. On which team are you least likely to play?

The cards below are turned over and mixed up. You are to pick one card.

14. Which letter are you most likely to pick?

15. Which letter are you least likely to pick?

16. Which color of card are you most likely to pick?

17. Which color of card are you least likely to pick?

Chance

You are to pick one of these tickets without looking.

You might pick any one of the tickets. How many tickets are there?

How many green tickets are there?

Your **chance** of picking a green ticket is

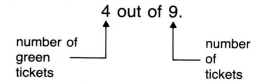

4 out of 9.

number of green tickets — number of tickets

What is your chance of picking a white ticket?

What is your chance of picking a brown ticket?

Exercises

You put your money in a milk machine and push one of these buttons without looking.

What is your chance of getting each of these?

1. chocolate milk

2. skim milk

3. whole milk

You spin the pointer so that it stops on one of the numbers.

What is your chance of getting

4. 4

5. 5

6. 2

7. 3

8. an even number

9. a number less than 4

10. an odd number

11. a number greater than 3

These cards are turned over and mixed up.

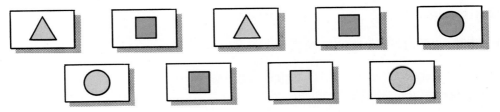

You are to pick one card. What is your chance of getting a

12. blue figure

13. red figure

14. red circle

15. circle

14. square

17. blue triangle

18. triangle

19. blue circle

20. red square

The cards below are turned over and mixed up.

You are to pick one card. What is your chance of getting

21. S

22. I

23. P

24. M

25. a red card

26. a blue card

27. a green card

Extra Practice—Set B, page 351   **309**

Heads or Tails

Flipping one coin:

When you flip a coin, it will land one of these two ways.

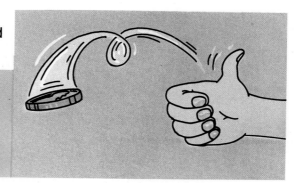

Heads   Tails

Your chance of getting *heads* is 1 out of 2.

1. Think of flipping a coin 10 times. Guess how many times you will get *heads.*

2. Make a table like this.

Heads
Tails

3. Get a coin. Flip it 10 times. Keep track of *heads* and *tails* in the table. Was your guess correct?

4. Think of flipping a coin 50 times. Guess how many times you will get *heads.* Try it. Was your guess correct?

5. Guess how many times you will get *heads* in 100 flips. To get 100 flips, add your results of 50 flips to those of a classmate for 50 flips. Was your guess correct?

6. Your chance of getting heads is 1 out of 2. Does that tell you *exactly what will happen* or *what will most likely happen?*

Flipping two coins:

Think of flipping a dime and a penny at the same time.

The coins will land one of these four ways.

both heads

dime heads and penny tails

dime tails and penny heads

both tails

In one flip, what is your chance of getting

7. both heads

8. both tails

9. both coins alike

10. dime heads and penny tails

11. dime tails and penny heads

12. a head and a tail

13. Guess how many times you will get *both heads* in 20 flips. Try it. Was your guess correct?

14. Guess how many times you will get *a head and a tail* in 20 flips. Try it. Was your guess correct?

SKILLS REVIEW

Would you use *centimeters, meters,* or *kilometers* to find the length of

1. a school bus
2. a caterpillar
3. a river

Would you use *grams* or *kilograms* to find the weight of

4. yourself
5. a pencil

Could each of these hold a liter of water?

6. a drinking glass
7. a quart bottle
8. a bathroom sink

Copy and complete.

9. $\frac{6}{8} = \frac{\blacksquare}{4}$

10. $\frac{2}{3} = \frac{\blacksquare}{6}$

11. $1 = \frac{\blacksquare}{5}$

12. $2 = \frac{\blacksquare}{6}$

Add. Write each answer in simplest form.

13. $\frac{1}{8} + \frac{3}{8}$

14. $\frac{5}{12} + \frac{5}{12}$

15. $2\frac{5}{8}$
$+3\frac{1}{8}$

16. $4\frac{7}{10}$
$+1\frac{8}{10}$

Subtract. Write each answer in simplest form.

17. $\frac{5}{6} - \frac{1}{6}$

18. $\frac{7}{8} - \frac{3}{8}$

19. $2\frac{9}{10}$
$-1\frac{3}{10}$

20. $5\frac{11}{12}$
$-3\frac{5}{12}$

Add or subtract.

21. $\quad 0.8$
$+0.7$

22. $\quad 13.2$
$-\ 6.4$

23. $\quad 29.67$
$+17.67$

24. $\quad 20.13$
-14.34

25. $\quad 48.98$
$+28.57$

26. $\quad 56.40$
-39.76

27. $\quad 15.7$
$+\ 8.4$

28. $\quad 92.00$
$-\ 6.54$

312

CHAPTER REVIEW

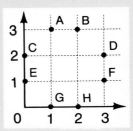

Write the letter for each ordered pair.

1. (3,1)   **2.** (1,3)   **3.** (2,0)

Write the ordered pair for each dot.

4. B   **5.** D   **6.** E

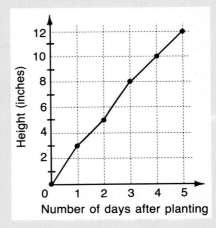

This line graph shows the growth of a tulip plant. How tall was the plant after this many days?

7. 1   **8.** $1\frac{1}{2}$ **9.** 2

10. 3   **11.** 4   **12.** 5

13. How tall do you think the plant will be after 6 days?

Use the bar graph of animal heights. How many meters taller is the giraffe than the

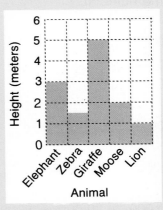

14. elephant   **15.** moose

16. How tall is the zebra?

17. Which animal is the shortest?

You pick one marble without looking. What is your chance of getting a marble that is

18. red   **19.** blue   **20.** yellow

REVIEW AND PRACTICE

Set A (Use after page 9.)

Write < or > for each ●.

    42 > 39   1. 13 ● 11   2. 9 ● 16   3. 28 ● 32

4. 21 ● 14   5. 31 ● 40   6. 18 ● 23   7. 57 ● 49

8. 52 ● 59   9. 61 ● 38   10. 72 ● 85   11. 39 ● 64

12. 80 ● 50   13. 71 ● 17   14. 45 ● 25   15. 89 ● 98

Set B (Use after page 15.)

Write the numeral.

    6000 + 200 = 6200   1. 2000 + 300 + 70 + 6

2. 3000 + 800 + 10   3. 5000 + 90 + 2

4. 7000 + 100 + 50 + 4   5. 20,000 + 5000 + 700

6. 10,000 + 300 + 20 + 7   7. 40,000 + 3000 + 5

8. 200,000 + 30,000 + 8000 + 900 + 60 + 9

9. 500,000 + 9000 + 800 + 10 + 3

10. 800,000 + 40,000 + 200 + 9

Set A (Use after page 17.)

	6 +8 14	1.	9 +4	2.	6 +7	3.	2 +8	4.	1 +9	5.	6 +6
6.	7 +7	7.	6 +9	8.	8 +5	9.	7 +8	10.	8 +9	11.	9 +9

Set B (Use after page 21.)

	27 +46 73	1.	15 +23	2.	38 +41	3.	19 +60	4.	52 +25	5.	61 + 8
6.	31 +19	7.	42 +28	8.	16 +25	9.	74 + 8	10.	49 +43	11.	57 +38
12.	57 +37	13.	15 +29	14.	39 + 6	15.	45 +45	16.	68 +18	17.	79 + 1
18.	88 + 7	19.	36 +26	20.	78 + 6	21.	17 +79	22.	59 +38	23.	68 +26

Set C (Use after page 23.)

	15 − 6 9	1.	8 −8	2.	12 − 5	3.	13 − 7	4.	12 − 6	5.	15 − 8
6.	11 − 4	7.	14 − 8	8.	16 − 7	9.	12 − 9	10.	10 − 3	11.	11 − 2
12.	16 − 8	13.	18 − 9	14.	17 − 8	15.	15 − 6	16.	14 − 7	17.	13 − 4

Set A (Use after page 27.)

	31 − 17 14	1.	18 − 11	2.	26 − 13	3.	49 − 6	4.	38 − 7	5.	90 − 50
6.	63 − 21	7.	55 − 43	8.	89 − 18	9.	77 − 26	10.	96 − 51	11.	46 − 46
12.	40 − 15	13.	71 − 28	14.	62 − 37	15.	53 − 44	16.	24 − 16	17.	41 − 9
18.	84 − 9	19.	20 − 18	20.	66 − 49	21.	85 − 7	22.	57 − 28	23.	86 − 68
24.	75 − 36	25.	81 − 64	26.	97 − 88	27.	80 − 23	28.	92 − 87	29.	70 − 6

Set B (Use after page 29.)

Write *odd* or *even* for each number.

7   odd   1. 4   2. 19   3. 83   4. 50

5. 118   6. 325   7. 200   8. 781   9. 2435

10. 4002   11. 3698   12. 6070   13. 35,792   14. 60,361

Set C (Use after page 32.)

Complete each number pattern.

47, 45, 43, _41_ , _39_   1. 57, 58, 59, ___, ___

2. 313, 312, 311, ___, ___   3. 85, 90, 95, ___, ___

4. 230, 220, 210, ___, ___   5. 994, 996, 998, ___, ___

Set A (Use after page 37.)

		1.		2.		3.		4.		5.	
	29		24		47		51		34		8
	37		20		15		19		28		28
	+16		+38		+12		+25		+13		+38
	82										

6.		7.		8.		9.		10.		11.	
	67		24		16		58		35		30
	11		39		46		20		15		28
	+18		+26		+36		+17		+49		+29

12.		13.		14.		15.		16.		17.	
	43		15		24		38		29		46
	27		69		26		42		35		17
	+18		+13		+25		+21		+34		+18

Set B (Use after page 39.)

		1.		2.		3.		4.	
	574		132		229		380		506
	+389		+346		+450		+617		+ 3
	963								

5.		6.		7.		8.		9.	
	172		353		288		549		867
	+634		+460		+653		+187		+ 75

10.		11.		12.		13.		14.	
	580		276		689		395		788
	+299		+471		+ 50		+595		+ 61

15.		16.		17.		18.		19.	
	236		463		574		807		341
	+416		+285		+ 6		+137		+309

20.		21.		22.		23.		24.	
	462		217		768		694		452
	+ 68		+285		+148		+208		+ 69

25.		26.		27.		28.		29.	
	648		299		657		897		388
	+197		+563		+ 59		+ 87		+256

Set A (Use after page 43.)

Round to the nearest ten.

75 ⟶ 80   1. 13   2. 38   3. 25

4. 67   5. 81   6. 92   7. 15   8. 44

Round to the nearest hundred.

449 ⟶ 400   9. 128   10. 273   11. 652

12. 99   13. 248   14. 850   15. 710   16. 464

Write an estimate.

$$\begin{array}{r} 392 \\ +518 \\ \hline \end{array} \longrightarrow \begin{array}{r} 400 \\ +500 \\ \hline 900 \end{array}$$

17. $\begin{array}{r} 72 \\ +19 \\ \hline \end{array}$ 18. $\begin{array}{r} 57 \\ +68 \\ \hline \end{array}$ 19. $\begin{array}{r} 85 \\ +23 \\ \hline \end{array}$

20. $\begin{array}{r} 205 \\ +615 \\ \hline \end{array}$ 21. $\begin{array}{r} 726 \\ +181 \\ \hline \end{array}$ 22. $\begin{array}{r} 374 \\ +526 \\ \hline \end{array}$ 23. $\begin{array}{r} 483 \\ +\ 98 \\ \hline \end{array}$ 24. $\begin{array}{r} 353 \\ +249 \\ \hline \end{array}$

Set B (Use after page 47.)

$$\begin{array}{r} 605 \\ -442 \\ \hline 163 \end{array}$$

1. $\begin{array}{r} 347 \\ -106 \\ \hline \end{array}$ 2. $\begin{array}{r} 788 \\ -245 \\ \hline \end{array}$ 3. $\begin{array}{r} 953 \\ -631 \\ \hline \end{array}$ 4. $\begin{array}{r} 268 \\ -\ 27 \\ \hline \end{array}$

5. $\begin{array}{r} 420 \\ -\ \ 7 \\ \hline \end{array}$ 6. $\begin{array}{r} 252 \\ -106 \\ \hline \end{array}$ 7. $\begin{array}{r} 614 \\ -563 \\ \hline \end{array}$ 8. $\begin{array}{r} 837 \\ -754 \\ \hline \end{array}$ 9. $\begin{array}{r} 300 \\ -\ 40 \\ \hline \end{array}$

10. $\begin{array}{r} 725 \\ -\ 95 \\ \hline \end{array}$ 11. $\begin{array}{r} 964 \\ -372 \\ \hline \end{array}$ 12. $\begin{array}{r} 400 \\ -210 \\ \hline \end{array}$ 13. $\begin{array}{r} 218 \\ -133 \\ \hline \end{array}$ 14. $\begin{array}{r} 695 \\ -576 \\ \hline \end{array}$

15. $\begin{array}{r} 397 \\ -318 \\ \hline \end{array}$ 16. $\begin{array}{r} 143 \\ -\ \ 9 \\ \hline \end{array}$ 17. $\begin{array}{r} 565 \\ -384 \\ \hline \end{array}$ 18. $\begin{array}{r} 446 \\ -173 \\ \hline \end{array}$ 19. $\begin{array}{r} 186 \\ -\ 94 \\ \hline \end{array}$

Subtract and check.

	500	114
	$-386 \longrightarrow$	$+386$
	114	500

1. 38
   -19

2. 85
   -47

3. 90
   -72

4. 927
   -406

5. 489
   -235

6. 246
   -113

7. 670
   -145

8. 508
   -240

9. 853
   -626

10. 390
    $-\ 82$

11. 551
    -247

12. 203
    $-\ 41$

13. 780
    -653

14. 318
    -129

15. 504
    -486

16. 286
    -199

17. 407
    $-\ 78$

18. 164
    $-\ 65$

19. 631
    $-\ 84$

20. 802
    -735

21. 214
    $-\ 8$

22. 926
    -327

23. 768
    -499

24. 300
    -171

25. 800
    -544

26. 900
    -293

27. 100
    $-\ 9$

28. 700
    $-\ 56$

Write an estimate.

	491	500
	$-186 \longrightarrow$	-200
		300

1. 82
   -31

2. 67
   -53

3. 95
   -28

4. 352
   -150

5. 810
   -418

6. 790
   -185

7. 473
   -269

8. 515
   -394

9. 604
   -287

10. 291
    -112

11. 933
    -526

12. 750
    $-\ 59$

13. 842
    $-\ 46$

Set A (Use after page 63.)

$4 \times 8 = 32$ 1. $6 \times 1 = \square$ 2. $5 \times 5 = \square$ 3. $7 \times 4 = \square$

4. $3 \times 9 = \square$ 5. $8 \times 2 = \square$ 6. $7 \times 5 = \square$ 7. $6 \times 4 = \square$

8.	9.	10.	11.	12.	13.
5 ×8	3 ×7	9 ×0	6 ×6	5 ×9	8 ×6

14.	15.	16.	17.	18.	19.
6 ×9	7 ×7	9 ×7	8 ×8	9 ×9	8 ×9

Set B (Use after page 65.)

	1.	2.	3.	4.
500 ×9 4500	40 ×6	80 ×1	10 ×7	90 ×3

5.	6.	7.	8.	9.
70 ×2	50 ×6	200 ×8	400 ×4	600 ×7

10.	11.	12.	13.	14.
500 ×4	800 ×6	100 ×3	700 ×9	900 ×8

Set C (Use after page 67.)

	1.	2.	3.	4.	5.
28 ×2 56	11 ×4	13 ×2	17 ×4	25 ×3	30 ×3

6.	7.	8.	9.	10.	11.
39 ×2	45 ×1	19 ×5	26 ×3	24 ×4	17 ×5

12.	13.	14.	15.	16.	17.
16 ×6	27 ×3	18 ×5	28 ×3	13 ×7	48 ×2

Set A (Use after page 69.)

	37 ×6 222	1. 42 ×3	2. 61 ×2	3. 53 ×3	4. 84 ×2	5. 71 ×3
6.	15 ×7	7. 18 ×6	8. 24 ×8	9. 33 ×4	10. 67 ×2	11. 58 ×4
12.	46 ×3	13. 52 ×5	14. 87 ×2	15. 45 ×6	16. 74 ×7	17. 67 ×8
18.	55 ×4	19. 98 ×8	20. 68 ×7	21. 66 ×9	22. 89 ×5	23. 99 ×9

24. A school uses 5 buses. Each bus holds 42 pupils. How many pupils can ride in all?

25. At a picnic, 38 people ate 3 hot dogs each. How many hot dogs were eaten?

Set B (Use after page 71.)

	142 ×4 568	1. 231 ×3	2. 142 ×2	3. 586 ×1	4. 110 ×8
5.	117 ×5	6. 439 ×2	7. 181 ×4	8. 263 ×3	9. 107 ×6
10.	109 ×9	11. 120 ×8	12. 388 ×2	13. 196 ×5	14. 279 ×3
15.	164 ×6	16. 124 ×8	17. 247 ×4	18. 285 ×3	19. 137 ×7
20.	359 ×2	21. 176 ×5	22. 128 ×7	23. 115 ×8	24. 299 ×3

Set A (Use after page 73.)

567 ×4 2268	1. 611 ×4	2. 523 ×2	3. 412 ×3	4. 201 ×8

5. 330 ×6   6. 451 ×5   7. 213 ×7   8. 408 ×4   9. 894 ×2

10. 935 ×3   11. 516 ×9   12. 370 ×8   13. 852 ×3   14. 197 ×4

15. 576 ×7   16. 982 ×5   17. 639 ×9   18. 458 ×6   19. 379 ×8

20. 745 ×6   21. 499 ×3   22. 808 ×8   23. 923 ×7   24. 681 ×9

Set B (Use after page 89.)

$\overset{9}{4\overline{)36}}$ 1. $1\overline{)8}$ 2. $2\overline{)6}$ 3. $4\overline{)8}$ 4. $3\overline{)9}$

5. $6\overline{)6}$ 6. $2\overline{)8}$ 7. $4\overline{)16}$ 8. $3\overline{)12}$ 9. $5\overline{)10}$

10. $2\overline{)14}$ 11. $3\overline{)18}$ 12. $8\overline{)16}$ 13. $9\overline{)18}$ 14. $6\overline{)24}$

15. $5\overline{)20}$ 16. $7\overline{)28}$ 17. $4\overline{)32}$ 18. $3\overline{)27}$ 19. $5\overline{)25}$

20. $4\overline{)36}$ 21. $6\overline{)36}$ 22. $7\overline{)35}$ 23. $5\overline{)45}$ 24. $8\overline{)40}$

25. $9\overline{)63}$ 26. $7\overline{)42}$ 27. $6\overline{)54}$ 28. $8\overline{)48}$ 29. $7\overline{)49}$

30. $8\overline{)56}$ 31. $7\overline{)63}$ 32. $8\overline{)64}$ 33. $9\overline{)72}$ 34. $9\overline{)81}$

Set A (Use after page 91.)

$$\frac{7}{5\overline{)38}} \text{ R3}$$

1. $2\overline{)7}$ 2. $3\overline{)10}$ 3. $5\overline{)15}$ 4. $2\overline{)13}$

5. $4\overline{)11}$ 6. $3\overline{)17}$ 7. $2\overline{)19}$ 8. $7\overline{)25}$ 9. $3\overline{)22}$

10. $5\overline{)28}$ 11. $6\overline{)18}$ 12. $8\overline{)23}$ 13. $9\overline{)26}$ 14. $6\overline{)14}$

15. $8\overline{)43}$ 16. $9\overline{)50}$ 17. $6\overline{)37}$ 18. $4\overline{)32}$ 19. $7\overline{)30}$

20. $3\overline{)29}$ 21. $4\overline{)35}$ 22. $7\overline{)55}$ 23. $8\overline{)68}$ 24. $6\overline{)47}$

25. $5\overline{)44}$ 26. $7\overline{)63}$ 27. $6\overline{)51}$ 28. $9\overline{)89}$ 29. $8\overline{)74}$

30. $4\overline{)37}$ 31. $9\overline{)68}$ 32. $7\overline{)60}$ 33. $5\overline{)45}$ 34. $6\overline{)56}$

Set B (Use after page 95.)

$$\frac{16}{6\overline{)96}}$$

1. $2\overline{)46}$ 2. $4\overline{)56}$ 3. $5\overline{)70}$ 4. $3\overline{)48}$

5. $6\overline{)72}$ 6. $9\overline{)90}$ 7. $2\overline{)58}$ 8. $7\overline{)77}$ 9. $4\overline{)60}$

10. $3\overline{)57}$ 11. $2\overline{)74}$ 12. $6\overline{)84}$ 13. $5\overline{)75}$ 14. $2\overline{)96}$

15. $4\overline{)88}$ 16. $7\overline{)91}$ 17. $3\overline{)93}$ 18. $9\overline{)99}$ 19. $8\overline{)80}$

20. $5\overline{)90}$ 21. $6\overline{)90}$ 22. $8\overline{)96}$ 23. $7\overline{)98}$ 24. $4\overline{)92}$

25. $2\overline{)82}$ 26. $4\overline{)76}$ 27. $3\overline{)87}$ 28. $8\overline{)88}$ 29. $6\overline{)96}$

30. $4\overline{)68}$ 31. $5\overline{)95}$ 32. $6\overline{)78}$ 33. $7\overline{)84}$ 34. $3\overline{)81}$

Set A (Use after page 97.)

18 R1
4)73 1. 2)39 2. 2)57 3. 3)74 4. 5)84

5. 4)77 6. 6)81 7. 3)89 8. 4)49 9. 7)97

10. 5)73 11. 6)73 12. 7)79 13. 8)95 14. 4)80

15. 3)98 16. 5)99 17. 6)83 18. 7)82 19. 2)57

20. 4)64 21. 8)98 22. 6)69 23. 3)72 24. 7)99

25. 6)97 26. 2)94 27. 5)93 28. 7)86 29. 8)89

Set B (Use after page 101.)

146 R4
6)880 1. 2)256 2. 4)992 3. 4)488 4. 3)375

5. 3)368 6. 4)521 7. 8)992 8. 8)928 9. 2)329

10. 4)620 11. 5)561 12. 6)713 13. 3)820 14. 4)725

15. 7)917 16. 2)999 17. 8)894 18. 5)655 19. 9)999

20. 6)742 21. 4)592 22. 3)560 23. 7)783 24. 8)979

25. 5)824 26. 2)687 27. 4)929 28. 3)837 29. 6)890

30. 8)944 31. 7)865 32. 6)941 33. 5)930 34. 4)879

35. 3)793 36. 6)887 37. 7)936 38. 8)896 39. 7)999

Set A (Use after page 103.)

$$\overset{\text{88 R3}}{4)\overline{355}}$$

1. $5)\overline{369}$ 2. $4)\overline{152}$ 3. $3)\overline{195}$ 4. $2)\overline{164}$

5. $3)\overline{142}$ 6. $4)\overline{288}$ 7. $6)\overline{270}$ 8. $8)\overline{456}$ 9. $4)\overline{231}$

10. $5)\overline{258}$ 11. $5)\overline{374}$ 12. $8)\overline{616}$ 13. $4)\overline{315}$ 14. $6)\overline{119}$

15. $7)\overline{410}$ 16. $7)\overline{357}$ 17. $9)\overline{684}$ 18. $5)\overline{370}$ 19. $4)\overline{329}$

20. $2)\overline{173}$ 21. $3)\overline{288}$ 22. $6)\overline{487}$ 23. $4)\overline{196}$ 24. $9)\overline{591}$

25. $7)\overline{358}$ 26. $5)\overline{498}$ 27. $8)\overline{620}$ 28. $6)\overline{581}$ 29. $4)\overline{272}$

30. $9)\overline{763}$ 31. $8)\overline{591}$ 32. $9)\overline{690}$ 33. $7)\overline{336}$ 34. $9)\overline{890}$

Set B (Use after page 105.)

Divide and check.

$$\overset{\text{147 R5}}{6)\overline{887}} \longrightarrow \begin{array}{r} 147 \\ \times 6 \\ \hline 882 \\ +5 \\ \hline 887 \end{array}$$

1. $3)\overline{54}$ 2. $5)\overline{94}$

3. $7)\overline{81}$ 4. $4)\overline{73}$

5. $2)\overline{134}$ 6. $7)\overline{476}$ 7. $6)\overline{351}$ 8. $8)\overline{916}$

9. $4)\overline{729}$ 10. $3)\overline{264}$ 11. $5)\overline{440}$ 12. $8)\overline{692}$

13. $6)\overline{852}$ 14. $4)\overline{890}$ 15. $7)\overline{654}$ 16. $6)\overline{354}$

17. $5)\overline{736}$ 18. $3)\overline{877}$ 19. $8)\overline{984}$ 20. $9)\overline{820}$

21. $7)\overline{924}$ 22. $6)\overline{401}$ 23. $8)\overline{750}$ 24. $9)\overline{487}$

Solve each problem.

1. You buy a bicycle decal for 39¢ and a patch for 54¢. What should you pay the clerk?

2. April has 30 days. How many weeks does April have? How many extra days are left?

3. You need 2 pounds of rock salt to make a quart of ice cream. How much rock salt do you need to make 8 quarts of ice cream?

4. How much longer is the flatcar?

Boxcar   Flatcar

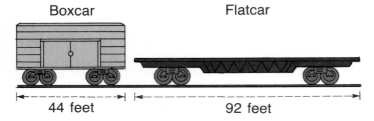

44 feet   92 feet

Use the table for problems 5–7.

5. How much faster is the car than the bicycle?

6. How much slower is the car than the train?

7. How much faster is the jet than the train?

| | Speed |
Vehicle	(miles per hour)
Bicycle	13
Car	55
Train	70
Jet	464

8. Some scouts hiked 7 miles a day for 12 days. How many miles did they hike?

9. A talent-show ticket costs 15¢. How much money do you need to buy 6 tickets?

10. 520 orange trees are planted in rows of 8 each. How many rows are there?

11. 384 erasers are packed in boxes of 4 erasers each. How many boxes are there?

Write what else you need to know to solve each problem.

1. Your math test score is 94. Your science test score is higher. What is your science test score?

2. You have 2 boxes of colored pencils. How many pencils do you have altogether?

3. 36 pupils separated into teams of the same size. How many teams were there?

4. You buy a notebook for 68¢ and a pen. What is the cost of both items?

Set B (Use after page 121.)

Use the picture. Make up a problem in which you must do this.

1. Add

2. Subtract

3. Multiply

4. Divide

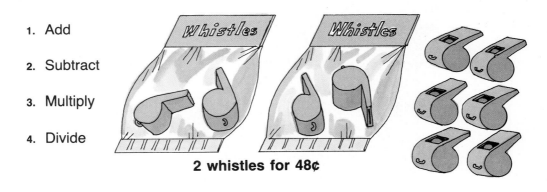

2 whistles for 48¢

5. Add

6. Subtract

7. Multiply

8. Divide

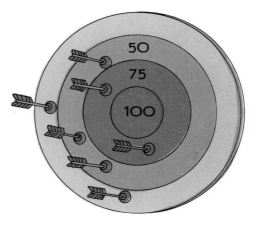

Color of ring	Total points
Yellow	50
Green	―
Blue	―
Red	0
Game Total	―

Set A (Use after page 123.)

Solve each problem.

1. Apples cost 17¢ each. Oranges cost 12¢ each. You buy 3 apples and 4 oranges. How much do you spend?

2. You buy a comic book for 49¢ and a pencil for 18¢. You give the clerk 75¢. How much change should you get?

3. A wagon costs $37. You have $8. Mother gives you $15. How much more money do you need?

4. 40 boys and 32 girls will be put on teams of 6 pupils each. How many teams will there be?

5. Anne has 17 nickels and 15 pennies. How many cents does she have?

6. Stan has 3 quarters and 2 dimes. How many cents does he have?

Set B (Use after page 133.)

Name the shape of each object.

1.  2.   3.   4.

5. soccer ball

6. piece of pipe

7. sugar cube

8. sun

9. die

10. juice can

Write one of these names for each shape.

triangle   quadrilateral   pentagon

11.   12. 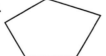 13.   14.

328

Set A (Use after page 135.)

Write *P* for parallel lines. Write *I* for intersecting lines.

1.

2.

3.

4.

5.

6.

Set B (Use after page 139.)

a   b   c   d   e   f

1. Write the letter of each figure above that is a square.

2. Find two sides of this rectangle that have the same length.

3. Find two more sides that have the same length.

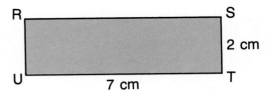

4. How long is side RS?

5. Which side looks parallel to side RS?

6. How long is side RU?

7. Which side looks parallel to side RU?

8. How many right angles does the rectangle have?

Set A (Use after page 143.)

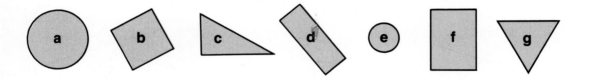

Write the letter of each figure that is a

1. triangle

2. rectangle

3. circle

4. square

5. right triangle

Set B (Use after page 145.)

Which figure has the same size and shape as the red one?

1.   a    b   c

2.   a   b   c

3.   a   b 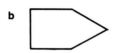   c

4.   a    b   c

330

Set A (Use after page 155.)

Would you use *centimeters, meters,* or *kilometers* to find these?

1. length of a comb

2. distance across a room.

3. height of a house

4. distance across your town

5. length of a nail

6. distance across a lake

7. length of your foot

8. distance across your state

Complete.

9. 1 m = ___ cm

10. 400 cm = ___ m

11. 1 km = ___ m

12. 7000 m = ___ km

13. 5 m = ___ cm

14. 200 cm = ___ m

15. 6 km = ___ m

16. 8000 m = ___ km

Set B (Use after page 163.)

Would you use *inches, feet,* or *miles* to find these?

1. height of a drinking glass

2. length of a kite string

3. height of a bookcase

4. distance between 2 towns

5. length of a pen

6. distance around the moon

Find each perimeter in the units shown.

7. 11 cm 6 cm 6 cm 11 cm

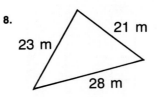

8. 23 m 21 m 28 m

9. 35 ft 35 ft 35 ft 35 ft

hese figures are *not* actual size. Find each area in the units shown.

1.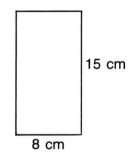
3 cm
6 cm

2.
4 in
4 in

3.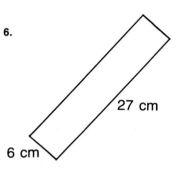
9 m
13 m

4.
7 ft   7 ft

5.
15 cm
8 cm

6.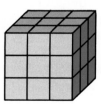
27 cm
6 cm

Set B (Use after page 169.)

These figures are *not* actual size. Find each volume in cubic centimeters.

1.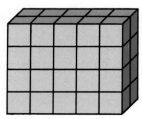

2.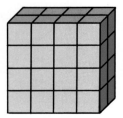

3.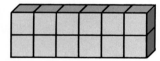

4.

5.

6.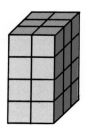

Choose the best answer.

1.

4 liters   40 liters   400 liters

2.

2 liters   10 liters   40 liters

Solve each problem.

3. The Gorman family drinks 3 liters of milk each day. How many liters do they drink in 7 days?

4. 56 liters of orange juice will be put into cartons of 2 liters each. How many cartons will there be?

5. You need 12 liters of paint. Each can of paint holds 4 liters. How many cans of paint do you need?

6. An aquarium can hold 80 liters of water. There are 46 liters in the aquarium. How much more water can be put in?

Set B (Use after page 173.)

Complete.

1. 1 gallon = ___ quarts

2. 1 quart = ___ pints

3. 1 pint = ___ cups

4. 1 gallon = ___ cups

5. 3 quarts = ___ pints

6. 12 quarts = ___ gallons

7. 12 cups = ___ pints

8. 2 gallons = ___ pints

9. 8 gallons = ___ quarts

10. 8 cups = ___ quarts

Solve each problem.

1. A penny weighs about 3 grams. About how much do 25 pennies weigh?

2. A book weighs about 1 kilogram. About how much do 11 of those books weigh?

3. A baseball weighs 225 grams. A golf ball weighs 49 grams. How much more does the baseball weigh?

4. Tara weighs 39 kilograms. Her older brother weighs 73 kilograms. How much more does her older brother weigh?

Complete.

5. 1 pound = ___ ounces

6. 1 ton = ___ pounds

7. 6 pounds = ___ ounces

8. 3 tons = ___ pounds

$$\begin{array}{r} 47{,}625 \\ +18{,}498 \\ \hline 66{,}123 \end{array}$$

1. $$\begin{array}{r} 7927 \\ +1464 \\ \hline \end{array}$$

2. $$\begin{array}{r} 5516 \\ +3796 \\ \hline \end{array}$$

3. $$\begin{array}{r} 2385 \\ +\ 980 \\ \hline \end{array}$$

4. $$\begin{array}{r} 1157 \\ +4364 \\ \hline \end{array}$$

5. $$\begin{array}{r} 3076 \\ +\ \ \ \ 4 \\ \hline \end{array}$$

6. $$\begin{array}{r} 5822 \\ +1498 \\ \hline \end{array}$$

7. $$\begin{array}{r} 8657 \\ +1947 \\ \hline \end{array}$$

8. $$\begin{array}{r} 4066 \\ +4973 \\ \hline \end{array}$$

9. $$\begin{array}{r} 1465 \\ +7539 \\ \hline \end{array}$$

10. $$\begin{array}{r} 5285 \\ +\ 645 \\ \hline \end{array}$$

11. $$\begin{array}{r} 6978 \\ +\ 823 \\ \hline \end{array}$$

12. $$\begin{array}{r} 60{,}421 \\ +19{,}653 \\ \hline \end{array}$$

13. $$\begin{array}{r} 58{,}662 \\ +24{,}502 \\ \hline \end{array}$$

14. $$\begin{array}{r} 34{,}074 \\ +41{,}938 \\ \hline \end{array}$$

15. $$\begin{array}{r} 59{,}528 \\ +\ 3{,}509 \\ \hline \end{array}$$

16. $$\begin{array}{r} 45{,}843 \\ +27{,}199 \\ \hline \end{array}$$

17. $$\begin{array}{r} 96{,}726 \\ +\ \ \ \ 387 \\ \hline \end{array}$$

18. $$\begin{array}{r} 27{,}979 \\ +\ 2{,}041 \\ \hline \end{array}$$

19. $$\begin{array}{r} 44{,}687 \\ +\ 8{,}656 \\ \hline \end{array}$$

Set A (Use after page 187.)

Round to the nearest thousand.

6793 → 7000

1. 2400	**2.** 8600

3. 5290	**4.** 3810	**5.** 1166	**6.** 9318
7. 3472	**8.** 4500	**9.** 2448	**10.** 6501
11. 4934	**12.** 961	**13.** 7050	**14.** 5782

Write an estimate.

$$\begin{array}{r} 6448 \\ +1567 \\ \end{array} \rightarrow \begin{array}{r} 6000 \\ +2000 \\ \hline 8000 \end{array}$$

15. $\begin{array}{r} 1892 \\ +3905 \\ \hline \end{array}$	**16.** $\begin{array}{r} 8065 \\ +952 \\ \hline \end{array}$

17. $\begin{array}{r} 4288 \\ +2743 \\ \hline \end{array}$	**18.** $\begin{array}{r} 5016 \\ +1299 \\ \hline \end{array}$	**19.** $\begin{array}{r} 3175 \\ +4908 \\ \hline \end{array}$	**20.** $\begin{array}{r} 1507 \\ +7466 \\ \hline \end{array}$

21. A theater sold 4076 tickets on Friday and 4813 tickets on Saturday. About how many were sold on both days?

22. One side of a theater seats 1485 people. The other side seats 1535 people. About how many people can both sides seat?

Set B (Use after page 191.)

$$\begin{array}{r} 7120 \\ -3251 \\ \hline 3869 \end{array}$$

1. $\begin{array}{r} 5489 \\ -2698 \\ \hline \end{array}$	**2.** $\begin{array}{r} 3722 \\ -1856 \\ \hline \end{array}$	**3.** $\begin{array}{r} 8360 \\ -570 \\ \hline \end{array}$	

4. $\begin{array}{r} 5271 \\ -4643 \\ \hline \end{array}$	**5.** $\begin{array}{r} 7105 \\ -1284 \\ \hline \end{array}$	**6.** $\begin{array}{r} 9440 \\ -6757 \\ \hline \end{array}$	**7.** $\begin{array}{r} 8276 \\ -8 \\ \hline \end{array}$
8. $\begin{array}{r} 4111 \\ -2935 \\ \hline \end{array}$	**9.** $\begin{array}{r} 2600 \\ -1542 \\ \hline \end{array}$	**10.** $\begin{array}{r} 3000 \\ -817 \\ \hline \end{array}$	**11.** $\begin{array}{r} 1025 \\ -936 \\ \hline \end{array}$

Set A (Use after page 194.)

Subtract and check.

20,100 − 13,486 6,614	6,614 + 13,486 20,100	**1.** 4039 − 2754	**2.** 7285 − 1638

3. 5743
 − 3986

4. 8000
 − 6459

5. 1136
 − 748

6. 9004
 − 527

7. 19,457
 − 12,903

8. 72,213
 − 51,270

9. 36,098
 − 549

10. 90,934
 − 57,865

11. 25,674
 − 15,988

12. 80,000
 − 62,417

13. 30,321
 − 1,448

14. 64,000
 − 8,096

15. The longest river, the Nile, is 4145 miles long. The Colorado River is 1450 miles long. How much longer is the Nile?

16. Mount Grays is 14,270 feet high. Mount Mitchell is 6684 feet high. How much higher is Mount Grays?

Set B (Use after page 197.)

Write an estimate.

8503 − 1618	9000 − 2000 7000	**1.** 7148 − 3929	**2.** 5396 − 1408

3. 6910
 − 2875

4. 3024
 − 1157

5. 7500
 − 4638

6. 4248
 − 950

7. 9165
 − 5887

8. 5500
 − 2713

9. 6436
 − 1449

10. 8004
 − 983

Set A (Use after page 203.)

	1.	2.	3.
8000 ×4 32,000	3000 ×6	9000 ×2	2000 ×5

4.	5.	6.	7.
1000 ×9	4000 ×7	8000 ×4	6000 ×6

8.	9.	10.	11.
8000 ×7	6000 ×5	9000 ×9	5000 ×8

12.	13.	14.	15.
8000 ×8	7000 ×6	8000 ×9	9000 ×7

16.	17.	18.	19.
7000 ×7	6000 ×8	9000 ×5	5000 ×7

Set B (Use after page 207.)

	1.	2.	3.
4723 ×7 33,061	3082 ×3	1630 ×5	2317 ×4

4.	5.	6.	7.
3586 ×2	1361 ×6	1524 ×8	4295 ×3

8.	9.	10.	11.
2054 ×9	3625 ×7	6734 ×4	5899 ×5

12.	13.	14.	15.
4961 ×8	6772 ×6	4393 ×9	8649 ×7

16.	17.	18.	19.
9274 ×3	4753 ×5	8366 ×4	7168 ×9

Set A (Use after page 208.)

	1.	2.	3.	4.
400 ×80 32,000	20 ×30	10 ×80	50 ×30	40 ×40

5.	6.	7.	8.	9.
30 ×60	40 ×80	50 ×20	70 ×40	60 ×50

10.	11.	12.	13.	14.
500 ×70	400 ×60	600 ×80	900 ×80	600 ×60

15.	16.	17.	18.	19.
800 ×90	500 ×40	400 ×80	600 ×70	900 ×90

Set B (Use after page 211.)

	1.	2.	3.	4.
65 ×43 2795	35 ×10	56 ×40	21 ×70	32 ×60

5.	6.	7.	8.	9.
87 ×20	68 ×30	47 ×50	55 ×80	98 ×90

10.	11.	12.	13.	14.
16 ×11	13 ×17	45 ×24	26 ×37	19 ×53

15.	16.	17.	18.	19.
36 ×48	88 ×29	57 ×37	65 ×61	78 ×49

20.	21.	22.	23.	24.
69 ×54	76 ×73	95 ×65	97 ×94	76 ×88

25.	26.	27.	28.	29.
83 ×47	64 ×95	58 ×77	86 ×98	65 ×74

Set A (Use after page 213.)

Write an estimate.

$$\begin{array}{r} 88 \\ \times 62 \end{array} \rightarrow \begin{array}{r} 90 \\ \times 60 \\ \hline 5400 \end{array}$$

1. $\begin{array}{r} 72 \\ \times 11 \\ \hline \end{array}$ 2. $\begin{array}{r} 27 \\ \times 58 \\ \hline \end{array}$ 3. $\begin{array}{r} 44 \\ \times 35 \\ \hline \end{array}$

4. $\begin{array}{r} 23 \\ \times 63 \\ \hline \end{array}$ 5. $\begin{array}{r} 82 \\ \times 39 \\ \hline \end{array}$ 6. $\begin{array}{r} 58 \\ \times 58 \\ \hline \end{array}$ 7. $\begin{array}{r} 91 \\ \times 43 \\ \hline \end{array}$ 8. $\begin{array}{r} 57 \\ \times 69 \\ \hline \end{array}$

9. $\begin{array}{r} 88 \\ \times 45 \\ \hline \end{array}$ 10. $\begin{array}{r} 62 \\ \times 74 \\ \hline \end{array}$ 11. $\begin{array}{r} 95 \\ \times 52 \\ \hline \end{array}$ 12. $\begin{array}{r} 89 \\ \times 66 \\ \hline \end{array}$ 13. $\begin{array}{r} 78 \\ \times 93 \\ \hline \end{array}$

14. There are 24 jars of peanut butter in a case. About how many jars are in 31 cases?

15. A train is going 78 kilometers per hour. About how far can the train go in 12 hours?

Set B (Use after page 215.)

$$\begin{array}{r} 607 \\ \times 32 \\ \hline 19{,}424 \end{array}$$

1. $\begin{array}{r} 112 \\ \times 44 \\ \hline \end{array}$ 2. $\begin{array}{r} 200 \\ \times 37 \\ \hline \end{array}$ 3. $\begin{array}{r} 125 \\ \times 36 \\ \hline \end{array}$ 4. $\begin{array}{r} 267 \\ \times 31 \\ \hline \end{array}$

5. $\begin{array}{r} 499 \\ \times 50 \\ \hline \end{array}$ 6. $\begin{array}{r} 503 \\ \times 42 \\ \hline \end{array}$ 7. $\begin{array}{r} 709 \\ \times 63 \\ \hline \end{array}$ 8. $\begin{array}{r} 354 \\ \times 83 \\ \hline \end{array}$ 9. $\begin{array}{r} 791 \\ \times 84 \\ \hline \end{array}$

10. $\begin{array}{r} 560 \\ \times 27 \\ \hline \end{array}$ 11. $\begin{array}{r} 800 \\ \times 56 \\ \hline \end{array}$ 12. $\begin{array}{r} 876 \\ \times 48 \\ \hline \end{array}$ 13. $\begin{array}{r} 309 \\ \times 62 \\ \hline \end{array}$ 14. $\begin{array}{r} 518 \\ \times 77 \\ \hline \end{array}$

15. $\begin{array}{r} 196 \\ \times 90 \\ \hline \end{array}$ 16. $\begin{array}{r} 988 \\ \times 79 \\ \hline \end{array}$ 17. $\begin{array}{r} 357 \\ \times 75 \\ \hline \end{array}$ 18. $\begin{array}{r} 700 \\ \times 66 \\ \hline \end{array}$ 19. $\begin{array}{r} 906 \\ \times 87 \\ \hline \end{array}$

20. $\begin{array}{r} 118 \\ \times 10 \\ \hline \end{array}$ 21. $\begin{array}{r} 654 \\ \times 98 \\ \hline \end{array}$ 22. $\begin{array}{r} 666 \\ \times 66 \\ \hline \end{array}$ 23. $\begin{array}{r} 505 \\ \times 46 \\ \hline \end{array}$ 24. $\begin{array}{r} 900 \\ \times 76 \\ \hline \end{array}$

25. $\begin{array}{r} 714 \\ \times 48 \\ \hline \end{array}$ 26. $\begin{array}{r} 643 \\ \times 81 \\ \hline \end{array}$ 27. $\begin{array}{r} 937 \\ \times 19 \\ \hline \end{array}$ 28. $\begin{array}{r} 492 \\ \times 56 \\ \hline \end{array}$ 29. $\begin{array}{r} 206 \\ \times 89 \\ \hline \end{array}$

204 R2
3)614

1. 2)406

2. 6)606

3. 3)618

4. 5)524

5. 5)900

6. 3)926

7. 4)833

8. 7)742

9. 6)720

10. 4)563

11. 2)607

12. 8)863

13. 9)978

14. 7)806

15. 5)504

16. 6)624

17. 4)818

18. 8)965

19. 9)998

Set B (Use after page 225.)

Find the average of each group of numbers.

63, 48, 54   Average is 55.

1. 36, 48, 33

2. 90, 93, 88, 97

3. 142, 203, 156

4. 41, 35, 28, 39, 27

5. 266, 389, 275

6. 89, 92, 95, 91, 88

7. 210, 217, 194, 187

8. 100, 80, 92, 0

9. 86, 86, 100, 92, 86

10. Debbie kept this record of how many minutes she practiced guitar. Find the average number of minutes practiced each day.

11. On which days did she practice less than the average?

12. On which days did she practice more than the average?

Sunday	35 minutes
Monday	35 minutes
Tuesday	40 minutes
Wednesday	50 minutes
Thursday	20 minutes
Friday	60 minutes

Set A (Use after page 227.)

$$\begin{array}{r} 600 \\ 9\overline{)5400} \end{array}$$

1. $2\overline{)6000}$

2. $3\overline{)9000}$

3. $4\overline{)8000}$

4. $5\overline{)1000}$

5. $4\overline{)2000}$

6. $7\overline{)1400}$

7. $8\overline{)2400}$

8. $9\overline{)3600}$

9. $6\overline{)3000}$

10. $8\overline{)4000}$

11. $5\overline{)3500}$

12. $7\overline{)4200}$

13. $4\overline{)3200}$

14. $9\overline{)8100}$

15. $8\overline{)5600}$

16. $8\overline{)6400}$

17. $5\overline{)4500}$

18. $7\overline{)6300}$

19. $6\overline{)5400}$

20. $7\overline{)5600}$

21. $6\overline{)4800}$

22. $9\overline{)7200}$

23. $8\overline{)7200}$

Set B (Use after page 231.)

$$\begin{array}{r} 1741 \\ 5\overline{)8705} \end{array}$$

1. $3\overline{)1116}$

2. $5\overline{)2310}$

3. $2\overline{)1940}$

4. $6\overline{)4428}$

5. $9\overline{)8604}$

6. $4\overline{)3220}$

7. $7\overline{)4963}$

8. $8\overline{)4096}$

9. $3\overline{)5493}$

10. $2\overline{)4670}$

11. $5\overline{)6825}$

12. $6\overline{)8982}$

13. $4\overline{)9000}$

14. $7\overline{)8113}$

15. $9\overline{)9081}$

16. $1\overline{)7742}$

17. $8\overline{)9576}$

18. $3\overline{)8721}$

19. $2\overline{)9950}$

20. $9\overline{)8181}$

21. $6\overline{)5304}$

22. $7\overline{)7623}$

23. $8\overline{)8032}$

24. 3200 oranges were put into packs of 8 oranges each. How many packs were there?

25. 6042 people went to the circus during 6 days. Find the average number of people at the circus each day.

Set A (Use after page 235.)

Find each quotient and remainder. Then check.

$$\begin{array}{r} 1386 \ \text{R6} \\ 7\overline{)9708} \end{array} \longrightarrow \begin{array}{r} 1386 \\ \times 7 \\ \hline 9702 \\ +6 \\ \hline 9708 \end{array}$$

1. $3\overline{)2495}$ 2. $5\overline{)1784}$

3. $4\overline{)3344}$ 4. $2\overline{)1009}$

5. $7\overline{)5856}$ 6. $9\overline{)6246}$ 7. $6\overline{)4121}$ 8. $5\overline{)3768}$

9. $8\overline{)6520}$ 10. $4\overline{)3029}$ 11. $9\overline{)8754}$ 12. $7\overline{)4932}$

13. $2\overline{)4160}$ 14. $3\overline{)5918}$ 15. $7\overline{)9336}$ 16. $6\overline{)7114}$

17. $4\overline{)6578}$ 18. $8\overline{)8655}$ 19. $5\overline{)7049}$ 20. $7\overline{)9136}$

21. $9\overline{)9122}$ 22. $6\overline{)8311}$ 23. $2\overline{)6012}$ 24. $8\overline{)9999}$

Set B (Use after page 237.)

$$\begin{array}{r} 6 \\ 40\overline{)240} \end{array}$$

1. $20\overline{)160}$ 2. $30\overline{)180}$ 3. $30\overline{)240}$

4. $40\overline{)160}$ 5. $50\overline{)200}$ 6. $40\overline{)200}$ 7. $50\overline{)350}$

8. $60\overline{)180}$ 9. $60\overline{)300}$ 10. $70\overline{)210}$ 11. $40\overline{)360}$

12. $80\overline{)320}$ 13. $60\overline{)480}$ 14. $90\overline{)360}$ 15. $80\overline{)480}$

16. $90\overline{)540}$ 17. $70\overline{)630}$ 18. $80\overline{)640}$ 19. $90\overline{)630}$

20. $30\overline{)150}$ 21. $50\overline{)450}$ 22. $70\overline{)350}$ 23. $90\overline{)810}$

Set A (Use after page 239.)

$$\begin{array}{r} 13 \\ 60\overline{)780} \end{array}$$

1. $10\overline{)600}$
2. $50\overline{)500}$
3. $20\overline{)400}$

4. $10\overline{)870}$
5. $20\overline{)360}$
6. $30\overline{)390}$
7. $50\overline{)800}$

8. $40\overline{)760}$
9. $60\overline{)660}$
10. $80\overline{)960}$
11. $70\overline{)840}$

12. $30\overline{)510}$
13. $50\overline{)950}$
14. $60\overline{)720}$
15. $40\overline{)600}$

16. $10\overline{)970}$
17. $70\overline{)980}$
18. $90\overline{)900}$
19. $60\overline{)960}$

20. A store has 200 pounds of ice in 10-pound bags. How many bags of ice does the store have?

21. 750 plastic cups are needed for a town picnic. Each package holds 50 cups. How many packages are needed?

Set B (Use after page 245.)

Write a fraction to tell how much is colored. Then write a fraction to tell how much is not colored.

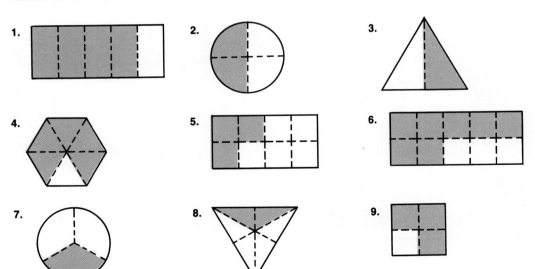

Set A (Use after page 251.)

Write <, >, or = for each ●.

1.

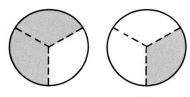

$\frac{2}{3}$ ● $\frac{1}{3}$

2.

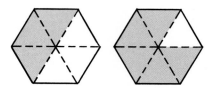

$\frac{3}{6}$ ● $\frac{5}{6}$

3.

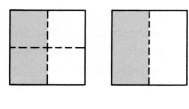

$\frac{2}{4}$ ● $\frac{1}{2}$

4.

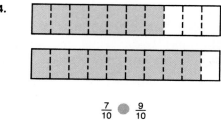

$\frac{7}{10}$ ● $\frac{9}{10}$

Set B (Use after page 253.)

Write a mixed numeral for each ___.

1.

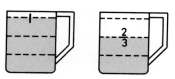

___ cups of juice

2.

___ gallons of cider

3.

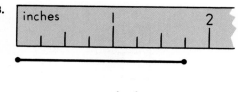

___ inches

4.

___ inches

Set A (Use after page 257.)

Write a decimal for each fraction and mixed numeral.

$2\frac{3}{100} = 2.03$

1. $\frac{1}{10}$

2. $\frac{7}{10}$

3. $8\frac{5}{10}$

4. $3\frac{9}{10}$

5. $16\frac{4}{10}$

6. $27\frac{3}{10}$

7. $\frac{4}{100}$

8. $\frac{8}{100}$

9. $\frac{10}{100}$

10. $\frac{22}{100}$

11. $1\frac{17}{100}$

12. $5\frac{2}{100}$

13. $13\frac{40}{100}$

14. $39\frac{83}{100}$

15. $87\frac{9}{100}$

Set B (Use after page 260.)

Use a $ and a decimal point to name each amount of money.

$6¢ = \$0.06$

1. 25¢

2. 50¢

3. 8¢

4. 91¢

5. 4 dollars, 5 dimes, 2 pennies

6. 7 dollars, 9 pennies

7. five dollars and twelve cents

8. three cents

9. sixteen dollars and forty-seven cents

10. twenty-eight dollars and eighty cents

Set C (Use after page 267.)

Add. Write each answer in simplest form.

$\frac{1}{12} + \frac{7}{12} = \frac{8}{12} = \frac{2}{3}$

1. $\frac{1}{4} + \frac{1}{4}$

2. $\frac{1}{3} + \frac{1}{3}$

3. $\frac{1}{6} + \frac{1}{6}$

4. $\frac{2}{5} + \frac{1}{5}$

5. $\frac{1}{8} + \frac{1}{8}$

6. $\frac{1}{10} + \frac{3}{10}$

7. $\frac{3}{8} + \frac{1}{8}$

8. $\frac{7}{10} + \frac{1}{10}$

9. $\frac{1}{12} + \frac{1}{12}$

10. $\frac{5}{12} + \frac{1}{12}$

11. $\frac{7}{12} + \frac{1}{12}$

12. $\frac{5}{8} + \frac{1}{8}$

13. $\frac{2}{5} + \frac{2}{5}$

14. $\frac{1}{8} + \frac{3}{8}$

Set A (Use after page 269.)

Subtract. Write each answer in simplest form.

$\frac{7}{10} - \frac{1}{10} = \frac{6}{10} = \frac{3}{5}$

1. $\frac{3}{10} - \frac{1}{10}$

2. $\frac{5}{6} - \frac{1}{6}$

3. $\frac{7}{8} - \frac{3}{8}$

4. $\frac{5}{12} - \frac{1}{12}$

5. $\frac{7}{8} - \frac{1}{8}$

6. $\frac{7}{12} - \frac{1}{12}$

7. $\frac{9}{10} - \frac{3}{10}$

8. $\frac{11}{12} - \frac{5}{12}$

9. $\frac{9}{10} - \frac{1}{10}$

10. $\frac{11}{12} - \frac{1}{12}$

11. $\frac{7}{8} - \frac{5}{8}$

12. $\frac{7}{12} - \frac{5}{12}$

13. $\frac{9}{10} - \frac{7}{10}$

14. $\frac{11}{12} - \frac{7}{12}$

Set B (Use after page 273.)

Add. Change each sum to a whole number or a mixed numeral.

$\frac{3}{10} + \frac{9}{10} = \frac{12}{10} = 1\frac{2}{10} = 1\frac{1}{5}$

1. $\frac{3}{4} + \frac{1}{4}$

2. $\frac{4}{5} + \frac{2}{5}$

3. $\frac{2}{3} + \frac{1}{3}$

4. $\frac{5}{6} + \frac{5}{6}$

5. $\frac{1}{8} + \frac{7}{8}$

6. $\frac{3}{10} + \frac{9}{10}$

7. $\frac{11}{12} + \frac{1}{12}$

8. $\frac{5}{12} + \frac{11}{12}$

9. $\frac{7}{10} + \frac{7}{10}$

10. $\frac{7}{12} + \frac{5}{12}$

11. $\frac{7}{8} + \frac{5}{8}$

12. $\frac{9}{10} + \frac{7}{10}$

13. $\frac{7}{12} + \frac{11}{12}$

14. $\frac{9}{10} + \frac{9}{10}$

Add.

$\begin{array}{r} 4\frac{1}{12} \\ + \ 6\frac{7}{12} \\ \hline 10\frac{8}{12} = 10\frac{2}{3} \end{array}$

15. $\begin{array}{r} 2\frac{1}{6} \\ +2\frac{5}{6} \\ \hline \end{array}$

16. $\begin{array}{r} 5\frac{2}{3} \\ +1\frac{2}{3} \\ \hline \end{array}$

17. $\begin{array}{r} 4\frac{1}{5} \\ +3\frac{3}{5} \\ \hline \end{array}$

18. $\begin{array}{r} 5\frac{3}{8} \\ +8\frac{3}{8} \\ \hline \end{array}$

19. $\begin{array}{r} 7\frac{3}{4} \\ +9\frac{1}{4} \\ \hline \end{array}$

20. $\begin{array}{r} 6\frac{9}{10} \\ +6\frac{7}{10} \\ \hline \end{array}$

21. $\begin{array}{r} 4\frac{5}{12} \\ +8\frac{5}{12} \\ \hline \end{array}$

22. $\begin{array}{r} 6\frac{3}{10} \\ +9\frac{1}{10} \\ \hline \end{array}$

23. $\begin{array}{r} 5\frac{5}{8} \\ +7\frac{1}{8} \\ \hline \end{array}$

24. $\begin{array}{r} 8\frac{7}{12} \\ +2\frac{7}{12} \\ \hline \end{array}$

25. $\begin{array}{r} 9\frac{3}{10} \\ +9\frac{7}{10} \\ \hline \end{array}$

Set A (Use after page 275.)

$$17\tfrac{7}{8}$$
$$-\ 8\tfrac{1}{8}$$
$$9\tfrac{6}{8} = 9\tfrac{3}{4}$$

1. $5\tfrac{3}{4}$
$-4\tfrac{1}{4}$

2. $7\tfrac{2}{5}$
-2

3. $4\tfrac{5}{6}$
$-1\tfrac{1}{6}$

4. $8\tfrac{3}{8}$
$-2\tfrac{1}{8}$

5. $10\tfrac{2}{3}$
$-\ 6\tfrac{1}{3}$

6. $11\tfrac{1}{2}$
$-\ 4$

7. $9\tfrac{3}{10}$
$-3\tfrac{1}{10}$

8. $10\tfrac{5}{12}$
$-\ 5\tfrac{1}{12}$

9. $12\tfrac{3}{5}$
$-\ 3\tfrac{1}{5}$

10. $18\tfrac{5}{8}$
$-\ 7\tfrac{3}{8}$

11. $13\tfrac{4}{5}$
$-\ 7\tfrac{1}{5}$

12. $11\tfrac{7}{10}$
$-\ 2\tfrac{3}{10}$

13. $8\tfrac{7}{12}$
$-6\tfrac{5}{12}$

14. $15\tfrac{7}{8}$
$-\ 7\tfrac{1}{8}$

15. $12\tfrac{7}{12}$
$-\ 6\tfrac{1}{12}$

16. $13\tfrac{7}{8}$
$-\ 8\tfrac{3}{8}$

17. $16\tfrac{7}{10}$
$-\ 9\tfrac{1}{10}$

18. $17\tfrac{4}{5}$
$-\ 8\tfrac{2}{5}$

19. $14\tfrac{11}{12}$
$-\ 7\tfrac{7}{12}$

20. $11\tfrac{9}{10}$
$-\ 3\tfrac{3}{10}$

21. $15\tfrac{11}{12}$
$-\ 6\tfrac{5}{12}$

22. $16\tfrac{9}{10}$
$-\ 8\tfrac{1}{10}$

23. $18\tfrac{11}{12}$
$-\ 9\tfrac{1}{12}$

Set B (Use after page 277.)

$$24.3$$
$$+18.8$$
$$43.1$$

1. 0.3
$+0.5$

2. 0.8
$+0.5$

3. 0.6
$+0.7$

4. 5.0
$+0.5$

5. 3.8
$+7.0$

6. 0.9
$+2.6$

7. 1.2
$+4.6$

8. 3.7
$+2.4$

9. 6.9
$+5.8$

10. 7.5
$+9.2$

11. 3.4
$+6.8$

12. 4.7
$+9.6$

13. 16.3
$+41.5$

14. 23.2
$+17.9$

15. 13.7
$+47.8$

16. 36.3
$+28.9$

17. 59.8
$+35.8$

18. 87.3
$+\ 7.7$

19. 36.5
$+46.5$

Set A (Use after page 279.)

| | $10.45
+ 29.87
$40.32 | 1. | $0.56
+ 0.42 | 2. | $0.83
+ 0.17 | 3. | $0.39
+ 0.61 |

4. $1.29
+ 0.95

5. $2.36
+ 0.87

6. $1.04
+ 6.99

7. $4.38
+ 0.75

8. $2.19
+ 8.96

9. $7.44
+ 9.56

10. $13.54
+ 0.68

11. $11.98
+ 0.33

12. $24.78
+ 35.77

13. $20.25
+ 19.75

14. $37.11
+ 42.93

15. $14.57
+ 5.88

16. $17.68
+ 19.86

17. $15.04
+ 67.39

18. $58.95
+ 25.95

19. $89.41
+ 1.59

20. $23.65
+ 18.49

21. $38.87
+ 28.92

22. $62.25
+ 17.75

23. $79.09
+ 8.94

Set B (Use after page 281.)

| | 42.8
− 16.9
25.9 | 1. | 0.8
− 0.3 | 2. | 0.7
− 0.2 | 3. | 1.9
− 0.1 | 4. | 3.4
− 0.8 |

5. 6.2
− 0.9

6. 7.5
− 4.6

7. 8.1
− 2.8

8. 14.0
− 9.5

9. 18.3
− 0.6

10. 21.1
− 15.7

11. 30.4
− 7.6

12. 73.6
− 49.8

13. 10.7
− 4.9

14. 50.5
− 23.7

15. 39.4
− 9.7

16. 82.3
− 5.6

17. 61.7
− 42.8

18. 96.5
− 88.9

19. 40.2
− 34.5

	$80.00 − 17.23 $62.77	1.	$0.52 − 0.31	2.	$0.48 − 0.09	3.	$0.84 − 0.25

4. $5.95
   − 3.47

5. $8.25
   − 2.75

6. $9.44
   − 0.77

7. $3.26
   − 0.89

8. $7.21
   − 0.85

9. $9.07
   − 4.50

10. $18.30
    − 5.32

11. $11.62
    − 7.84

12. $12.00
    − 3.33

13. $21.00
    − 16.75

14. $40.00
    − 27.12

15. $60.00
    − 9.54

Set B (Use after page 295.)

Write the letter for each ordered pair shown on this grid.

(0,2)   E   1. (0,0)   2. (1,4)

3. (5,3)   4. (2,0)   5. (3,5)

6. (2,2)   7. (4,1)   8. (3,3)

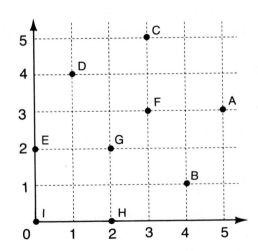

Write the ordered pair for each dot on this grid.

D   (1,4)   9. I   10. B

11. F   12. A   13. C

14. E   15. H   16. G

Use the heights of the bean plant. Copy and complete the table.

	Age (days)	Height (inches)
1.	0	0
2.	3	
3.	6	
4.	9	

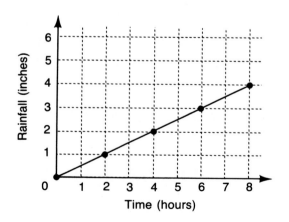

3 days   6 days   9 days

1 in   2 in   3 in

5. How much taller was the bean plant at 9 days than at 3 days?

6. Make a line graph from the table you made.

Set B (Use after page 301.)

This line graph shows the amount of rainfall. How much rain had fallen at the end of

1. 2 hours   2. 4 hours

3. 6 hours   4. 8 hours

5. 1 hour   6. 5 hours

After how many hours was the rainfall

7. 1 inch   8. 2 inches

9. 3 inches   10. 4 inches

11. $1\frac{1}{2}$ inches   12. $3\frac{1}{2}$ inches

Set A (Use after page 303.)

How many pupils collect

1. stamps   2. cards

3. coins   4. shells

5. rocks

6. What is collected by the most pupils?

7. What is collected by the fewest pupils?

8. How many more pupils collect cards than stamps?

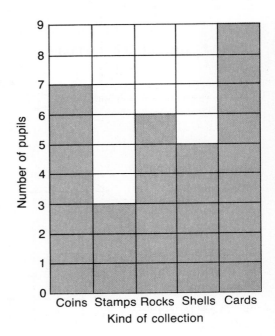

Set B (Use after page 309.)

You are to pick one card without looking. That card tells the position you will play.

1. Which position are you most likely to play?

2. Which position are you least likely to play?

What is your chance of being

3. the pitcher   4. an outfielder

5. an infielder   6. the catcher

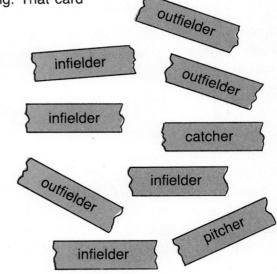

Glossary

addend Any of the numbers to be added.

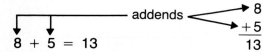

8 + 5 = 13

addends

$$\begin{array}{r} 8 \\ +5 \\ \hline 13 \end{array}$$

angle A figure that looks like this.

area The number of square units that fit inside a figure. The area of this figure is 12 square inches.

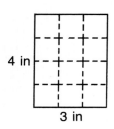

4 in

3 in

average The quotient obtained when the sum of a set of numbers is divided by the number of addends.

centimeter A unit of length in the metric system (one hundredth of a meter).

1 centimeter or 1 cm

circle A curved figure (in a plane) with all points the same distance from a point called the *center.*

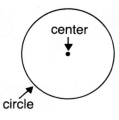

center

circle

cone A figure that is shaped like this.

cube A figure that is shaped like this. Each of its six faces is a square.

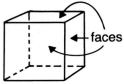

faces

cylinder A figure shaped like this.

decimal A numeral with place values based on ten. The following are decimals:

5.6   12.48   342

denominator The bottom number in a fraction. In the fraction $\frac{3}{4}$, the denominator is 4.

diameter A line segment that joins two points on a circle and passes through the center.

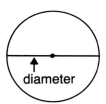

diameter

difference The number you get by subtracting one number from another.

48 − 29 = 19

difference

$$\begin{array}{r} 48 \\ -29 \\ \hline 19 \end{array}$$

digit Any of the symbols 0, 1, 2, 3, 4, 5, 6, 7, 8, and 9.

dividend A number that is divided.

$$32 \div 4 = 8 \qquad\qquad 4\overline{)32}^{\,8}$$

$32 \div 4 = 8$ — dividend — $4\overline{)32}^{\,8}$

divisor A number by which another number is divided.

$32 \div 4 = 8$ — divisor — $4\overline{)32}^{\,8}$

equivalent fractions Two or more fractions that name the same number or amount.

$\frac{1}{3}$, $\frac{2}{6}$, and $\frac{3}{9}$ are equivalent fractions.

estimate To guess a result before doing the computation.

even number Any whole number with 0, 2, 4, 6, or 8 in the ones place.

factor Any of the numbers to be multiplied.

$6 \times 12 = 72$

factors $\begin{array}{r} 12 \\ \times\, 6 \\ \hline 72 \end{array}$

fraction A name for numbers like $\frac{1}{2}$, $\frac{5}{6}$, $\frac{8}{3}$, and $\frac{4}{4}$.

gram A unit of mass (weight) in the metric system (one thousandth of a kilogram).

graph A diagram that shows how two sets of information are related (bar graph, line graph, circle graph, picture graph).

is greater than A comparison to show that one number is more than another number.

$8 > 5$ is read "8 is greater than 5."

is less than A comparison to show that one number is less than another number.

$7 < 9$ is read "7 is less than 9."

is more than See *is greater than.*

kilogram A unit of mass (weight) in the metric system (1000 grams).

kiloliter A unit of capacity in the metric system (1000 liters).

kilometer A unit of length in the metric system (1000 meters).

line segment Any part of a line that joins two points.

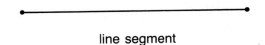

line segment

liter A unit of capacity in the metric system (1000 milliliters).

meter A unit of length in the metric system (100 centimeters).

milligram A unit of mass (weight) in the metric system (one thousandth of a gram).

milliliter A unit of capacity in the metric system (one thousandth of a liter).

millimeter A unit of length in the metric system (one thousandth of a meter).

mixed numeral A numeral formed by naming a whole number and a fraction. Numerals like $1\frac{1}{2}$ and $54\frac{5}{8}$ are mixed numerals.

multiple A product of two whole numbers is a multiple of each number. The following numbers are multiples of 5:

0, 5, 10, 15, 20, and so on.

numeral A name for a number. A name for the number eight is 8.

numerator The top number in a fraction. In the fraction $\frac{5}{8}$, the numerator is 5.

odd number Any whole number with 1, 3, 5, 7, or 9 in the ones place.

ordinal number *First, second, third, fourth,* and so on are ordinal numbers. They are used to tell order.

parallel lines Two or more lines (in the same plane) that never meet or cross.

parallel lines

perimeter The distance around a figure. The perimeter of this figure is 16 feet.

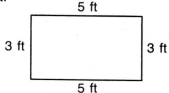

place value The value of the place or position of a digit in a numeral.

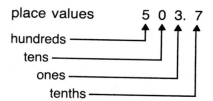

product The number you get when two or more numbers are multiplied.

$$3 \times 15 = 45$$

product

$$\begin{array}{r} 15 \\ \times 3 \\ \hline 45 \end{array}$$

quadrilateral A figure that has four sides.

quadrilaterals

354

quotient The number you get when one number is divided by another.

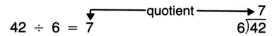

$$42 \div 6 = 7 \qquad 6\overline{)42}$$

radius A line segment that joins the center of a circle with any point on the circle.

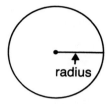

rectangle A figure with four sides and four right angles.

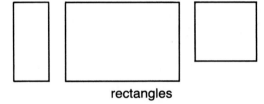

rectangles

remainder The number that is left over, or remains, after a division is completed.

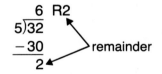

remainder

right angle An angle formed by a square corner.

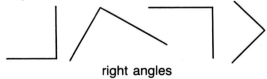

right angles

simplest form (1) A fraction is in simplest form if 1 is the only whole

number factor of both the numerator and the denominator. (2) A mixed numeral is in simplest form if the fraction is in simplest form and names a number less than 1.

sphere A figure shaped like this.

square A rectangle with all four sides the same length.

square

sum The number you get when two or more numbers are added.

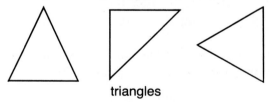

$$33 + 28 = 61 \qquad \begin{array}{r} 33 \\ +28 \\ \hline 61 \end{array}$$

sum

triangle A figure with three sides.

triangles

volume The number of cubic units that fit inside a figure. The volume of this figure is 12 cubic centimeters.

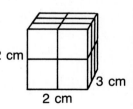

2 cm
3 cm
2 cm

whole number Any of the numbers 0, 1, 2, 3, 4, 5, and so on.

Table of Measures

Length

1 centimeter (cm) = 10 millimeters (mm)

1 meter (m) = 1000 millimeters

1 meter (m) = 100 centimeters

1 kilometer (km) = 1000 meters

1 foot (ft) = 12 inches (in)

1 yard (yd) = 3 feet

1 mile (mi) = 5280 feet

Capacity

1 liter (L) = 1000 milliliters (mL)

1 kiloliter (kL) = 1000 liters

1 cup = 8 fluid ounces

1 pint (pt) = 2 cups

1 quart (qt) = 2 pints

1 gallon (gal) = 4 quarts

Weight

1 gram (g) = 1000 milligrams (mg)

1 kilogram (kg) = 1000 grams

1 pound (lb) = 16 ounces (oz)

1 ton = 2000 pounds

Time

1 minute (min) = 60 seconds (sec)

1 hour (h) = 60 minutes

1 day = 24 hours

1 week = 7 days

1 year = 365 days

1 leap year = 366 days

1 year = 12 months

1 decade = 10 years

·1 century = 100 years

Index